Alphanumeric Displays

Alphanumeric Displays

Devices, Drive Circuits and Applications

G. F. Weston
Philips Research Laboratories

R. Bittleston
G.E.C. Hirst Research Centre

McGraw-Hill Book Company

New York   St. Louis   San Francisco   Auckland   Bogotá
Hamburg   Johannesburg   London   Madrid   Mexico
Montreal   New Delhi   Panama   Paris   São Paulo
Singapore   Sydney   Tokyo   Toronto

Library of Congress Cataloging in Publication Data

Weston, G. F. (George Frederick)
   Alphanumeric displays.

   Includes bibliographical references and index.
   1. Information display systems. I. Bittleston, R.
II. Title.
TK7882.I6W47   1983   621.3819'532   82-22846
ISBN 0-07-069468-0

McGraw-Hill edition, 1983

First published in Great Britain 1982 by Granada Technical Books Ltd.

1234567890   KGP/KGP   89876543

ISBN 0-07-069468-0

Contents

Preface

The man—machine interface has become one of the more important areas of research and product development in the last decade. This can be mainly attributed to the very rapid development of low cost, high reliability electronic devices which have brought 'intelligence' to even the simplest domestic equipment. As the equipment we use becomes more complex, so in turn the interface between it and its interpreter — ultimately a human being — has to become more capable.

This book examines the visual interface, the display, and in particular those which provide numeric or textual information, commonly referred to as alphanumeric displays. This interface is probably the most important as it provides the most rapid transfer of information between the machine and its operator. Alphanumeric information can be concise, consisting of a limited number of characters and has been the area of greatest activity especially for the newer technologies where large, high density displays are still some way off. Graphic information offers the possibility of even faster data transfer in certain applications and is essential in many circumstances. However the graphic display market is almost exclusively the province of the cathode ray tube and requires a different approach to alphanumeric displays. Since, in a book of this size it is necessary to make some restrictions, graphics are only dealt with in outline. We have chosen to discuss alphanumeric display devices from three points of view, perceptual, technology including the drive circuits and applications. Perceptually, we consider what factors govern the viewability of a display and how we measure them? This is the principal subject of the first two chapters.

The largest portion of the book is devoted to the display technologies themselves. These are examined by detailing their construction and their electrical properties including important factors such as durability and optical maintenance.

The techniques by which displays may be addressed is the subject of chapter three whilst chapters four, five and six elaborate on their principles of operation, fabrication and performance. Chapter seven considers the drive circuits pertinent to each technology and chapter eight completes the picture by considering the display system as a whole. The final chapter considers the applications for these displays by examining the various requirements placed upon them. This acts as a consolidation of the information set out in the preceding chapters, as it puts the various attributes of each display technology in context. In writing this book, we have tried to avoid highly theoretical material. Instead the emphasis has been on presenting an overall picture of display systems technology and how this relates to real applications, i.e. cost effective reliable solutions to the presentation of visual information. It is hoped that presenting the information in this way will help the engineer, who wishes to incorporate display in his equipment, to a better understanding of the devices and facilitate interpretation of manufacturers data. Most of the display devices discussed in this book have been with us for some time. The real changes have come about in the control and drive electronics and consequently we have made a special effort to look at this area. The applicability of the integrated technologies in such areas as high voltage systems is covered, as this has shown itself to be a deciding factor in the practical realisation of the display system. The impact of dedicated large scale integrated circuits as well as that of the micro-processor to the complete system is also examined.

There is a great deal that has been written about displays over the last twenty-five years. Several societies have been formed to look specifically at displays as well as an uncountable number of conferences. We have tried to acknowledge our sources of reference in every instance but it is inevitable that some references will have been missed for which we apologise in advance.

Chapter 1

Presentation of visual information

1.1 Introduction

Of the human senses, sight is the most sophisticated and versatile. Not only can one assimilate a wide angle, high resolution colour image of one's surroundings over a range of ambient light intensities, but also most people can match colours and light intensity levels with surprising accuracy. Presenting information visually, therefore, from electronic equipment to the user, across the so called man—machine interface, offers greater scope than any other communicating method. The information may be presented pictorially, as in television, graphically, as alphanumeric data, or as a combination of these methods. This book, however, is limited to alphanumeric display with brief mention of its applications to graphics. Alphanumeric display still covers a wide range of technologies and applications, and the scope has been further restricted to those forms of display in which the characters are presented by electronic devices with the visual output controlled by electrical signals and in which the output can be changed. This is taken to exclude static signs, hard copy and electromechanical displays, although mention of recent signboard displays will be made under matrix technologies in chapter 6.

1.2 Display criteria

Ideally, we should like to have an electronic alphanumeric display with a font as versatile as the printed character in a book and with full colour capability, and which is self-illuminated to any brightness level. In practice such an idealised system does not exist, and for technical and economic reasons we have to settle for much simpler formats with limitations on colour and brightness.

As a minimum criterion the display should be readable without error or eye strain or indeed undue fatigue. The ease and thus speed with which it can be read, and whether or not there is any fluctuation, or distortion, or any restriction on ambient lighting conditions, will affect its viability in the market-place. Also there will be preferences on colour, format, dimensions, etc and arguments as to whether the display should be active, emitting its own illumination, or passive, reflecting the ambient light.

Most of these criteria are subjective and cannot be quantified or measured with a scientific instrument. However, there are certain parameters which can be measured on which some of the criteria depend. For example, the readability depends not only on the size and format of the characters and their spacing, but also on the contrast between the character and its background. These parameters can be defined and measured. In turn the contrast will depend on the ambient lighting, colour and, for self-illuminating displays, on the brightness of the display; again, parameters which can be measured. To be able to compare the various electronic displays currently available or likely to be available in the future, it is necessary to understand these parameters and be able to measure them.

1.3   Photometric parameters

Let us first consider what one might call the photometric parameters which have evolved over the years for defining and measuring illumination. Since illumination must be defined in terms of its effect on the eye, the radiation energy must take into account the spectral response of the eye. This leads to some confusion, since we may have two light sources emitting the same radiation energy but which because of their frequency spectrum show a vast difference in light intensity. There is also confusion on the terminology and units of the photometric parameters which have varied over the years and from country to country. Throughout this book we use the definitions and units adopted by the C. I. E. (Commission Internationale de l'Éclairage), but conversion values are given in the Appendix to cover other units which are likely to be still in use. The terms used are luminous intensity, luminous flux, illuminance and luminance. Although not strictly photometric, colour and contrast ratio are included under this heading. For more detailed information the reader is referred to books on photometry, for example the book by Stimson.[1]

1.3.1   Luminous intensity

If we measure the amount of light energy per second, L, falling on an area of surface, a, at a distance, d, from a light source, where d is large compared with the source dimensions so that the source could be considered as a point, then we would find that L would vary with d according to the inverse square law and that

$$\frac{Ld^2}{a} = \text{constant } (I).$$ (1.1)

This constant can be considered as representing a measure of the power or luminous intensity of the source in the given direction, and we note that a/d^2 is the solid angle, ω. Thus luminous intensity is defined as the light power per solid angle for a very small cone in the given direction, i.e.

$$I = \frac{L}{\omega} \lim (\omega \to 0).$$ (1.2)

The unit of luminous intensity in international units is the candela (cd), and is derived from the luminous intensity of a 'black body' (perfect) radiator at the temperature of the solidification of platinum, which is taken as 60 candela/cm^2.

It should be stressed that the definition only tells us something about the luminous intensity in a given direction; the luminous intensity of a source is undefined unless it is a uniform source radiating equally in all directions. Otherwise we need to know the radiation in all directions to define the source completely. For practical purposes most sources of light in a display will be sufficiently symmetrical for measurement in a single plane to give the required information which can then be represented on a polar diagram. This plot of luminous intensity against angle allows direct comparison between sources.

1.3.2 Luminous flux

The luminous flux is the passage of light energy per second, L in equation 1.1, but related to its capacity to produce visual sensation, i.e. it cannot be expressed directly in watts. The unit of luminous flux is the lumen (lm) and is defined as the flux emitted in unit solid angle by a uniform point source of one candela. Thus in equation 1.2, if I is measured in candela and ω in steradians, L will be in lumens. It follows that the total luminous flux emanating from a uniform point source of 1 cd is 4π lm.

1.3.3 Illuminance

When the luminous flux falls on the inner surface of a sphere around the point source the surface is said to be illuminated. The illuminance, E, is defined in terms of the luminous flux and surface area as

$$E = \frac{L}{a} = \frac{I}{d^2}. \tag{1.3}$$

The international unit is the lux (lx) and is the illumination produced by one lumen falling on an area of one square metre. It follows that an illuminance of 1 lux is produced on an area of 1 m^2 at a distance of 1 m from a point source of 1 candela.

In practice one is mainly concerned with the illuminance of flat surfaces. Providing a is small compared with d^2 the error entailed in ignoring the difference between flat and concave surfaces is negligible. However, if the surface subtends a large angle then the fact that the light waves are incident at an angle has to be considered. Equation 1.3 can be extended to include any area where the normal makes an angle of θ with the direction of the incident light by considering the projected area, in which case

$$E = \frac{L \cos \theta}{a} = \frac{I \cos \theta}{d^2}. \tag{1.4}$$

To give some idea of values, direct sunlight gives about 10^5 lux, daylight 5×10^3 lux, and a brightly lit office around 500 lux.

1.3.4   Luminance

For defining displays, luminance is the most important photometric parameter, as it relates to a light emitting or light reflecting surface. A surface will appear more or less bright according to the amount of light coming from it. Further, since both the image area on the retina of the eye and the flux entering the eye vary inversely with the square of the distance, the illumination of the retinal image is unaffected by distance and therefore the brightness of a surface is independent of the distance of the viewer from that surface. Brightness is usually considered to be the subjective concept depending on ambient light, surroundings, etc. whereas the luminance is used to define the actual quantity of light emitted or reflected per unit area of surface. Luminance, B, is therefore the luminous intensity per unit area, which in metric units is measured in candelas per square metre, cd/m^2, sometimes termed the nit. It refers to a given direction, but if the surface is uniformly diffusing such that the luminous intensity at an angle θ to the surface normal, I_θ, is $I \cos \theta$ (i.e. it obeys the cosine law) then, since the area concerned is the projected area $a \cos \theta$ in the given direction (fig. 1.1), the luminance is the same in all directions:

$$B_\theta = \frac{I_\theta}{a \cos \theta} = \frac{I}{a} = B .$$ (1.5)

Such a surface is known as a Lambertian surface after the scientist who first propounded these ideas, and although it is an idealised surface, many diffuse surfaces in practice obey the cosine law over a reasonable range of θ.

Since the intensity varies as the cosine of θ, the total flux from a Lambertian surface will differ from that of a point source. By integrating over the hemisphere in front of the surface it can be shown that the total flux from a Lambertian surface B' is given by

$$B' = \pi B$$ (1.6)

where B' is expressed as lumens per square metre of surface area.

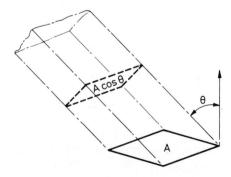

Fig. 1.1 Luminance at an angle of θ for a Lambertian surface

For a Lambertian reflecting surface illuminated by E lux the luminance will then be given by

$$B = \frac{r}{\pi} E \tag{1.7}$$

where r is the reflectivity and B is expressed in cd/m^2.

For a display the luminance may well be directional and this must be borne in mind when comparing displays whose photometric quantities are expressed by different parameters.

The practical values of luminance required for a display depend very much on the contrast as explained later (section 1.3.7). Nevertheless an indication of the order of the luminance values can be derived, if it is assumed that the display should not have a luminance which is greatly above or below the luminance of the surroundings. Average room lighting gives about 300 lux and assuming reflectivities of less than 50% (white surfaces tend to be higher) the general background luminance would be below 48 cd/m^2. Luminance values around this figure are therefore required for an 'indoor' display. The reflectivity of the immediate surroundings of the characters should be as low as possible for a good contrast active display.

1.3.5   Luminous efficiency of radiation

As already stated, the photometric parameters measure the radiation parameters in so far as they affect the eye. Although it is not necessary to understand the detailed complexity of the human visual system to appreciate the relationship between the photometric parameters and the radiation in terms of energy and wavelength, it is nevertheless useful to outline the functioning of the detection part of the eye, namely the retina, at this point.

The retina is a delicate film covering the back of the eye, consisting chiefly of nerve cells and fibres spreading out over the surface from the main optic nerve which feeds the information to the brain. These nerve cells consist of a large number of light sensitive elements, of the order of 120 million, which are divided into two types, 'rods' and 'cones'. The rods are distributed evenly over the whole surface, but the cones are more closely packed around the centre. The rods' diameters are around $1-2$ μm depending on position whilst the cones are all around 1.5 μm. The rods and cones behave differently to light stimulation. The rods have no colour sensitivity, but on the other hand they have a very much lower threshold to illumination. The cones are divided in roughly equal proportions between those sensitive to green, those sensitive to red and those sensitive to blue light, and thus are able to distinguish colours. They cease to respond to light levels below 3 x 10^{-4} cd/m^2, but under ordinary conditions of brightness the rods become overloaded and cone vision predominates. Since it is this area of light conditions that concerns display, we only need to consider the cone vision, the so-called photopic region, and in particular the variation of sensitivity to radiation of a given power level with wavelength, i.e. the spectral response. Although the spectral response of individuals' eyes varies, the variation for normal sighted people is relatively small. A mean

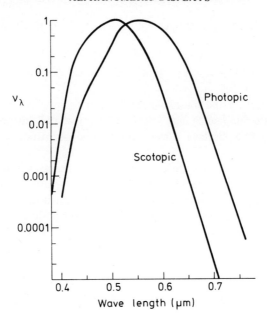

Fig. 1.2 Sensitivity of the eye to light of various wavelengths for cone vision (photopic) and for rod vision (scotopic)

sensitivity curve can therefore be used to represent the behaviour of the average eye. Such a curve of relative sensitivity against wavelength, adopted internationally, is shown in fig. 1.2. This curve allows us to convert the luminous flux measured in lumens to the radiation flux measured in watts, the so-called luminous efficiency of radiation, K. K is a maximum at a wavelength 0.55 μm and the value for any other wavelength is found by multiplying this maximum value, K_m, by the relative efficiency for that wavelength, v_λ, from fig. 1.2. K_m can be determined from the standard 'black body' of 60 cd/cm^2, since the spectral distribution for such a radiator is determined by its temperature according to Planck's radiation formula. The value of K_m from such measurements has been found to be 680 lm/W.

1.3.6   Colour

The consideration of the spectral response of the eye brings us on to considerations of colour. The eye is sensitive to two effects: (1) differences in hue such as those noticed between neighbouring portions of the spectrum, and (2) differences in saturation in which one colour differs from another by the addition of a small amount of white light. The sensitivity to hue varies somewhat irregularly with the spectrum and there are quite wide differences between individuals, whilst the sensitivity to saturation, as might be expected, follows more or less the spectral response curve of the eye.

Experimentally it has been found that the colour of any light can be matched in hue and saturation by a suitable mixture of three dissimilar colours. This has led to the trichromatic system of defining colour, wherein three reference colours of red, green and blue are specified and the colour vision characteristics of a 'standard' observer defined. The colour is then defined by the relative amounts of the three reference colours. Normally the colour can be expressed by three numbers which are quantities of each colour required to match unit quantity of the light specified. These numbers are known as the chromaticity co-ordinance of the colour, x, y and z. If $x + y + z = 1$, the values of two of the co-ordinates fixes the third, and the colour can be represented on a Cartesian co-ordinate system by plotting y against x. The particular reference colours adopted by the C. I. E. are such that the locus of monochromatic light spectrum points is located within the (01, 00, 10) triangle. This spectrum locus is illustrated in fig. 1.3. All real visible emitting sources are additive mixtures of two or more monochromatic radiations and lie within the locus. The C. I. E. reference colours are therefore hypothetical. Since the locus is

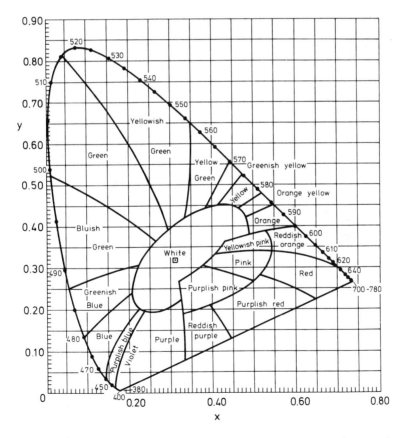

Fig. 1.3 C.I.E. chromaticity diagram showing the spectrum locus for wavelengths from 380 to 780 nm

convex, not all real colours can be produced by the same three real colours located on the spectrum locus, but provided colours are chosen close to the extremities, as in colour television, sufficient range can be obtained for practical purposes (see chapter 5).

Defining the colour does not give any indication as to the desirability of specific colours for displaying information. This is very much a subjective matter and can only be assessed by statistical methods using a sample of 'typical' observers. Several studies of this type have been carried out but the results are far from conclusive. Early experiments suggested that green or yellow light emitting displays corresponding to the maximum sensitivity of the eye were preferred to red, but often different devices were used for different colours and other factors were present which could affect the results. A study by Ellis et al.[2] using a simulated emissive display with filters in high brightness surroundings showed that the error rate for red characters was below that for green by almost a factor of three for the same luminance. What is fairly conclusive is that colours near the edge of the visible spectrum are undesirable, as the cut-off frequency for individuals varies considerably. The red emission of the light emitting diodes (l.e.d.s) comes into this category. Some individuals, particularly those with astigmatism, have difficulty in focussing on red l.e.d. displays, and for a small percentage the emission lies beyond their cut-off frequency and they cannot see the display at all.

The desirability of multi-coloured alphanumeric display is also controversial; some workers have found that the extra information given by colour effectively increases operator performances, whilst others find that it yields no advantage and can be a distraction. Given a choice most people will prefer a colour display and it is then a matter of whether this in itself justifies the extra cost. Although the eye is sensitive to small colour variations, when colours are presented in isolation only a limited number of colours can be distinguished without error; Halsey and Chapanis suggest ten to twelve.[3] The seven most distinctive colours are blue, green, yellow (red + green), red, cyan (blue + green), magenta (red + blue), and white (blue + red + green). In general the fewer the colours required the better and it should be borne in mind that about 20% of the male population are partially colour blind.

1.3.7   Contrast ratio

The visibility of a character depends on its luminance compared with that of its surroundings. This is expressed as the contrast ratio and is basically given by

$$C_R = \frac{B_C}{B_B} \qquad (1.8)$$

where B_C is the total luminance of the character and B_B the total luminance of the background, which is assumed to be less than that of the character. If the reverse is true then the inverse B_B/B_C is taken as the contrast ratio. If the display is passive C_R will be equal to the ratio of reflectivities (see equation 1.7). If the character and/or background in an active display is illuminated B_C and B_B will also include a contribution from ambient light reflected from the surface. Although contrast ratio is sometimes used for other parameters, the above is adhered to in this book.

Above brightness levels of 10 cd/m^2 the eyes can perceive luminance variations in adjacent areas of less than 5%, i.e. a contrast ratio of 1.05. This, however, depends on the size of the areas being compared and for practical purposes of reading characters the minimum contrast ratio is around two with preferably values above five. Indeed Sheer[4] suggests a figure of ten to ensure high accuracy in character recognition. For an active display this could mean luminance values of two or three hundred cd/m^2 in a reasonably lit room.

If the character and background are of different colour then a lower contrast ratio becomes acceptable. In the extreme, two reflecting surfaces of contrasting colour (red and green for example) can be distinguished even with the same brightness, as demonstrated in tests for colour blindness. The effect depends on the degree of saturation, and the C. I. E. has defined the colour difference between two colours in terms of a mathematical formula involving their x, y, z colour co-ordinates.[5] However, although the C. I. E. definition is in line with general observation unfortunately there is no simple measurement criterion on colour which can be applied to the colour contrast effect in terms of readability.

The contrast of an active display can normally be enhanced by the use of filters, albeit at the expense of luminance. If a colour filter is used which more or less matches the emission spectrum of the display the attenuation of the emitted light will be small, whereas the ambient white light reflected from those parts of the display device making up the surroundings of the character will be considerably reduced. In some devices the 'off' components of the character and other constructional detail are clearly visible in the ambient light and detract from the display. If the light level is reduced by a neutral density filter the structure detail will be masked and the appearance improved. Of course this will also reduce the luminance of the emitted light, but since most of the ambient light passes through the filter twice the contrast will also be improved. A combination of a colour filter and a neutral density filter may be recommended for some displays to give the optimum contrast.

Since some of the reflected light will be specular rather than diffuse some of it will be plane polarised. By using a circularly polarised filter the plane polarised component can be virtually cut off, improving the contrast. Such filters, however, tend to be rather more expensive than colour or neutral density filters.

Most of the display technologies have a glass front plate and contrast is often degraded by specular reflection from the front surface, particularly of light from lamps or windows. Filters in general are plastic with similar reflecting surfaces and do not necessarily overcome this problem. The only filter effective in reducing this problem is obtained by coating the surface with an interference $\lambda/4$ antireflection coating (blooming). The specular reflected light can be reduced by 80% or more without reducing the emitted light by this means. However, it is an expensive process and vulnerable to damage such as scratching. In general one tries to avoid such reflections by positioning of the display relative to the ambient light source so that its reflected image is not observed by the user.

1.4 Legibility

1.4.1 Size and shape of the character

The contrast ratio relates to distinguishing an object from its background and, as already stated, the smaller the object the greater must be the contrast ratio. In identifying the object or in our case reading the character (legibility), the size, shape and edge sharpness of the character as well as character spacing play important roles which are not necessarily related to the contrast ratio.

The size requirements are related to the resolving power of the eye, which may be defined as the minimum separation of two point objects which are just resolvable by the eye, i.e. that can be distinguished as two separate objects. The resolving power is limited by the cone diameters relative to the retinal image of the objects and therefore will depend on the distance of the objects from the eye. It is normal, therefore, to express the resolving power in terms of the minimum angle subtended by the point objects which can just be resolved. For the average eye the value is about 1 minute of arc in the photopic region. Alternatively, the reciprocal of the resolving power is used, termed the visual acuity, expressed in reciprocal minutes of arc, i.e. visual acuity is one for the average eye. It could be said therefore that any line or dot of a character can be distinguished providing it subtends an angle greater than 1 minute of arc at the eye, about 0.075 mm at a distance of 25 cm. This would imply character heights of less than 1 mm and although the eye could read such characters if well formed with good contrast, it would put a considerable strain on the reader. Printing in most books, where the font can be optimised, employs character heights for upper case letters of around 2.5 mm. To produce similar font characters using a dot pattern requires a resolution of at least 12 dots/mm (300 dots/inch), the resolutions aimed at for high quality matrix printers. Further, the number of dots required per character for reproducing printing fonts would be well over 1000. For comparison the colour dot resolution on a colour t.v. tube is around 4 dots/mm with the beam diameter covering two or more dots of the same colour. Even if it were technically possible to produce an electronic display device with such resolution the cost of the device and the encoding circuit would be prohibitive.

For technical and economic reasons, therefore, much simpler fonts are resorted to in electronic displays. The simplest font uses a fixed pattern of bars to make up the character. Seven bars can be used to depict the numerals, whilst thirteen to sixteen bars (star burst) are required to give a full range of upper case letters and numerals. The slight incline of the format appears to give a better representation. These formats are illustrated in fig. 1.4. The seven-bar numerical configuration is commonly used for numerical displays where each bar is a light emitting or light modulating element and the combination is suitably selected by seven 'gates' (see chapter 3). The rather square format has become not only acceptable but fashionable. The main criticism is that failure of a particular segment (off or on) can give a false reading. However, it has been suggested by Tannas[6] that alternative fonts adding extra bars could overcome this problem making them fail safe, in that failure

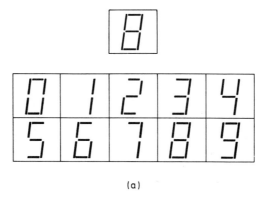

(a)

(b)

Fig. 1.4 Bar-matrix formats for display, (a) for numerics only (seven-bar), (b) for alphanumerics (thirteen-bar)

of a segment will produce an unintelligible character. An example of an eight-segment numerical display which is fail safe is shown in fig. 1.5.

Representation of letters on the star-burst pattern is not particularly good and certainly larger characters are required than in print, a minimum of 3 mm in height at optimum reading distance. For most alphanumeric applications a dot-matrix pattern is preferred and normally employed. A 5 x 7 matrix (five columns, seven rows) as illustrated in fig. 1.6 will give all upper case letters and numerals and if the matrix is extended to 5 x 9 lower case letters can be presented with the tails of letters such as g dropping below the line. A better font is obtained by using a 7 x 9 (7 x 12) matrix, and the choice is between good character representation and

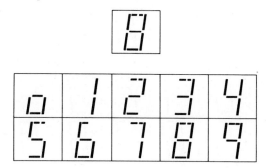

Fig. 1.5 Fail-safe eight-segment bar-matrix display for numerals according to Tannas.[6] (Permission for reprint, courtesy Society for Information Display)

economy. Several subjective studies have been made on such fonts looking at dot size and shape, mark to space ratio, and font sets.[7-10] Generally there is agreement that although a 5 x 7 dot matrix is acceptable, the 7 x 9 format is superior especially for lower case letters and symbols such as £ and $. There is also evidence which suggests that the provision of extra dots for the tail of the lower case letters improves legibility, especially for the 5 x 7 matrix format. The dots should be round or square and not elongated in any direction[9] and spacing between dots should not be greater than the dot diameter. Spacing between characters of one dot appears adequate for the 5 x 7 format but evidence favours a two-dot spacing for 7 x 9 format. The space between character rows should be at least 50% of the character height and some workers suggest > 100% of the character height. Unlike the bar-matrix design, inclining the character to the vertical decreases legibility. The character height should subtend at least 16 minutes of arc. However, this does depend to some extent on the use of the display. For searching a menu, Snyder and Maddox[9] found that larger characters gave faster search times. An alternative approach which can be used on the Cathode ray tube (c.r.t.) is to build the character up with strokes equivalent to drawing lines between the dots in a dot matrix. Often referred to as random position stroke matrix, the system allows a greater number of orientations than obtained with a fixed matrix. Fig. 1.7 shows a set of characters where sixteen

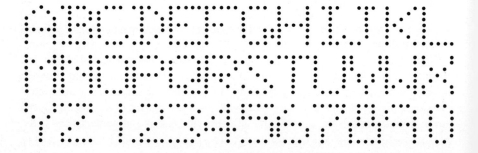

Fig. 1.6 Thirty-five element dot-matrix array for alphanumeric presentation

ABCDEFGHIJKLMNOPQRSTUVWXYZ
Ø123456789

Fig. 1.7 Random position stroke matrix using sixteen orientations

orientations are used. Failure of a segment in this system or a dot in the dot matrix format will not normally produce a false reading (see section 1.4.2).

Another factor affecting the legibility is the sharpness of the edge of a character. If the image is fuzzy, reading errors and eye strain might be expected as the observer strives to focus the image. The edge sharpness is known as acutance and is usually expressed as the mean square of the gradient of the luminous flux with distance from the edge. For most display technologies it does not appear to be a problem, but very little study has been made of either the measurement of acutance or its effect on legibility of alphanumeric displays.

1.4.2 Defects and blemishes

It has already been pointed out that for a bar-matrix display, failure of a bar to operate or activation of an unwanted bar could produce an erroneous reading which would have serious consequences in some applications. For a dot-matrix display the presence of an unwanted dot or a missing dot will not normally cause a reading error, but it could happen if more than one dot in a character position is affected. The probability of more than one dot failing in a character position can be related to the overall number of dots failing in a panel from statistical considerations providing there are no identifiable 'bad' areas of the display panel. In fig. 1.8 the probability that not more than one dot in a character position will be defective is plotted against the failure rate, assuming a Poisson distribution. It is seen that 95% assurance that not more than one dot will fail in a character is obtained with 1% failure of dots over the panel. The effect of defective dots in a 480-character panel is simulated in fig. 1.9. Using random numbers, 1% of the dots have been designated inoperative, i.e. causing missing dots when they occur at a character position, and ¼% of the dots are considered on when they should not be. The missing dots are hardly noticable, but, because of the larger background area, one is aware of the unwanted dots even at the lower percentage. Neither defect is likely to cause reading errors, but how far they may cause eye strain or fatigue has not been investigated as far as the authors are aware.

Such failures could be caused in matrix displays by constructional defects or defects in the display media. They could also be caused by circuit defects or bad matching of the circuit to the device. In a c.r.t., missing dots could be caused by blemishes on the phosphor screen.

It is not necessary for segments of a display (bars or dots) to fail to degrade

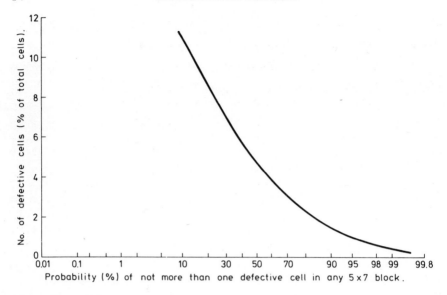

Fig. 1.8 Probability that not more than one dot in a character will be defective as a function of panel failure rate

the alphanumeric display. Variation in brightness or difference in segment area from segment to segment will detract from the performance of the display and might cause reading errors. Clearly there is wide scope here for subjective investigation.

1.4.3   Flicker and distortion

If the illumination level is changed the eye will take time to adapt to the new level. Because of this adaption time the eye acts as an integrator and if excited by light which is varying in intensity with time at a speed which is fast compared with the adaption time, the eye registers the average brightness. However, if the variation frequency is comparable with the adaption time, the eye will register the fluctuations, and the light is said to flicker. Flickering images are very disturbing, producing at best eye strain and at worst dizziness and sickness. It is important therefore in any display to reduce flicker to the minimum, ideally to eliminate it altogether. The critical frequency at which flicker ceases to be noticeable depends on the mean luminance and the amplitude and waveform of the variation; the greater the brightness and amplitude, the higher the critical value, with an upper limit around 60 Hz. The critical frequency is higher for the outer parts of the retina, and often an image which appears to be flickering when seen 'out of the corner of one's eye' ceases to flicker when viewed directly. The critical value for peripheral vision can be as high as 90 Hz. Thus in the U.K. with the normal television frame rate of 50 Hz flickering effect can be observed on c.r.t. displays and blinking or head movement can result in stroboscopic effects, particularly with fast decay phosphors.

With scanned displays such as the c.r.t. there is also the possibility of spatial movement, i.e. jitter, and distortion of the characters at the edges, both of which cause visual fatigue, although there is little or no information on this subject.

1.4.4   Angle of view

In some applications the display cannot be viewed along the normal, and restrictions on viewing angle can be detrimental. At wide viewing angles the characters would be foreshortened and difficult to read, and no one would suggest viewing at such angles. However, there are often other restrictions which make the viewing angle very much smaller than this. As already stated the luminance of displays is often directional and falls off with increasing angle from the normal, giving reduced contrast. In some displays screens or masks in front of the display elements present a further restriction and in the c.r.t. there is the curvature of the front face. How wide the viewing angle needs to be depends on the application, viewing distance and display size. In general a viewing angle of $\pm 30°$ to the normal would cover most applications, whilst anything less than $\pm 10°$ would severely limit the usefulness of the display.

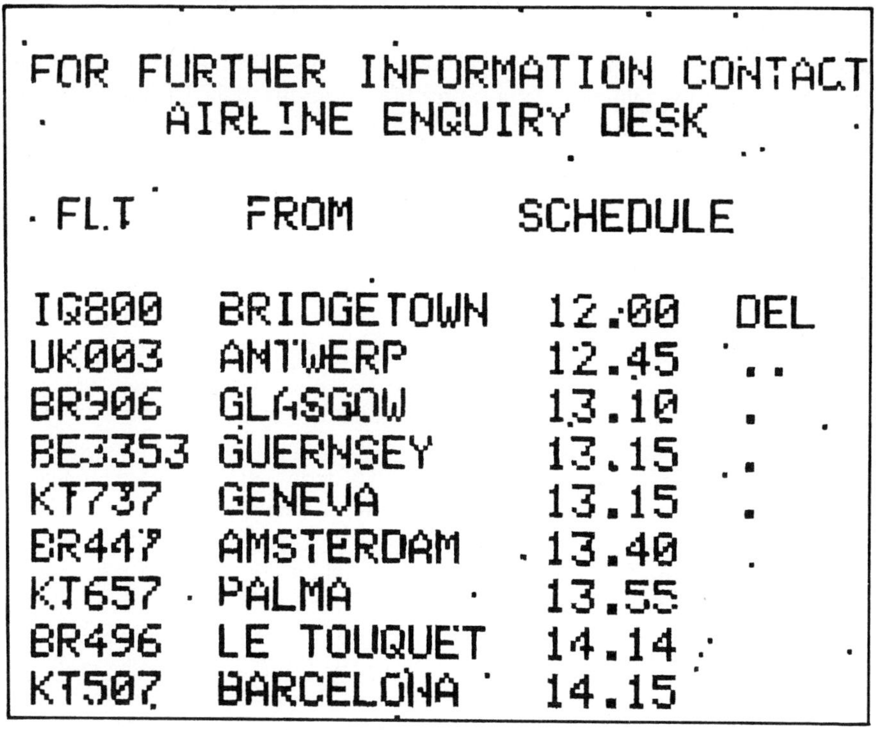

```
FOR FURTHER INFORMATION CONTACT
      AIRLINE ENQUIRY DESK

 FL.T       FROM          SCHEDULE

IQ800    BRIDGETOWN    12.00    DEL
UK003    ANTWERP       12.45
BR906    GLASGOW       13.10
BE3353   GUERNSEY      13.15
KT737    GENEVA        13.15
BR447    AMSTERDAM     13.40
KT657  · PALMA         13.55
BR496    LE TOUQUET    14.14
KT507    BARCELONA     14.15
```

Fig. 1.9 Simulated display with defective cells (1% failing to illuminate when addressed and ¼% illuminating when not addressed)

1.5   Parameter measurement and performance assessment

Ultimately the 'image quality' of a display must be judged subjectively by the user. However, no systems engineer would want to purchase a range of alternative display products and carry out statistical subjective tests on them before incorporating them in his equipment. The alternative is to define a set of the measurable parameters already discussed which will give the engineer a reasonable indication of the display device performance in the projected equipment and environment. Such a set should include

> Luminance (if active)
> Contrast ratio
> Angle of view
> Colour
> Character height
> Character format and interspacing
> Resolution
> Stability (flicker or jitter).

Luminance is the most pertinent photometric parameter for displays, but not the simplest to measure. Photocells with suitable correction filters can match the spectral response of the eye and measure the amount of light incident on the cell. Incorporated with suitable optics, such instruments are known as photometers and can measure the light intensity of a source in a given direction. They are normally calibrated against a standard source to give accuracies up to ± 1%. To measure luminance the source area must be defined. The most satisfactory method is to ensure the the display element being measured 'overfills' the aperture of the photometer. Since the elements may be small this usually means mounting the photometer on a microscope which is then focussed onto a small area of the display. Such photometers are commercially available suitable for measuring down to areas of 50 μm diameter. Since the amount of light available is low, they normally incorporate a photomultiplier rather than a photocell. Such instruments can measure the luminance variation over the display and also luminance with viewing angle. Under continuous light emission the accuracy can be up to ± 1% providing frequent calibration is made against a standard lamp. The time constant of the photometer is usually arranged to be large compared with say 50 Hz so that the average luminance value is recorded for fluctuating sources. However, for large capacity alphanumeric displays the duty ratio (on time to off time) is very low for each element, with high peak light intensities during the on period. Under these circumstances it is possible that the pulses will overload the detector and it is dangerous to assume that a photometer claiming to read average values for a.c. activated light sources will give the correct value for such duty cycles. For matrix displays it would be useful to know the variation of luminance over the different elements, which is possible with these photometers.

    A similar photometer can be used for measuring the contrast ratio, by first measuring the luminance of the character and then the luminance of the surroundings. It is important when making the measurements to specify the ambient illumination or better still to make a series of measurements over a range of ambient lighting conditions. The ambient lighting condition can be obtained by measuring the luminance of a Lambertian surface of known reflectivity and applying equation 1.7 to find the illuminance.

It is also important to know how the luminance and contrast ratio vary with viewing angle, and whether there are any other restrictions on viewing angle such as masks in front of the display.

Ideally the colour should be specified, either in terms of the values of the C. I. E. chromaticity diagram or by the spectral distribution. The latter is easy to measure with a spectrometer and probably more useful as it enables the best filter to be selected and can be compared with the eye response.

Measurement of the character height, format and spacing is fairly straightforward and in matrix displays will be defined by the mechanical structure. The resolution is relevant in displays having fine structure and for graphics. It is particularly important for scanned displays such as the c.r.t. A number of methods are employed for measuring the resolution of a c.r.t., for example by use of a t.v. test card or by measuring spot diameter. However, the method which gives the most objective measurement is the use of the modulation transfer function (m.t.f.), a method which has become established for defining the resolution of optical systems. The m.t.f. is a measure of the sine wave response of a system. A 100% modulated sine wave is applied to the brightness control electrode of the c.r.t. to give a series of light and dark bars on the raster with a sinusoidal spatial brightness variation. The frequency is varied and the depths of modulation measured with a photodetector. By relating the modulation frequency to the scan frequency the photodetector can be fixed and the pattern scanned across it. The resulting plot of modulation depth against spatial frequency is typically of the form shown in fig. 1.10. On the same figure is plotted the depth of modulation required for visually resolving lines at optimum reading distance. The cross-over point represents the limit of resolution. The m.t.f. of the system can be expressed as the spatial frequency (cycles per millimetre) at a given percentage modulation or for example the depth of modulation at the limit of resolution.

The stability, particularly flicker, is difficult to define but at least one should know the refresh rate and other variations that are likely to occur.

The above indicates the data that the engineer might expect the manufacturer of display devices to provide. Unfortunately no standards for defining display devices have been accepted and the engineer is presented with manufacturers' specifications which are often confusing and sometimes misleading. For example, although for many displays luminance is given, it is often expressed in non-standard units. For l.e.d.s it is more normal to give the luminous intensity in microcandelas rather than luminance, and unless full dimensions are given the luminance cannot be derived. Some manufacturers simply use terms such as 'high brightness' or 'visible under normal room lighting'. Similarly, contrast ratio is often given without any reference to the ambient lighting conditions and the definition is not always specified. Some manufacturers quote the contrast ratio with a filter whilst the luminance is given without the filter. Very few manufacturers give details of the variation of

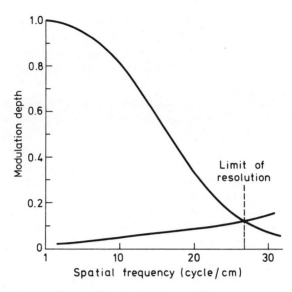

Fig. 1.10 Typical m.t.f. curve for a cathode ray tube

luminance and contrast ratio with viewing angle. Colour is normally quoted in general terms and one is unlikely to find spectral emission curves; the exception is for c.r.t. phosphors. The character dimensions, particularly for matrix displays, are normally specified adequately, although the width of the bars in bar-matrix displays is sometimes absent. Stability is rarely quoted. For most parameters, typical values will be given without minimum or maximum values and samples can deviate markedly from these typical values. Hopefully as the market grows and becomes more competitive the manufacturers will provide the information from which comparisons can be made. In the meantime the user is left to make such measurements for himself.

Given the information on the relevant parameters there is still the question of which display gives the least errors in reading and/or eye strain when continuously viewed. There is a considerable amount of research devoted to this subject and no doubt, with time, criteria will be arrived at which will help the design engineer. It is, however, not just a matter of readability; such factors as posture and positioning of input keyboards also affect the results.[11] The criteria are also likely to depend on the application. In the following chapter the various applications are outlined and the visual parameters required for the applications are discussed.

References

1. Stimson, A. (1974) *Photometry and Radiometry for Engineers*, N. York: Wiley.
2. Ellis, B., Burrell, G. J., Wharf, J. and Hawkins, T. D. F. (1974) 'The format and colour of small matrix displays for use in high ambient illumination'. *Digest of Technical Papers, S. I. D. International Symposium* **5**, 106–107.

3. Halsey, R. M. and Chapanis, A. (1951) 'On the number of absolutely identifiable spectral hues'. *J. Opt. Soc. Amer.* **41**, 1057–1058.
4. Sheer, S. (1979) *Electronics Displays*, New York: Wiley, 45.
5. Pauli, H. (1976) 'Proposed extension of the CIE recommendation on uniform colour spaces, colour difference equations and metric colour terms'. *J. Opt. Soc. Amer.* **66**, 866–867.
6. Tannas, L. E. (1977) 'Fail-safe matrix fonts'. *Digest of Technical Papers, S. I. D. International Symposium* **8**, 54–55.
7. Huddleston, H. F. (1971) 'An evaluation of alphanumerics for a 5 x 7 matrix display'. *Proc. I. E. E. Display Conference*, Loughborough. I. E. E. conference publication no. 80, 145–147.
8. Shurtleff, D. A. (1974) 'Legibility research'. *Proc S. I. D.* **15-2**, 41–51.
9. Snyder, H. L. and Maddox, M. E. (1980) 'On the image quality of dot matrix displays'. *Proc. S. I. D.* **21-1**, 3–7.
10. Suen, C. Y. and Shiau, C. (1980) 'An iterative technique of selecting an optimum 5 x 7 matrix character set for display in computer output systems'. *Proc. S. I. D.* **21-1**, 9–15.
11. Stewart, T. F. M. (1979) 'Eyestrain and visual display units: a review'. *Displays* **1**, 25–32.

Chapter 2

Display requirements

2.1 Background

The introduction of counting circuits in the 1940s and the need to register the count, saw the introduction of counting and positional indicator tubes whereby a spot of light could be produced at any of ten positions, either on a 'clock face' or on a line, to define the numerical value of each decade. By the middle of the 1950s the possibility of displaying the count with numerals in each decade position which could be electrically altered was being actively pursued. Most of the devices which were developed depended on an array of indicator lamps which either projected an image of the numerals on to a small display screen or illuminated sectors of a seven-bar matrix. One exception was the gas discharge numerical indicator tube (n.i.t.) in which a stack of numeral shaped cathodes could be 'picked out' with a glow to select the numeral. First introduced by the Burroughs Corporation in the late 1950s, the n.i.t. dominated the market for the next decade.

With the growth of digital circuits in the 1960s, the market for numerical displays expanded rapidly with a wide range of equipment featuring digital readout in the form of a single row of numerals, mostly for professional or industrial markets. Other technologies were being investigated and by the beginning of the 1970s seven-bar devices were on the market using l.e.d., liquid crystal and vacuum fluorescent technologies as well as gas discharge devices – and the market expanded into the domestic area.

The need to display letters as well as numerals arose with the growth of the computer business, and especially in areas where an on-line interactive terminal was required as, for example, in airline ticket reservations. For such applications it was necessary to write up several sentences and so the full alphanumeric displays tended to be those with a capacity of at least 1000 characters. Circuits for generating characters on a c.r.t. were investigated in the 1950s but early exploitation of alphanumeric displays was limited by cost. It has only been over the last few years, with the introduction of cheap integrated circuits, that a worthwhile market has built up for such displays.

Today the major market is still for numerical displays of up to 16 characters but, with the introduction of viewdata such as 'Prestel' into the home and word processing systems into the office, the display of a large number of alphanumerics could become the dominant market requirement of the future.

2.2 Applications

Table 2.1 summarises the main display applications, activities for which data displays are needed. The first column catalogues the application area and successive columns categorise the displays, first according to the equipment in which they are used, then by physical characteristics. Since the large majority are used for the presentation of numerics or alphanumerics, the number of characters displayed is given. Those displays which are not strictly alphanumeric are nevertheless still

Table 2.1 Applications for alphanumeric displays

Applications	Equipment	Number of characters	Size (mm)
Computers	V.D.U.	1000+	$150^2 - 250^2$
	Teletype	500+	150^2
	Data entry	80	150
	Programme keys	6—10	25
Word processing	Memory typewriter	300+	250 x 60
	Full page editor	6000	$A4 - 350^2$
Instruments	Oscilloscope	—	100 dia.
(including	Digital meters	8—16	60—120
medical)	Calculators	8—16	60—100
	Industrial controllers	1000	250^2
Retail	Weighing machine	16+	100+
	Cash registers	16	75—100
	Point of sale	250+	100^2
	Petrol pumps	12	150
Domestic	Watches	4—6	12—25
	Clocks	4—6	
	White goods' indicators	2—8	<100
	T. V. indicator	2	<20
	Viewdata	800+	$150^2 - 300^2$
Telephony	Dial indicators	8—16	50—100
	Exchange displays	250	
	Prestel	1000	200^2
Automobile	Dashboard	up to 200	150 x 100
	Taxi meter	4—8	10
Military	Large area display (radar etc.)	3000+	$>250^2$
	Cockpit displays	up to 200	150 x 100
	Mobile radio	100+	small
Public address	Signboards	1000+	up to 3m x 10m

categorised in numbers of characters since this can indicate the number of elements available for other presentations such as graphics. The size of the display is expressed in millimetres, which for the small displays indicates the length of the register. For larger displays the area is given. The last two columns are based on the current state of the art, and not necessarily on the ideal display for the application. The figures should be taken as indicative rather than definitive.

It is seen from table 2.1 that the display application area is in no way restricted to the specialised professional market but covers industrial, military and domestic appliance applications. To cover this wide field of interest the display requirements range from a single numeral to over 6000 characters, with a noticeable gap between 16 and 200 characters. The overall display dimensions vary from 10 mm² to several metres square and, although not shown, the applications cover character heights varying from a few millimetres to several centimetres.

For applications using up to 16 characters the demand is mainly for numerics. There is an emerging demand for the display of a limited number of alphanumeric characters, fewer than 200, but most alphanumeric display applications require rather more than this, with an upper limit around 6000 characters, equivalent to a full A4 page of typescript.

The relative importance of the various applicational areas in terms of market size is difficult to ascertain and figures quoted in market surveys vary considerably. In general the turnover of professional c.r.t.s is about a quarter of the turnover for other readout devices. Since some of the c.r.t.s will be used for oscilloscopes and similar displays and most of the other readout devices are destined for the numerical display market, one can say that the demand for numeric display is at least five times that for alphanumerics in terms of market value. This is largely because numeric displays have found wider application and have penetrated the large domestic market in clocks, watches and pocket calculators. On the other hand alphanumeric displays at present are confined to the professional market.

The growth of the market is fairly fast; for example, turnover in the display field practically doubled over the years from 1977 to 1980, and no doubt further expansion with new applications emerging will occur in the future. Table 2.1, however, represents the range of applications at the end of 1981 and does not include possible future trends.

The equipment applicable to the various display areas makes certain demands of the display devices used and these requirements in turn influence the technologies which are appropriate. In section 2.3 we consider these demands over the spectrum of applications as a prelude to discussing in later chapters the various technologies and drive circuits available.

2.3 Display specifications

The display device plus its drive circuit represents a system that converts electrical input information into visual output information. Thus it has two interfaces, that with the viewer and that with the information source, and both of these impose requirements on the display system. The visual output has already been considered

in chapter 1, and concerns luminance, contrast, colour, resolution and character shape and size. The input information interface requires consideration of address and erase time, power dissipation, storage facilities and electrical tolerances. There is also the question of the transcoding requirements by which is meant the need to convert the input information which would normally be in binary form into a 'pattern' to represent the characters. Finally, there are requirements unrelated to the interfaces such as ruggedness, life, reliability and cost.

The various applications listed in table 2.1 obviously place different requirements on the visual output in terms of number, size and shape of the characters. Differing requirements may be imposed on other visual parameters; for example, the luminance of an aeroplane cockpit display needs to be considerably higher than for a similar display in an office environment. The equipment needed for each application can also be expected to differ in overall conception and output circuitry and therefore impose separate restrictions on the input interface. Unfortunately there is no suitable universal display system that can be adapted to all equipment. The most suitable system for each application has to be determined from the requirements.

To examine all the applications and discuss the most suitable display for each would be neither practicable in a book of this type nor indeed very profitable. Some typical applications have therefore been selected to cover the main areas of the display spectrum, which will illustrate the factors involved in specifying the display system and which can then be adapted to other applications.

The display requirement for five pieces of equipment are considered, two numeric, two alphanumeric and one where graphics can be displayed, and these are listed in table 2.2.

The pocket calculator is typical of small hand held instruments including watches, where up to eight numerals are required with possibly the facility for some symbols. The numerals can be fairly small because the instrument can normally be held at optimum reading distance. The instrument must be run from a small battery and for reasonable battery life the power should be kept as low as possible; a figure of 5 mW has been taken as desirable, but a lower figure would be required for displays which are continuously 'on', such as in a watch. Also it would be convenient to run the display from the battery direct, without the need to up-convert the voltage. For the digital meter, a larger instrument is envisaged which although portable would not be hand held in use. Larger numerals would be required since it could not always be placed at a convenient reading distance. However, since it may be mains operated or have a heavier battery, a higher power dissipation has been allowed and a higher operating voltage can be tolerated. Nevertheless it would be desirable to drive the display from the logic chip without amplifiers and this is reflected in the voltage switching listed in table 2.2. For both these numerical display applications a seven-bar format would be acceptable, indeed desirable, in terms of encoding and driving circuit costs. The normal method of addressing the display would be by sequentially switching the numerals using a common decoder; alternatively the corresponding segments in all the numerals would be interconnected and addressed sequentially. In the former system the duty cycle would be 1 in n, where n is the number of digits in the display, whilst in the latter system the duty cycle would be 1 in 7 (see chapter 3).

Table 2.2 Specification for five typical alphanumeric displays

	Pocket calculator	Digital meter	Banking terminal	Alphanumeric/ graphic v.d.u.	Page editor for word processor
Character capacity	8–16	4–8	300–600	3000	6000–8000
Characters per line	8–16	4–8	40–64	80	80–126
Number of lines	1	1	8	32	64–80
Character height	3 mm	10–15 mm	4 mm	4 mm	3 mm
Format	7-bar	7-bar	7 × 5 dots	7 × 5 dots	11 × 7 dots
Element pitch (mm)	—	—	0.63 (40 lines/inch)	0.42 (60 lines/inch)	(80 lines/inch)
Display area (max)	6 cm × 0.5 cm	10 cm × 1 cm	25 cm × 15 cm	28 cm × 21 cm	30 cm × 40 cm
Power	5 mW	1 W	2 W	2 W	10 W
Switching potential	1.5 V	<30 V	<60 V	<60 V	<60 V
Luminance	340 cd/m^2	340 cd/m^2	340 cd/m^2	340 cd/m^2	340 cd/m^2
Efficiency	5.6 lm/W (16 char)	0.4 lm/W (8 char)	0.8 lm/W (600 char)	1.0 lm/W	1.5 lm/W (8000 char)
Write time	250 μs	500 μs	25 μs	6 μs	1.6 μs
Erase time	10 ms	10 ms	10 ms	10 ms	10 ms

The bank terminal is taken to represent the low cost end of the data-terminal market. Full alphanumerics are required but upper case letters only using a 5 × 7 dot-matrix format would be acceptable. Again this is a matter of economy. The 300 or so characters allow interactive messages to be received and sent, which is the main requirement of this type of terminal. The message would be displayed on a scanned display or a cross-bar matrix, and would be addressed by either a dot or a line at a time sequence (see chapter 3). The latter would give a duty cycle of around 1 in 60. It is unlikely that the terminal would be battery operated and therefore higher power and voltages are possible. Two watts has been suggested as a desirable target, but a higher dissipation could be tolerated which would then make less demand on efficiency. For a fixed matrix display with cross-bar address it would be desirable to address the display from integrated circuits and a figure of < 60V is quoted for the switching voltage.

The low cost graphics visual display unit (v.d.u.) envisaged is one that would be connected to a main computer to present the output data in the form of graphical plots or representative line drawings with appropriate labelling. The 3000-character capability implies a matrix of about 500 x 500 dots all of which must be addressable. A feature of the graphic display must be spatial linearity which should be around 1%. A 5 x 7 matrix could be used for the labelling and the duty ratio for a line at a time would be 1 in 500.

The word-processing display represents the upper requirement for a high performance terminal. The capacity would allow a full A4 size page of typescript with upper and lower case letters. A 7 x 9 dot-matrix format is desirable with extra lines for the tails of certain lower case letters. It could be argued that the display should be of A4 dimensions with letters of typescript size. However, it is considered that the 3 mm character height suggested in table 2.2 would be acceptable or even desirable bearing in mind that the display will be rigidly mounted and the distance between display and observer cannot always be set at optimum. The duty ratio for line at a time would be about 1 in 1000.

The luminance of 340 cd/m^2 has been assumed for all the displays. This allows the display to be read in a reasonably lit room but not in direct sunlight. It applies only to active displays; for passive displays the contrast ratio is the important criterion. A figure of ten is given for the contrast ratio as defined in chapter 1. This would give a very good contrast display but a lower figure in the region of five would probably be acceptable, certainly for displays which were not continuously being viewed. The lumens required per element for the light emitting displays have been deduced from the luminance values, and the efficiency expressed as lumens per watt obtained by multiplying the lumens per element by the number of active elements in the display and dividing the results by the mean power. Thus the required efficiency is deduced for the case where all the elements are illuminated, a condition rarely reached in practice. The figure for a large data display could be a factor of four lower for a 'white on black' display. If the display were required to be viewed outdoors on a bright day (e.g. petrol pump displays) a luminance of at least 1000 cd/m^2 would be needed, with a corresponding increase in efficiency.

For displays which are continuously refreshed, which make up the bulk of displays, the peak luminance would be given by the mean value multiplied by the duty factor (ratio of 'off' time to 'on' time). For the word processor this would mean a peak luminance of 340 000 cd/m^2 even for a line addressed system. The colour of the display is probably not important providing the output is not close to the limits of the visual spectrum. For the five systems specified a monochrome display is suitable, although there could be advantage in changing colours to draw attention to parts of the display. For example a change in colour of a numerical display on reaching a critical value or going negative could act as a useful warning signal. Also key words and headings could be given a different colour in the alphanumeric displays and there would be obvious advantages for graphics in having plots of different colours. The desirability of such colour variation in the display would depend on the economics of providing such a facility.

The writing time is taken as that time required for an element to achieve maximum output when switched from the off or zero state. If the display is continuously refreshed then it must be addressed at a field rate of at least 50 Hz for a flicker free presentation. The writing time is taken to be 10% of the on time. Thus for an eight-character display sequenced a numeral at a time, the on time per character is 2.5 ms and a writing time of less than 250 μs is required. For the high performance terminal the line on time would be 20 μs at most and the write time would have to be below 2 μs. The erase time is the time taken for an element to return to zero light output after removal of the address pulse, and therefore can be up to 20 ms for a 50 Hz refresh rate. If storage could be incorporated into the display, a delay of say half a second could be tolerated when data are changed and the write time could be correspondingly increased. The problem of peak luminance and flicker would also be alleviated.

In specifying the display dimensions, only the viewing screen size is given. Ideally one would like a flat panel display for all the applications, to give the greatest flexibility of design. However, for console type equipment a flat panel is not absolutely essential, although one would not like the depth to be much greater than the diameter of the screen.

Factors such as ruggedness and life have not been tabulated, since the same criteria apply more or less to all five applications. The display must stand up to reasonable handling and last several years, say 50 000 hours. It is only when military applications are considered that much more robust displays are needed and shorter operational lives can be accepted. For example, displays mounted in motor vehicles would have to stand up to considerable vibration and shock, but they would only be in operation for say 500 hr per annum.

The equipment manufacturer of course would like the cost of the display to be as low as possible, but as a rough guide the cost of the display device and its drive circuit should not represent more than 10% of the total equipment cost.

Chapter 3

Addressing techniques

3.1 Introduction

As an introduction to the succeeding chapters which examine displays and their
supportive systems in some detail, it is useful to outline the various addressing
techniques. Fortunately, despite the very large number of display systems available,
the majority are addressed using one of three basic techniques. The few exceptions
are peculiar to particular display needs and are covered in chapter 7 which discusses
the specific requirements of each display type in detail. The three addressing
techniques to be discussed are direct addressing, multiplexing and scanning. Because
the book concentrates on character displays, the greatest emphasis has been given
to multiplexing which has become the standard method of accessing the more
recently developed display devices.

Before we look at these addressing modes, it is important to understand how we
can classify the performance and capabilities of a display panel that determine the
suitability of any one technology for one or other of the addressing systems.

3.2 Display characteristics

The most important display characteristic to the systems engineer is that of a
display's optical response to electrical stimulus. Several different measurements are
possible to examine the performance of a display under varying conditions of drive.
Because each of the addressing techniques makes use of different properties for any
given display, these tests can be quite extensive. Here we shall consider the main
body of these tests generally defined as a set of curves called the $L-IV$ (luminance,
current and voltage) characteristics which provide most of the important information
in cryptic form.

Characterisation of a display is most simply done with a single element rather
than a more complex configuration. Experience has shown that reasonable extra-
polations may be made, although very large displays have proved a law unto themselves for reasons which we will consider later.

The term luminance is not applicable in the context of passive displays. For
these displays we can interpret the term luminance as optical response or
transmissivity.

We can test simple display elements in several ways. The following are the most useful:

Optical response to applied voltage
Optical response to applied current
.Optical response to applied power
The current—voltage characteristic.

It is necessary to consider all of these with respect to time. The response of a display to short electrical pulses is important when considering multiplexing and the long term effects reflect the life expectancy of the panel. Additionally we need to examine the optical and electrical rise times of each display.

3.2.1 Luminance—voltage (L−V) characteristic

Fig. 3.1 shows the features of the $L-V$ characteristic. Voltage is plotted along the x axis. This may be a d.c. or a.c. excitation depending on the device under test. The plot depicts the steady state response of the display element, rather than the pulse response which is somewhat modified. In fig. 3.1 we can note three significant profiles. With no voltage applied L is zero. Unless there was a passive storage mechanism (see section 6.6 on electrochromic displays) we would not expect to have something for nothing. As V is increased, very little happens until we reach a point (a), where a further small increase in voltage causes a much larger change in the value of L. At some point (b in fig. 3.1) the sharp increase in L starts to flatten out. A further increase could permanently damage or even destroy the device. The sharp transition at (a) is generally called the threshold or 'knee' and its magnitude, slope and linearity are a function of the display under consideration. The term 'knee' is borrowed from zener diode terminology, where knee has a very similar meaning. The flattening out at voltages greater than (b) is generally referred to as the saturation point. The display is behaving less efficiently at this point and inputting larger voltages is not yielding a pro rata increase in L.

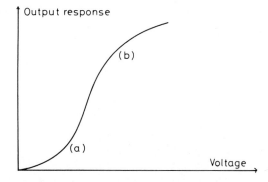

Fig. 3.1 General $L-V$ characteristic

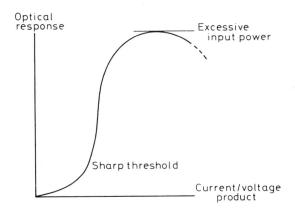

Fig. 3.2 Typical $L-IV$ response curve

3.2.2 $L-IV$ characteristic

This is often very similar to the $L-V$ characteristic, but here we are examining the response of an element to power (the product of V and I) and this provides some additional information, namely the efficiency of the display element. There are many different levels of efficiency that we would discuss with respect to displays. Here we are interested in the electrical input to optical output transfer as this gives us the needed information for actual display drive. Usually for an emissive display, efficiency of this type is expressed in lumens/watt (see chapter 1). Fig. 3.2 shows the general form of the $L-IV$ characteristic. The significant difference between this and the $L-V$ characteristic is that the saturation is much more pronounced. In most other respects there is very little difference between the two measurements. The efficiency characteristic that can be calculated from this $L-IV$ curve is shown in fig. 3.3. In practice, it should be borne in mind that real display efficiencies can vary greatly in both their magnitude and slope functions. All displays have some input power at which their optical response for a given input power is optimum. This peak is clearly shown in fig. 3.3. Its value with respect to the voltages (a) and (b) of figs 3.1 and 3.2 are important and these are shown as values on the x axis.

3.2.3 $I-V$ characteristic

At first glance, one might be forgiven for thinking that the measure of a characteristic which takes no account of the optical performance of a display could not be of much use. Actually, the opposite is true because it is the system engineers' direct measure of the display drive requirements. From this, he can evolve the equivalent circuit of the display element and hence determine the likely electrical performance of more complex structures such as a matrix array. $I-V$ measurements are used to obtain indirect parameters such as capacitance or inductance. It is usually important to measure $I-V$ performance under several conditions (static and dynamic current/ voltage measurements) if a precise picture of the device behaviour is to be obtained.

3.2.4   Optical and electrical rise and fall times

The optical rise and fall time is one of the many factors that determine the kind of drive that is required for any particular display technology. We shall examine its precise effect when we come to look at the various addressing techniques. However, in general we can say that on application of the appropriate electrical signal the optical rise and fall or decay time will be exponential, with a time constant depending on the display technology. It can vary from nanoseconds for l.e.d.s, for example, to milliseconds for some c.r.t. phosphors. More important, however, may be the electrical rise and fall time. Many of the display technologies depend on the build-up of charges or charged particles transported through the medium and this can introduce a considerable delay. Not only does this rise and fall of the electrical characteristics affect the optical output, but also the fall time in particular could affect the repetition rate at which electrical signals can be supplied when changing the information.

3.3   Addressing methods

Having given a brief outline of display characteristics in terms of the response to electrical stimulation we can now return to consideration of the driving techniques. As already hinted, the fact that these characteristics are common to many of the displays currently being developed has meant that the actual addressing techniques employed fall into a handful of categories, indeed the three listed in section 3.1.

Before expanding these further it should be pointed out that few device technologies can be addressed by all three methods. The first two techniques, direct

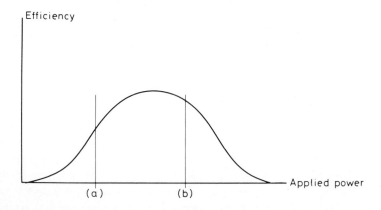

Fig. 3.3 Efficiency as a function of applied power

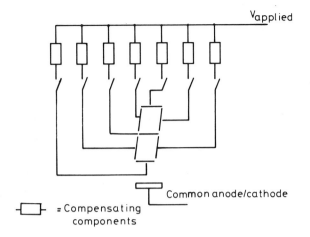

$V_{applied}$

Common anode/cathode

⊣▭⊢ = Compensating components

Fig. 3.4 Direct connection of a seven-segment display

addressing and multiplexing, apply only to those displays where the 'picture' is built up from discrete display elements which are activated separately, whereas scanning applies only to those displays where the display medium or screen can be uniformly activated over its whole area and the picture elements are defined by an incident beam, be it electrons or light. Direct addressing and scanning are relatively straightforward. The former is limited to the display of a small number of characters, mainly on economic grounds, whilst the scanning technique offers a large character capacity display, the number of picture elements being limited only by the beam diameter relative to the screen area. Multiplexing is, as its name implies, a more complex approach. It is of great importance since it offers the opportunity of bridging the gap between direct addressing and scanning to produce large character capacity displays in technologies which cannot be adapted to scanning techniques. It thus warrants a more detailed discussion.

3.4 Direct addressing

This is the simplest display drive mode. Each display element is driven by its own driver. Fig. 3.4 shows this for a seven-segment display. The drivers may be simple switches or they could incorporate compensation circuitry to minimise ageing or adjust for particular operating conditions. The displays themselves are usually driven continuously and the drive voltages and currents will depend on the display in question.

Direct addressing is simple to use and integrated circuit display drivers can make this form of addressing economical, for a small number of display elements.

There are many reasons why direct addressing should not be dismissed as a trivial addressing mode, and the fact that many commercial displays use this approach bears this out.

The main advantage is the simple control of the display; simple systems are reliable. This can be important for displays used in critical environments, e.g. aeroplanes, military vehicles and failure warning systems, and it is not difficult to incorporate a back-up drive system (commonly termed redundancy) by duplicating the driver.

The one to one correspondence between drivers and elements offers the gain that device failure has only local impact. A failure of a driver usually only affects the driven element. Other forms of addressing (multiplexing is the important one) rely more heavily on each driver, and a failure can cause several elements to be 'lost'. With careful display design, single element failures can be tolerated and legibility retained. Another benefit of one driver, one element, is that any compensation needed to prolong the life of a display element can be included. Most displays 'age'; that is, their light output (or transmissivity) decreases with time. In many cases the change is trivial, but for applications where the life of the display is critical or where the performance must be maintained some compensation is essential. Complicated addressing techniques rarely allow for compensation because the driver is remote from the element and it is then necessary to address the display directly.

There are also other advantages, for example interference. The noise due to the comparatively high energy switching transients required to address multiplexed displays is occasionally undesirable. Direct addressing is a method by which such electrical noise can be minimised. In critical environments (where delicate measuring gear is employed) radio frequency noise is a hazard. The infrequent switching of direct addressing is often used to overcome this problem.

There is also a cost advantage in the low processing overheads which we will only touch on here, as it is really the province of chapter 8. Basically, when we are considering the drive system needed to support the display drivers, it is often useful to minimise the time required to service a display. This is the case with many microprocessor controlled displays. Directly addressed displays are 'static', that is, they do not require refreshing or updating except when new information has to be displayed. This can allow the microprocessor to devote itself to more important tasks, and not expend useful time managing the display.

The benefits of directly addressed displays are quickly offset by the large number of drivers required to address the more complex displays. Table 3.1 compares the number of drivers needed to address a display directly and using a common alternative, i.e. matrix multiplexing, when each element is addressed by two electrodes which are commoned with other elements. Table 3.1 has three columns; number of elements, number of drivers required to address each element and number of drivers required when addressing with the best arrangement available when matrix multiplexing. As is quite clear, even when we require to address six elements, it is more economical (in terms of the number of drivers required) to multiplex the display. We have said nothing about the differences in the actual drivers between the two addressing modes, and it is important to consider the increase in driver complexity when making a full comparison. For some display technologies, the difference in driver requirement is only nominal, and here it is quite common to see multiplexing employed. For large displays (more than 400 elements), direct addressing is rarely feasible, except possibly for very stringent applications.

Table 3.1 Comparison of direct and multiplexed addressing

Number of elements	Number of drivers in direct addressing	Number of drivers when multiplexing
1	1	2
3	3	4
4	4	4
6	6	5
8	8	6
10	10	8
20	20	9

3.5 Multiplexing

Most larger electronic displays are driven using one or other form of an addressing technique known as multiplexing. The principal exception is the cathode ray tube, which is scanned.

The goals of multiplexing are twofold: to reduce the number of drivers required to address a particular display and to reduce the number of connections needed to interconnect the display and its drive system. Both these goals are in the interests of producing an economical end product. No display currently available offers ideal characteristics for multiplexing, and in almost every example multiplexing imposes restrictions on performance. Some displays do not possess the optoelectrical characteristics for multiplexing. In all instances multiplexing is a compromise. The analysis of these restrictions is of general interest and forms the main topic of this next section.

3.5.1 Operation of matrix multiplexing

The word matrix is used to describe display multiplexing because multiplexing is generally explained and understood in terms of a two-dimensional matrix consisting of several elements which are selected by accessing their x or y axes.

Consider an array of six display elements, this being the minimum number one would consider multiplexing, as shown in table 3.1. For matrix multiplexing, the six-element array would be interconnected through five lines, three lines on the x axis and two on the y axis as shown in fig. 3.5. They could of course be connected the other way round with three vertical lines and two horizontal; at this stage it makes no difference. The elements could for example be l.e.d.s, in which case a positive voltage could be applied to the x axis and a current sink to the y axis to activate an element. The important requirement of any alphanumeric display system is to select the elements required to make up the characters and only those

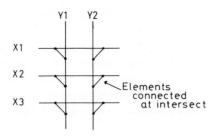

Fig. 3.5 Basic matrix

elements and to display them in such a manner that, as far as the eye is concerned, the information is continuously presented. We can examine how multiplexing our six-element matrix of fig. 3.5 can satisfy these requirements.

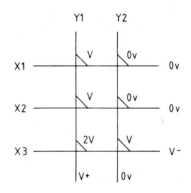

Fig. 3.6 Voltage distribution across the matrix

Access to any element in the six-element array must be through the interconnecting paths. The technique is to select an element by applying a voltage (or current) to two of the connectors in such a way that only the element at the intersection of these conductors is selected. This can be done by applying a small voltage to each of the axis drivers such that the sum of the voltages (which only appears at the intersection) is enough to select the desired element and hence cause it, and only it, to switch on. However, there is a complication. Several other elements will 'see' one of the fractional voltages (depending to some extent on the voltages on unaddressed lines). Fig. 3.6 shows the distribution of voltages if we connect all of the unselected lines to a zero potential. Two possibilities should be considered. These are generally referred to as 'part' selection and 'sneak path' effects. Several elements in fig. 3.6 are half selected, that is, a half voltage has appeared across them as a result of selecting the element $(y_1 x_3)$. The affected elements are $(y_1 x_1)$, $(y_1 x_2)$ and $(y_2 x_3)$. It is important that these voltages do not cause a partial selection of the elements which results in a background glow (or in the case of passive displays, a loss of contrast). This relates back to the discussion on $L–IV$ curves as we can see that the elements of fig. 3.6 should not become selected until very nearly the full selecting voltage is applied. There exists therefore the need for an asymmetrical 'knee'. In this example we should like the knee to be as sharp as possible. The ideal characteristic is shown in fig. 3.7. This figure shows an infinitely sharp characteristic which lies between the half voltage and the full selecting voltage. This would ensure that there was no chance of a background glow. The earlier L–IV characteristic of fig. 3.1, which is rather more like reality, shows that in practice partial selection is inevitable.

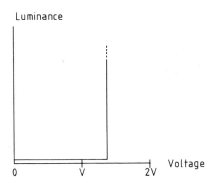

Fig. 3.7 Ideal optical response

In many displays the knee occurs at or close to the half voltage point with which we have elected to address our display. In effect, this will almost certainly lead to a loss of contrast. The value at which this becomes unacceptable depends on several factors such as the ambient illumination and the ratio of background glow to the selected elements' light output. In the instance of passive displays, the effect of partial selection is seen as a simple loss of contrast, which can make the display difficult to read.

The second consideration in this example of display addressing is that of 'sneak paths' or reverse voltage conduction. Fig. 3.8 redraws fig. 3.6 but including possible

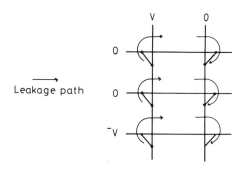

Fig. 3.8 'Sneak' paths due to leakage

alternative current paths. These sneak paths can arise because of the poor reverse insulation characteristic of the display elements allowing current to flow in reverse through the display. The end result could be loss of contrast or damage to the display.

If we only require to address one element at any one time, the simplest way of preventing these sneak paths is to connect all unused lines to the most negative potential in the system, which ensures that currents return to the display drive through the shortest route.

Having established that it is feasible to address elements uniquely provided that we can tolerate partial voltages within the display, it is necessary to demonstrate that full addressing is possible. This raises several other important and often limiting factors in this form of display addressing. There are two main types of matrix multiplexing, real time multiplexing and storage techniques. The most commonly occurring of these two is real time multiplexing, so we shall consider this first.

3.5.2　Real time multiplexing (light emitting displays)

Returning to our six-element array (fig. 3.6), supposing we wish to display elements at the intersection of x_1y_1, x_2y_1 and x_3y_2. We could select each element in turn by applying voltage pulses to x_1 or y_1, then to x_2 and y_1 and lastly to x_3 and y_2, and repeat this sequence at a repetition rate fast enough to give an apparent continuous display of the three elements as a result of the persistence of vision. This is known as dot sequential addressing. Alternatively we could apply first a half voltage pulse to y_1 and simultaneously pulses to x_1 and x_2 and then apply pulses of half voltage to y_2 and x_3. This is known as a line dumping system and is more clearly seen if we go to the familiar dot matrix of a 5 x 7 array used for alphanumeric application (see chapter 1).

The build-up of a character on a 5 x 7 dot matrix is shown in fig. 3.9. Here we are applying a fractional voltage (a half voltage in most cases) to each y line in turn and as we do this the x axis lines are receiving a further half voltage. As we have already seen, we expect the elements at the intersect of the x and y lines to be selected. The difference here is that several x lines can be driven simultaneously, en-

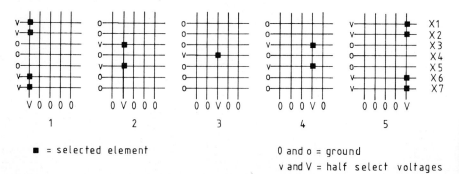

Fig. 3.9 Building up the character X cycle by cycle

abling several elements to be selected. If we do this in the manner depicted in fig. 3.9 we are able to control elements in any one column at any one time. The history of one cycle is shown in fig. 3.9, in which the character X is displayed one column at a time. Array addressing in this way has several implications. Again it is important to emphasise that we are talking generally, and that terms such as luminance and contrast will have different inferences depending on the technology in question. The following topics can be considered in these more general terms:

    Optical requirements
    Contrast optimisation
    Matrix addressing limitations.

3.5.3 Optical requirements

The most important feature of real time multiplexing is of course that elements cannot be continuously lit. The amount of time that any one element can be illuminated depends on the rate at which the display is being scanned and the number of lines in the array. If we assume that the display is continuously scanned (which is generally the case), the time that any one element is on per cycle is

$$\frac{1}{n} t \quad \text{seconds}$$

where n is the number of lines being scanned and t is the time of one cycle (i.e. all lines scanned once). To obtain a luminance comparable to that obtained with a directly addressed display involves driving the elements of the display in a quite different mode, that of short pulse operation. During this short pulse it may be necessary to apply much greater inputs of electrical stimulation so that the mean level of luminance can be achieved. This implies that the peak luminance will have to be greater by a factor of n if this is to be achieved.

If we were to look at the general $L-IV$ characteristic of fig. 3.2 the effect described as saturation would appear to be a limiting factor as it is clear that as the power is increased above moderate levels of input power there is a decrease in display efficiency. However, under short duration pulsed conditions most displays show a markedly different behaviour to that illustrated for continuous electrical stimulation in fig. 3.2. This difference is shown in fig. 3.10 which again is a general representation of the most frequently occurring $L-V$ characteristics. Fig. 3.10 contrasts the continuous characteristic with a short pulse drive. The duty ratio of the element is about 1%. As the duty ratio ('on' time to 'off' time) decreases, so there is a general tendency for the level at which saturation occurs to increase. The principal reason for this is that the total power being input to the element is not increasing; consequently the heating effect which is an important cause of saturation is avoided. The picture given here is simple, and there are other factors to consider. Firstly 'short', as applied to short pulse drive, is not quantitative and can vary from nanoseconds to seconds depending on the technology. A secondary limitation is due to the absolute or quantum efficiency of the technology in question. This parameter ultimately determines how many lines we can address before the maximum level of luminance obtainable falls below a level acceptable for the particular application.

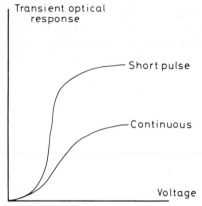

Fig. 3.10 Overdrive at reduced duty ratios

Many of the concepts just described apply equally to light modulating displays, but here we cannot talk of luminances or peak brightness as these do not apply. The important requirement is to establish a technique of addressing which will ensure the maintenance of contrast when multiplexing. The most commercially interesting light modulating display is the liquid crystal and the considerations relating to pulse addressing are so different for this technology that a detailed discussion of this aspect of multiplexing is deferred to later chapters.

3.5.4   Contrast optimisation

Contrast for a light emitting display is taken here to mean the ratio of luminance of 'on' elements to that of 'off' elements when measured in a dark room (see section 1.3.7). The reason for interest in this particular form of contrast measurement is that it is a direct measure of the effectiveness of matrix multiplexing in the unique selection of display elements. Similarly for a passive display it is the 'on' element to 'off' element contrast and not that of the background which we need to measure. We have already looked at ways in which contrast can be degraded as a consequence of sneak paths and partial selection of elements. We should also look at the problem caused by sneak paths when several elements are being addressed. Contrast can also be degraded by the phenomenon of crosstalk.

Sneak paths in fully multiplexed displays are not always easy to avoid because several lines (the data lines) have to be driven simultaneously leading to a more complicated distribution of voltages. The end effect is that several alternative paths for current flow can be set up. A well defined $L-IV$ curve and a good reverse insulating characteristic is the best way of ensuring that these paths cannot arise. In large matrices even a small leakage of current through undesirable paths often leads to a degradation in contrast.

Crosstalk is important and amenable to optimisation. It can be controlled with good design. Crosstalk can be due to either poor addressing or charge storage.

Fig. 3.11 demonstrates how crosstalk can occur by mistiming when scanning. The 4 x 4 matrix illustrated here is scanned along its axis and no time has been left between consecutive line addresses. For many reasons this can lead to crosstalk. If the drivers supplying the data to the display (the x axis drivers in fig. 3.11) are slow to change, or there is some other delay in the system electronics, then there is a strong possibility that the same data will appear on more than one line. Information will be diverted to the wrong elements for a part of each line time. The effect will be a loss of contrast as a result of faulty timing. Provided time is allowed for the display and its drive system to 'settle down' then this form of crosstalk is quite easily avoided.

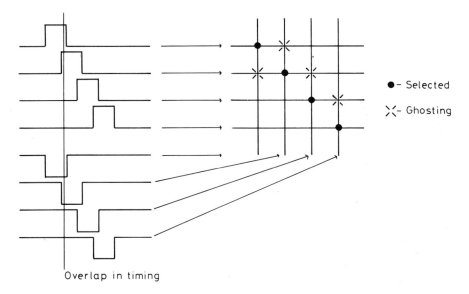

Overlap in timing

Fig. 3.11 Crosstalk due to mistiming

Crosstalk due to charge storage is rather more common. The construction of most matrix displays is such that there is inevitably some inductance and/or capacitance associated with the axis drive lines. In many cases the display is a matrix of capacitances as each element possesses some local capacitance. Fig. 3.12 shows a matrix with these storage elements included. The left half of fig. 3.12 shows the top x axis line being selected with some of the elements turned on through the y axis. The capacitances will be charged up as a result of this. When we move on to the next line, any residual charge will be passed on to the element of that line. This is shown in the right half of fig. 3.12. The ghosting effect that this causes will vary in severity depending on factors such as capacitance and the rate at which the display is scanned. It can often be avoided by leaving a 'wait' time between each line scan to allow the stored charge to dissipate. In large matrices, delays such as this would

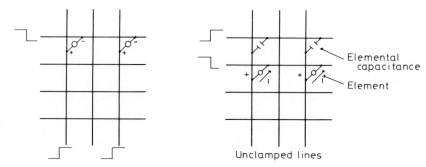

(Top line selected - two elements on)   (Residual charge passed to next line)

Fig. 3.12 Crosstalk due to capacitative coupling

severely limit brightness levels and alternative techniques are used, the most usual being actively to discharge the display between each scan eliminating the possibility of charge build-up.

The charge storage effect is not always a disadvantage. It can be used in a storage addressing mode which we explore later.

3.5.5   Matrix addressing limitations

The factors limiting matrix size vary for light emitting and light modulating displays. The discussion of specific limitations is deferred to chapter 7. Peak brightness under certain pulse conditions and the possibility of limitations due to contrast diminution are two limiting factors which we have already covered. Other considerations are the efficiency of the technology, limitations on the drive circuit and interconnections, and temporal effects in both the device and the circuit.

In table 2.2 we saw that a limit must be put on the total power dissipated in any practical display. The figures quoted for the alphanumeric panels were fairly conservative and amount to an average dissipation over the display of around 5 mW/cm^2. However, for this dissipation an efficiency of 1 lm/W is required. Most of the practical light emitting matrix displays fall short of this target, usually less than 0.5 lm/W, and the power dissipation is at least doubled. The upper limit is reached when the display reaches an unacceptable temperature of say 50°C which roughly corresponds to a dissipation of 20 mW/cm^2. The total watts dissipated in a panel, i.e. that quoted in table 2.2, also represents the peak power taken per line in a line addressed system. The implications of the efficiency on the peak power and on the drive circuit and connections is illustrated in table 3.2.

In table 3.2, R^* is the maximum resistance of the connecting lead to ensure the voltage drop along it is less than 5% of the device switching voltage.

There is thus a need to provide drivers with greater current output capabilities for matrix displays than for direct drive. The lower the switching voltage, the greater this current has to be. Also the current required to change any capacitance caused by the geometry of the matrix display has to be taken into account.

Table 3.2 Drive requirements for a 300-character data panel (see table 2.2)

Device voltage	Peak power (W)	Peak current per line	R^* (Ω)	Peak power (W)	Peak current per line	R^* (Ω)
2	2	1 A	0.2	10	5 A	0.04
10	2	0.2 A	5.0	10	1 A	1.0
50	2	40 mA	125	10	0.2 A	25
100	2	20 mA	500	10	0.1 A	100
200	2	10 mA	2000	10	50 mA	400

There is no great difficulty in providing a solid state drive circuit capable of meeting these requirements fairly easily although it is rather expensive for some display types. The limiting factor which we have to consider is precisely how the drive power is routed to the individual elements.

Up to this point, we have represented our matrix displays as a simple arrangement of elements at the crosspoints of address lines. These lines are undoubtedly resistive. Except where the current flow through the display is very low, it is not possible to ignore this. We usually use a distributed line as shown in fig. 3.13 to account for the effects of this resistivity. Bearing in mind that the elements of most displays comprise a non-linear resistor in parallel with a capacitor, we would expect that a pulse applied to one end of this line would be considerably modified at the other end. One might also expect a range of voltages along the line. The elements furthest away from the driving source will 'see' a lower voltage because of the potential division down the line. This is illustrated in table 3.2 where the value of resistance is calculated for a 5% fall in voltage assuming that all the elements are lit. We see that the problem gets larger the lower the switching voltage of the device. The effect at least will lead to a spread in luminance, but it could be a limitation to the number of elements that can be satisfactorily addressed. If the value of R in fig. 3.13 is small and the value of G is large, the effect will be small and vice versa. An added compli-

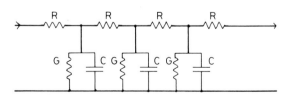

R	Element interconnection
C	Elemental capacitance
G	Non-linear elemental resistance

Fig. 3.13 Transmission line equivalent. R, interelectrode resistance; G, non-linear elemental resistance; C, elemental capacitance

cation of display capacitance is the introduction of a time constant which could cause even more non-linearity along the display line. The maximum length of line is governed by the ability to provide a good connection between elements causing the minimum loss along its length. One simple method of increasing the number of elements that may be driven in any one line is to drive the line from both ends. Generally capacitance is not a major consideration in limiting the maximum line length, and tends to play a more important role in limiting the maximum frequency at which a given display can be refreshed.

Finally we have the limitation due to the optical and electrical rise and fall times.

The theoretical maximum duty ratio for any dot-matrix display is the reciprocal of the number of lines in the display, $1/n$. In practice this can rarely be achieved owing to delays to minimise crosstalk, delays to allow lines to charge and discharge and delays in the drive circuitry and in the device.

As these are all nearly constants, i.e. not a strong function of display size, the easiest way to get as close as possible to the theoretical maximum duty ratio is to scan the display as slowly as possible. This will inevitably involve a compromise between visual needs and drive capability. In general it is the duty ratio and not the number of lines which limits the matrix display character capacity. Partly as a result of the rise and fall times of the display technology there will be an optimum pulse length requirement. Many of the display technologies show a wide variation in efficiency when subjected to a range of current/voltage pulse drive conditions. Some of these variations are peculiar to the particular display technology but there are a few general characteristics. If the pulse is too short the light output may not reach its maximum level; also, there will be more energy expended in charging any storage component within the display. If it is too long, heat effects may cause saturation, as we have already seen (section 3.3).

From this we can infer that there is a range of desirable voltage/current pulse widths with which the matrix should be driven. There is a connection between this and the largest matrix size that can be driven, because the pulse width times the number of lines dictates the refresh rate and this must be fast enough to present an apparently flicker free continuous display.

3.5.6 Real time matrix displays in other forms

Although the most important new displays take the form of a dot-matrix display, multiplexing is used in many displays some of which look nothing like a dot matrix. All the principles and considerations of array type displays apply, although because the displays usually have far fewer elements there are correspondingly fewer problems in addressing them. The main examples of simple multiplexed displays are multi-digit numeric displays, simple pictorial displays and bar/graphic displays.

Multi-digit numeric displays became commonplace with the advent of the pocket calculator where small size and ease of assembly were paramount in bringing a low cost product to the market-place. The scheme for multiplexing a set of four digits is shown in fig. 3.14. This will be quite familiar to many readers. Using the dot matrix as an analogy, the seven segments of each digit are interconnected and represent the data lines. The common anodes (or cathodes) are scanned as the x axis lines of

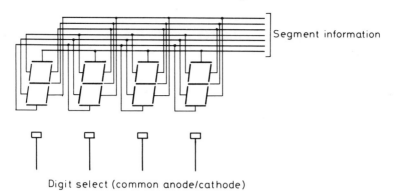

Segment information

Digit select (common anode/cathode)

Fig. 3.14 Four-digit multiplexing

fig. 3.5. Most of the considerations applicable to a dot matrix apply to digit displays, especially in the case of crosstalk. This is most easily avoided by leaving a gap between consecutive digit addresses, which should be easily accomplished as there are no severe constraints on refresh rate owing to the limited number of digits. It is often desirable to scan simple displays like this at quite a high refresh rate (significantly greater than the 50 Hz minimum) to allow for movements of the observer. A full timing diagram of one cycle for the four digits incorporating all the desirable features just described is shown in fig. 3.15.

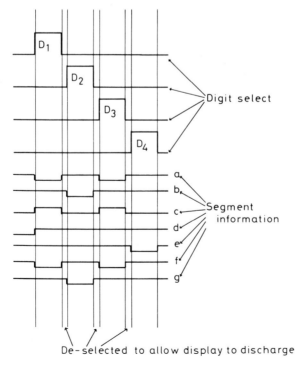

D_1

D_2

D_3

D_4

Digit select

a
b
c
d
e
f
g

Segment information

De-selected to allow display to discharge

Fig. 3.15 Time division multiplexing

There are many instances where matrix multiplexing can be used even when the display is made of most un-matrix-like legends. By way of an example look at fig. 3.16 which is a multi-legend display interconnected such that it can be multiplexed. The most common problem with this arrangement is as a result of uneven distribution of power along the multiplexed lines because of the range of element sizes. Care also has to be taken when accounting for the current pulse requirement as these displays are apt to be capacitive and/or draw large currents.

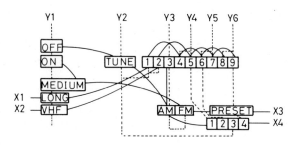

Fig. 3.16 Arranging a legend display for multiplexing

Bar graphs (used to simulate meter movements, etc.) are often multiplexed, as they have a large number of fairly small elements. The mechanical layout is shown in fig. 3.17, which is one of several possible arrangements. This technique offers a substantial saving in the number of drivers and is generally amenable to a more complete display system integration.

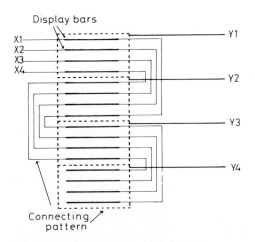

Fig. 3.17 Bar-display access for multiplexing

3.5.7   Multiple axis matrix multiplexing and storage

It is worth making a passing reference to an extension of the normal two-axis multiplexing technique if only because it highlights the need to find some better method of addressing displays. In a few instances it is possible to reduce the number of drivers still further by using an additional axis (and sometimes several). The principles are broadly similar to those already discussed, but instead of applying two half voltages one would apply signals to all three lines such that the device will only be activated at the crosspoint where all three signals are applied. The technique has been demonstrated in conjunction with flat screen c.r.t.s which are discussed in more detail in chapters 5 and 7, and also for gas discharge panels. The latter have characteristics which allow the lines to be scanned by a small number of pulses (see chapter 6).

Alternative display addressing techniques have been in the melting pot for some time. The most important of these is storage addressing. Some displays have an intrinsic storage capability and these are discussed later. For others it is necessary to introduce more components into the display to achieve the same effect. Not all display technologies are amenable to these modifications, and in those that have been redesigned as storage displays there have often been significant problems.

The two main types of external storage technique are latched display control and capacitive multiplication. There are many ways of achieving both; the following serve only as examples of the principle.

Fig. 3.18 shows how we might consider a latched matrix array. At the crosspoint of each drive line is an element and a latching device (which is usually a semi-conductor). The latching action of a thyristor could be used.

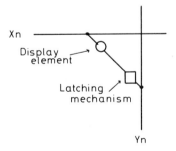

Fig. 3.18 Crosspoint latch

Fig. 3.19 illustrates one practical implementation of such a system. If we supply a sufficiently large voltage to the anode of the circuit, the thyristor will switch on, and only when the supply is removed (or significantly lowered) will the latching effect be lost. This type of latch could well be used in fig. 3.18. The method of addressing is somewhat different to that used in real time displays, as we have to provide the necessary latching pulses and sustain voltages. The write cycle is as

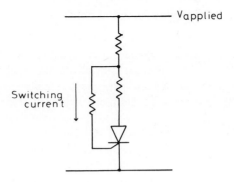

Switching current

$V_{applied}$

Fig. 3.19 Thyristor action

follows. Initially all drivers are off. The display is not addressed. This has the effect of clearing the latches. The next phase is to provide a 'holding' voltage to the elements. This is a voltage which is not great enough to switch any elements on, but will sustain elements which become switched on subsequently. The matrix can now be addressed very much as for real time multiplexing except that the half voltages are superimposed upon the holding voltage. The elements at the crosspoints of the full select voltage would now be triggered and the holding voltage ensures that they stay on. This type of display only requires updating when information on the screen has to be updated, and of course the screen is its own memory which offers savings in the system electronics. The timing and sequencing for such a display is shown in fig. 3.20. There are many advantages to this method of display drive. The main ones arise from the fact that the display is on continuously. This means that there is only one write cycle, there is no flicker for most of the time, and the luminance is not degraded by the duty ratio. The problems of pulsed operation are minimised, and with an optimised driver arrangement it is possible to reduce driver costs to a minimum. Some examples are given in chapter 7. Lastly, electrical noise is reduced.

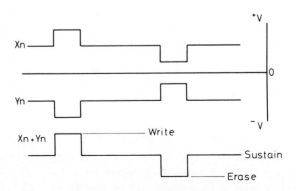

Fig. 3.20 Memory in d.c. systems

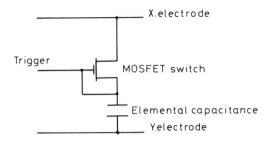

Fig. 3.21 Storage using capacitance multiplication

The second class of memory display is that which uses a capacitive multiplication circuit. This is a way of making the most of the inherent capacitance of many dot-matrix displays by using it to store information. The multiplication is achieved by incorporating a transistor, usually field effect, in the way shown in fig. 3.21. If a charge is placed on the capacitor C (which can be the elemental capacitance, the transistor's gate capacitance or a discrete capacitor), then the transistor will switch on. The transistor provides isolation between the capacitor and the display in such a way that the charge will hold the transistor on for some considerable time. If we include such devices in a display we can select elements by charging the appropriate capacitors. These will then act as a memory. In practice the capacitors have to be refreshed periodically as leakage of charge is inevitable. The rate of refresh is considerably lower than that needed for real time addressing. Many of the benefits associated with latched displays can be realised. It is quite difficult to make fault free areas of thin film transistors (which is the most common substrate for this type of storage of display). Several examples of this form of addressing exist mainly where the drive requirements are nominal; such is the case with liquid crystal displays.

3.5.8 Summary of matrix multiplexing

Matrix multiplexing offers several advantages over direct addressing:

The number of drivers required is reduced.
The number of display connections is reduced, making a remote siting of the display simpler.
Multiplexing is more compatible with integrated circuit technology.

The following considerations are important:

Flicker has to be minimised by adequate scanning rates.
Contrast is likely to be poorer than that obtainable with direct addressing because of partial element selection and crosstalk effects.
The x/y matrix connections must be such that they can carry higher pulse currents without undue voltage drops which would cause non-uniformity.
Display elements need to operate under short pulse conditions. We have to

consider the effects of saturation and thermal dissipation and delay times.
Display drivers may have to tolerate surge currents to cope with display capacitance.
The maximum matrix size is always limited by these restrictions. One method of increasing matrix size is to use a storage technique, where the refresh requirements are much less stringent.

There is much more that can be said about this form of display addressing, but this is best discussed in context, i.e. chapter 7.

3.6   Scanning

Scanning is an addressing technique that has been employed for some time in the cathode ray tube. It is one of the most economical forms of display addressing because only two drivers are required, one for each axis. As this form of addressing is so well explained elsewhere, we shall not consider its operation in any detail. It is useful to understand its principal characteristics as these serve as a comparison with the addressing techniques that we have already looked at.

Essentially scanning involves the deflection of a beam of light or electrons over a target so that an image may be built up on the target. The raster scan is often used and this is illustrated in fig. 3.22. The requirements of scanning drivers are that they must be able to deflect the beam accurately and rapidly. The picture must appear stable, and unless we employ a storage technique (below) we will have to refresh the target regularly.

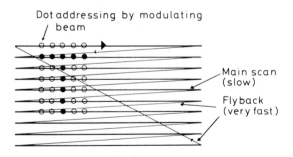

Fig. 3.22 Dot matrix using a raster scanned display

The intensity of the transmitted beam will have to be high to accommodate the very low duty ratios which will be encountered. In matrix multiplexing the duty ratio was shown to be 1/(number of lines). In scanned displays, the duty ratio is 1/(number of elements). Fig. 3.23 shows a comparison between the two addressing modes, which gives a clear indication of the large overdrive needed to scan successfully.

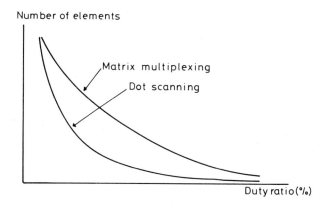

Fig. 3.23 Comparison of duty ratios. Scanning versus line dumping

The electron beam fulfils these requirements, and more recently examples of optical beam scanned displays have emerged as a result of advances in laser technology. The difficulties of deflecting optical beams has led to the development of memory or storage systems where the beam speed and intensity can be conceded. The analogies between this and the application of memory techniques to matrix multiplexing is clear. Fig. 3.24 outlines this technique. The target is made of a storage material which retains the information supplied by the scanning beam. There only needs to be one write cycle, and some mechanism for erasure. In many applications the picture can be 'built up' relatively slowly.

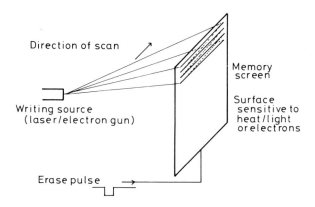

Fig. 3.24 Principles of memory screen operation

Scanning is undoubtedly a successful technique. Its longevity is assured, but there are many areas where multiplexing or direct addressing have become the preferred approach. The drawbacks of scanning can be summarised as follows:

Although only two drivers are used, these can be quite elaborate and consequently expensive. Integrated drivers and simple interconnection to multiplexed displays is causing bigger and bigger arrays to become cost competitive.

Most scanning systems take up space, which is at a premium in much modern equipment. Again the inherent thinness of many other technologies is attractive. Very few scanned display systems exist. Although it is generally agreed that it is a desirable addressing system, it is not easy to apply to many display technologies. The ratio of multiplexed to scanned displays will become quite clear in the next few chapters.

Chapter 4

Display technologies

4.1 Classification

Essentially the display system is set by the technology of the display device itself, and in the following two chapters the display device technologies are considered in some detail.

The interest and market size of alphanumeric display has prompted the investigation of a wide variety of phenomena potentially capable of producing or modulating light. The former are classed as active displays and the latter as passive. As a result of these investigations there has emerged a number of technologies that offer practical systems for electronic alphanumeric display; several of these are commercially available, others are in development or research.

Most of the technologies are unrelated and each must be discussed separately. However, a broad grouping can be made by considering the address methods (see chapter 3). There are two basic methods of presenting alphanumeric information electronically; in one the viewing screen is scanned by an electron beam or a light beam which is modulated to produce the necessary pattern, and in the other the display screen is made up of a number of elements (a two-dimensional matrix) and the pattern is obtained by electrically activating the required elements. These two groups, termed scanned and matrix displays, are covered respectively in chapter 5 and chapter 6.

4.2 General survey

Table 4.1 lists the main technologies that will be discussed further under the appropriate headings in chapters 5 and 6. Also listed are some of the parameters pertinent to their display applications. The information given, however, should be treated with some caution because much of it is indicative rather than absolute, and some needs qualification. For example, as already discussed, the contrast ratio depends on the duty factor and on the ambient light and can be improved by filters at the expense of luminance. Also display is very much a field of on-going development and device characteristics are continuously being improved, so that information in table 4.1 is likely to become dated.

Table 4.1 Display technologies and their characteristics

Address method	Technology	Operation mode	Display type		Electrical characteristics					Visual characteristics		
			Small numeric	Large alphanumeric	Operating potential	Switching potential	Storage	Switching speed		Colour	Efficiency (1 m/W)	Contrast ratio†
								On	Off			
Electron beam	C.R.T. (conventional)	Active	No	Yes	10–50 kV		No	100 element per µs	100 µs	Any	10–50	40:1
	Cathodochromic	Reflective	No	Yes	10–50 kV		Yes	1 element per µs		Blue on white	–	
	Titus	Transmissive	No	Yes	10–50 kV		No	100 element per µs			–	
	Eidophor	Transmissive	No	Yes	10–50 kV		No	100 element per µs		Full colour possible	– –	
Light beam	Laser scan	Active	No	Yes	(100–500 V)		No					
Matrix	L.E.D.	Active	Yes	Limited	2 V	2 V	No	10 ns	10 ns	Red (yellow, green)	0.1	40:1
	Gas discharge	Active	Yes	Yes	100–200 V	<100 V	Possible	20 µs	10–100 µs	Orange	0.2	40:1
	Electro-luminescent	Active	Yes	Yes	100 V +	100 V	No	500 µs	500 µs	Yellow	0.5	20:1
	Vacuum fluorescent	Active	Yes	Limited	25 V	25 V	No	<1 µs	<1 µs	Green	⌐1.2*	40:1
	Filament	Active	Yes	No	2–5 V	2–5 V	No			Red	1 to 5	40:1
	Liquid crystal	Reflect or transmit	Yes	Limited	5–25 V	5–25 V	Possible	10 ms	500 ms	(Grey)	–	20:1
	Electrochromic	Reflective	Yes	No	1.5 V	1.5 V	Yes	100 ms	100 ms	Mauve or blue	–	20:1
	Electrophoretic	Reflective	Yes	Possible	100 V	100 V	Yes	10 ms	10 ms	Any	–	50:1
	Ferroelectric	Reflect or transmit	Yes		50 V	50 V	Yes	10 ns	10 ns	(Grey)	–	10:1

* This includes heater dissipation.
† Contrast ratio for emissive displays are at low ambient light.

The operation mode describes whether the display technology produces an active or a passive display. Passive displays can be ones in which transmitted light from an auxiliary light source is modulated by the device or they can produce a pattern which is viewed by reflected light rather like a printed page. In the latter case the ambient light is utilised and the power consumption is likely to be low. Also there will be no upper limit to the illumination; the display will be readable in direct sunlight. Some passive displays can be used in either mode.

Under display types it is observed that the scanned displays are aimed at large character capacity displays, and are generally not suitable for a limited register of numerals. The conventional cathode ray tube dominates this area of application. Some of the matrix displays, particularly gas discharges, are challenging the supremacy of the c.r.t., mainly for medium capacity displays of 200 to 1000 characters. Their main application, however, is for numeric displays of up to twenty numerals, where seven-bar format devices predominate and where scanned displays do not compete.

The importance of the operational voltage is in the economy of the circuit. The actual supply voltage to the device is less important than the switching voltage since this must be driven from the logic circuit. In matrix displays a large number of drivers are required and there is a great deal of advantage if these can be integrated. The higher the voltage the more difficult and expensive become the integrated drivers.

The facility for storage in the display can be important for some applications. It allows slower switching speeds to be employed and alleviates problems of peak luminance and flicker. A further advantage can be exploited if the storage is non-volatile, that is the display remains visible even when the power supply to the display device is switched off.

Unless storage is available the switching speed dictates the number of elements that can be sequentially addressed and thus the character capacity of the display. The efficiency can also be a limitation to the display capacity both by the mean power required and by the pulsed power. It is particularly important for battery operated displays.

The contrast ratios given in table 4.1 are purely indicative. In particular, the values given for emissive displays are those quoted for low ambient light conditions and basically indicate the amount of light coming from the unlit elements when the rest of the display is operational. In other words the reflected ambient light is considered to be small or negligible. In a well lit room the values could drop down to less than 4:1.

4.2.1 Scanned displays

The scanned display technologies were essentially developed for television and have been adapted or modified for alphanumeric or graphic display application. In the conventional c.r.t. the electron beam scans a phosphor screen, the electron energy activating the phosphor to give light output, so called cathodoluminescence. There are, however, other methods of employing a scanned electron-beam for producing a display as will be discussed in chapter 5. Of particular interest are the technologies where the electron beam impinges on a material or structure acting as a light valve. The energy of the electron beam changes the material from opaque to transparent or vice versa and the pattern set up by the electron beam is then projected onto a screen by a subsidiary light source. There are also some types of cathode ray tube designed specifically for alphanumeric display, an example being the 'charactron' whereby the character is formed by passing the beam through a stencil (see chapter 5).

Light beam displays became possible with the invention of the laser. The laser produces a well collimated, high intensity beam which is well adapted for projecting a scanned picture onto a screen. The problem is in modulating and deflecting the beam. Various systems have been described using rotating precision mirrors or electro-optic crystals. They are all rather expensive and complex. There is also a problem in obtaining a laser with reasonable efficiency. The systems have been mainly aimed at large screen television but special deflecting techniques for alphanumeric displays have been described. It is also possible to use the energy in the laser beam to activate a light valve as with the electron beam.

Scanned displays in general scan a dot at a time and therefore the duty factor is n where n is the total number of display elements. For an emissive display this implies a peak luminance of n times the mean luminance unless storage can be incorporated into the display. For a high resolution display giving 6000 or so characters n would be 10^6 and a peak luminance of 340×10^6 cd/m^2 would be required. There is also the problem in high character capacity displays of response time; each dot or element will only be activated for 20 μs every 20 ms for a 50 Hz field rate. Such factors therefore as efficiency, ability to focus the beam to a small spot size, writing speed, the ability to produce high peak output, and whether storage or a long decay time can be incorporated are important to this type of display. Problems of resolution, contrast and stability are unique to the scanned display, and may be measured in a different way to the matrix displays. There is also the possibility of spatial distortion and jitter, which places constraints on the circuit to produce linear scans which are stable. To focus and scan the beam a certain depth is required either behind or in front of the viewing screen, which can be an embarrassment for some applications. It is particularly true of the c.r.t. where the bulky vacuum envelope can take up valuable space. Attempts to obtain flat versions are being carried out in several laboratories and the various approaches will be described. However, a satisfactory solution has not yet been developed for commercial exploitation.

4.2.2   Matrix displays

Of the nine technologies listed five are commercially available and three others are in development, one being at a stage where development samples are available. The bulk of the market is shared almost equally by three of the technologies, namely light emitting diodes (l.e.d.s), liquid crystals and gas discharges. Their main competitors are the vacuum fluorescent and incandescent filament displays.

The devices offered are commonly in a seven-bar matrix configuration packaged as single-character devices or as multiples of up to sixteen characters in one unit. Some of the technologies are available in 5 x 7 dot-matrix format suitable for alphanumeric application, and a few offer the possibilities of a large dot-matrix panel for displaying several lines of alphanumeric characters. The gas discharge technology is unique in also offering formed characters, thus eliminating the need for a pattern encoder. The list is by no means exhaustive and there are several other technologies being investigated in research, mainly passive displays. The various technologies have little in common and, as can be seen from table 4.1, have rather different characteristics. They all have their advantages and disadvantages and none of them are ideal for all applications.

The l.e.d.s and electroluminescent devices depend on similar principles and are both solid state devices. However, whereas the l.e.d. is monocrystalline, the electroluminescent display is in the form of a powder layer or a thin film. Because of this, electroluminescent devices are more suitable for larger area displays and in fact are being developed as a contender to the c.r.t. for medium capacity alphanumeric panels. Ferroelectric devices are also solid state and, rather like a ceramic, they are formed by sintering at high temperature. They could offer the ideal medium for a solid state display but at present they are still at a research stage.

Liquid crystals, electrophoretic and electrochromic devices depend on phenomena in liquids and they must be contained in envelopes which are hermetically sealed. They tend to be similar in structure with the liquid held between two glass plates on which electrode patterns are deposited. The liquid crystal is the only one which has reached production, but the others are in the development area and could emerge as competitors in the near future. In some electrochromic devices an electrolytic gel is used instead of a liquid.

The vacuum fluorescent and incandescent filament technologies require a vacuum environment and gas discharge devices operate in inert gas at reduced pressure. All three therefore require a gas tight envelope with a viewing window. For the seven-bar numerical displays the structures tend to be similar for all three with glass envelopes in a flat pack configuration. The vacuum fluorescent device is essentially a cathodoluminescent device employing similar principles to the c.r.t. but using a low voltage activated phosphor. The commercial devices using this technology are mainly numeric but dot-matrix panels have been introduced with a limited character capacity. Gas discharges are the oldest display technology. Aimed first at the numerical market, they have been developed for large capacity alphanumerics and represent the main challenge to the c.r.t. Such displays are known as plasma panels and they have been constructed with matrixes up to 1000 x 1000 elements.

Finally there are several other ideas described in the literature for matrix type displays, such as suspended magnetic particles, magneto-optic and electrofluorescent displays. There is also a fixed matrix type of c.r.t. and matrix electromechanical devices aimed at large size characters for announcement boards. Such devices will be given a brief mention in chapter 6, but the chapter will chiefly cover the main technologies, giving details of the physical principles, device construction, characteristics and performance.

Since each technology could warrant a book in itself, the cover here is of necessity restricted. It is hoped, however, that the essential information for understanding the mechanism and appreciating the potential of the various devices will be adequate for those engineers wishing to exploit alphanumeric displays. For more comprehensive studies references are given to detailed investigations or textbooks on the individual technologies.

Chapter 5

Scanned displays

5.1 The cathode ray tube

The conventional monochrome cathode ray tube has been around for many years and is so well known and established that there is little need to delve deeply into the physics of the device or its characteristics. Backed by the huge domestic television market the c.r.t. has been continuously improved over the years and represents an economic display that is second to none in applications where a large number of picture elements are required.

Its main attribute is the simplicity of addressing, resulting from the beam scanning function, especially for serially fed information. This allows economic analogue circuits to be used with the minimum number of connections. Also mass production for the domestic market makes the c.r.t. itself a cheap device. Although it requires a dot sequential address system, the high efficiency, 40 lm/W, and the ability to emit high peak luminance, means that the c.r.t. can give adequate luminance at reasonable powers for most applications even though the duty factor is high.

Basically the c.r.t. consists of an electron gun, a beam focussing and deflection system, and a phosphor screen laid on the front face of the tube into which it is sealed. The whole is evacuated to a vacuum pressure of better than 10^{-5} N/m^2. The basic electron gun consists of a thermionic cathode biased negatively relative to the screen and two axial symmetric electrodes or grids in front of it; the first grid controls the current, i.e. modulates the beam, whilst the second accelerates the electrons. The grids are usually cup shaped with central apertures, and their shapes and spacing are designed to act as an electrostatic lens to produce a cross-over in the beam in front of the cathode. The beam is then focussed to give a small spot image of the cross-over on the phosphor screen by an additional focussing system. The raster on the screen is produced by two orthogonal deflecting systems between the focussing system and the screen. Both the focussing and the deflecting systems can be either electrostatic or magnetic and the arrangements for both systems are illustrated in the typical early designs of fig. 5.1.

The behaviour of electron beams in electrostatic and magnetic fields stems from the basic law relating the force on a moving electron F due to such fields expressed in vector notation as

$$F = e\epsilon + e\,(v \times B) \tag{5.1}$$

where e is the electron charge, ϵ is the electric field, v is the velocity of the electron

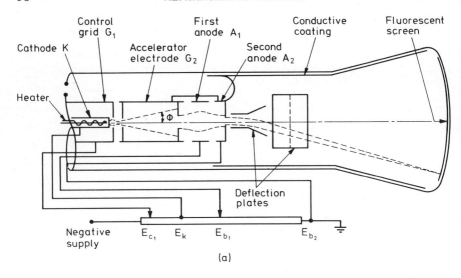

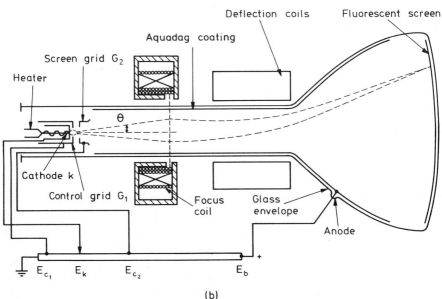

Fig. 5.1 Schematic diagram of early cathode ray tubes, (a) with electrostatic focusing and deflection, (b) with magnetic focusing and deflection

and B is the magnetic field. It has been extensively studied and is well documented in textbooks on electron optics, for example that by Paszkowski.[1] The design of the electron gun, focussing and deflecting systems in the c.r.t. is based on these well defined electron optic principles and for more details the reader is referred to the comprehensive book on the subject by Zworykin and Morton.[2]

Electrostatic deflection gives a good linearity of deflection against applied voltage and allows random access but requires a greater distance between the gun and screen than for a magnetic deflection system. It also has a limited deflection angle. Electrostatic deflection c.r.t.s are mainly restricted to oscilloscope applications, whilst for alphanumeric displays the magnetic deflection t.v. types are employed. The performance is comparable if not better than for electrostatic deflection but random access is not possible.

The modern tube has electrostatic focussing with normally 5 cup electrodes, the last three cup's, termed anodes number 2, 3 and 4, being used as a focussing lens. A schematic drawing of a modern tube is given in fig. 5.2. Anodes 2 and 4 are normally

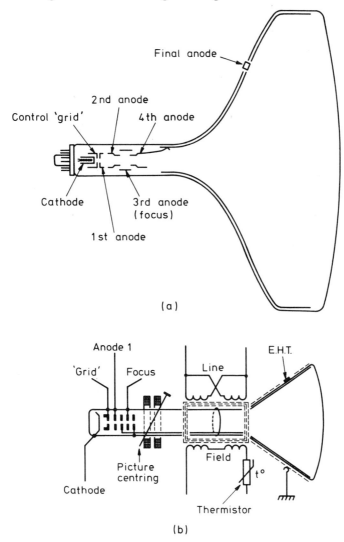

Fig. 5.2 Schematic diagram of modern television tube

connected to the graphic coating on the tube walls which contacts the phosphor screen and represents the final accelerating voltage electrode. The electron gun and focussing electrodes are compact, fitting into a tube neck of 20 to 36 mm diameter and about 10 cm in length. The deflection angle is commonly 110°, although 90° deflection tubes are also used; the angle refers to the maximum deflection, which for a tube having a rectangular faceplate will be along the diagonal.

The light from the screen is produced by cathodoluminescence, i.e. luminescence caused by the bombarding electrons. Luminescence is the general terms covering all phenomena in which light is emitted from matter on the absorption of energy but excluding thermal radiation. If the emission is immediate and ceases more or less directly the source of energy is removed, it is termed fluorescence, whereas if the emission persists for some time after the removal of energy it is called phosphorescence. Although several materials show cathodoluminescence, the materials which have sufficient effect for display purposes are the crystalline solids known as phosphors. Unlike thermal radiation where the emission is an averaged effect from all the atoms, fluorescence occurs at discrete emission sites known as 'activators' which are normally impurity atoms. The process of cathodoluminescence is complex, involving several steps. The fast electrons penetrate the solid, ionizing some of the atoms by ejecting electrons from the inner shells. These secondary electrons lose their energy to valence shell electrons producing electron–hole pairs with an energy equal to the bandgap plus their kinetic energy. Finally the electron–hole pairs thermalise and excite the 'activators' to produce the photons. According to the type of activator, two important classes of phosphors can be defined. First are the group II–VI and III–V semiconductors which include the widely used ZnS and CdS phosphors. In these semiconductors, luminance occurs by donor–acceptor recombination at impurity levels; an electron trapped at a donor level recombines with a hole trapped at an acceptor level, giving off photon emission. The other class consists of oxygen dominated lattices in which the activator has been introduced as an impurity. Among these phosphors are the oxides, phosphates, silicates and aluminates of Mg, Ca, Ba, Zn, Y and La. In this class the electron–hole pairs migrate to the activator to cause it to excite and decay to its ground state with the emission of light. For a more detailed description of cathodoluminescence the reader is referred to an article by Garlick.[3]

Considerable research and development has been carried out on phosphors for c.r.t.s. The most suitable phosphors are registered with the Joint Electron Devices Engineering Council (J.E.D.E.C.) in the U.S.A. and allocated a number, from P1 to P52. The details of these registered phosphors are published by the JEDEC[4] together with their characteristics. Some of the phosphors were developed for instrument applications or radar and are not pertinent to alphanumeric display tubes. Table 5.1 lists a selection of the registered phosphors with emphasis on those useful for alphanumeric or graphic display.

The terminology used, for example ZnS:Cu, refers to the host phosphor and activator, in this case zinc sulphide with copper impurity as activator. The colour co-ordinates are given rather than the peak wavelength as some of the phosphors have a wide bandwidth; they refer to the C.I.E. diagram fig. 5.3 (see also chapter 1). Since the behaviour of a phosphor depends on a number of factors such as the

J.E.D.E.C. number	Composition	Colour	C.I.E. chromaticity co-ordinate x	y	Luminous efficiency K (lm/W) of the radiation	Phosphor efficiency (%)	Decay time to 10%
P2	$ZnS:Cu$	Y–G	0.279	0.534	465	7	70 μs
P4 (all sulphide)	$ZnS:Ag$ / $ZnCdS:Ag$	(B) W / (Y)	0.270	0.300	285	15	50 μs
P11	$ZnS:Ag$	B	0.139	0.148	140	20	60 μs
P18	$CaMgSiO_3:Ti$ / $CaBeSiO_3:Mn$	(B) W / (Y)	0.333	0.347	240		55 μs
P20	$ZnCdS:Ag$	Y–G	0.426	0.546	480	15	60–250 μs
P22* (P1) (P27)	$ZnS:Ag$ / $Zn_2SiO_4:Mn$ / $Zn_3(PO_4)_2:Mn$	B / G / R	0.146 / 0.218 / 0.674	0.052 / 0.712 / 0.326	57 / 520 / 165	15 / 6 / 5	60 μs / 20 ms / 27 ms
P22	$ZnS:Ag$ / $ZnCdS:Cu$ / $Y_2O_2S:Eu$	B / G / R	0.155 / 0.326 / 0.623	0.067 / 0.591 / 0.342	85 / 514 / 265	20 / 18 / 13	60 μs / 1.0 ms / 1.0 ms
P23	Similar to P4	W	0.364	0.377	330	15	50 μs
P24	ZnO	G	0.245	0.441	365	5	1.5 μs
P31	$ZnS:Cu$	G (low current)	0.226	0.528	425	22	60 μs
		(high current)	0.193	0.420	350		
P39	$Zn_2SiO_4:Mn:As$	G	0.223	0.698	515	–	150 ms
P44	$La_2O_2S:Tb$	Y–G	0.300	0.596	548	11	1.2 ms
P45	$Y_2O_2S:Tb$	W	0.253	0.312	289	3	1.8 ms
P50† (8 kV)	$Y_2O_3:Eu$	R	0.655	0.340		7.5	1 ms
(15 kV)	$ZnCdS:Cu$	G	0.398	0.546	514	18	1 ms

* P22 covers the phosphors for colour television and only two from six sets are given here.
† P50 is a voltage dependent phosphor giving red at 8 kV, green at 15 kV and intermediate colours between.

particle size, the thickness, method of activation and operating characteristics of the electron beam, the efficiencies and decay times must not be taken as absolute but as an indication of the order of magnitude.

The common phosphor used for black-and-white television is P4 and consists of a mixture of two phosphors, a blue and a yellow. The shade of white depends on the ratio of the two constituents and over the years has tended toward a 'bluer' shade. All phosphors used for colour television are covered by P22. There have been six sets of the three colour phosphors registered between 1961 and 1975; the two given in table 5.1 are the first and the latest to be published. The main changes have been in the red phosphor and the rare earth activated phosphor supersedes the earlier phosphates or sulphides. The latest P22 phosphors are widely used today and the main advances have been in the depositing techniques to give enhanced contrast by either providing a black surround to the colour dots or pigmenting the phosphor. In the pigmented phosphor, the phosphor particles are coated with fine pigmentary-filter particles of the same colour as the light emitted by the phosphor. The colour points of the P22 phosphors are shown on the C.I.E. chart in fig. 5.3.

The most interesting development in cathodoluminescent phosphors has been

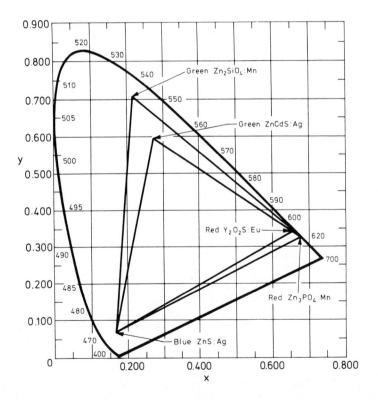

Fig. 5.3 C.I.E. chromaticity diagram showing the colour co-ordinates for colour television

the voltage dependent colour phosphors, an example of which is P50. Often referred to as 'onion skin' phosphors they consist of a 25 μm diameter core of one colour phosphor, with a layer of fine particle phosphor deposited around it of another colour, similar to the pigmented phosphor. The resultant phosphor mixture is then applied to the tube using normal techniques. The tube incorporating such a phosphor is known as the penetron tube. At low voltage the electrons do not penetrate the outer layer and the coating only fluoresces. At higher voltages the electrons also activate the core, and a critical value is reached where they pass through the outer layer and emission is obtained only from the core. For P50 the core is a green phosphor which is coated with a red phosphor, the required voltages for the two colours being given in table 5.1.

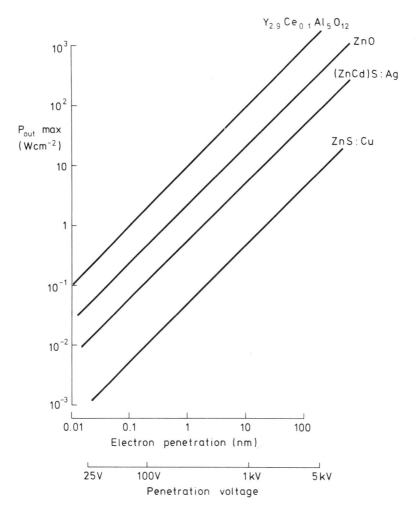

Fig. 5.4 Output power of a phosphor as a function of the energy or penetration of the bombarding electrons

The phosphors are deposited on the glass faceplate and have a high resistivity. In order to prevent them charging up under the electron bombardment a thin conducting layer, 0.2 to 0.5 μm thick, of aluminium is normally deposited onto the phosphor layer. This aluminium backing also improves the light output by reflecting the light from the phosphor which would normally be radiated back into the tube.

The luminance of the display depends on the input power and the efficiency. The efficiency figures given in table 5.1 are percentage power efficiencies and can be converted to lumens per input power by multiplying by K. The maximum luminance is limited by the total number of activating centres present, which in turn depends on the electron penetration. Increasing the voltage increases the maximum output power that can be obtained, illustrated in fig. 5.4. There is, however, another limitation due to the fact that the efficiency of the phosphor decreases with increasing temperature, a phenomenon known as thermal quenching. This can cause saturation of the emission before the maximum set by the number of activating centres is reached.

The description so far has referred to the monochrome c.r.t. and for most alphanumeric displays this fulfils the requirements. However, it is clear that with the expansion of the alphanumeric display applications the use of colour tubes to add extra information will take an increasing fraction of the market in the future. A full description of the shadow mask tube, the principal c.r.t. for colour television, is to be found in textbooks on television and will only be outlined here. Basically the tube has three electron guns, one modulated by the signal for the red constituent of the picture, one for the blue and one for the green. Beams from the three guns are focussed through an aperture plate (shadow mask) onto the phosphor screen. Since the beams emanate from different positions, they will focus at different points on the screen having passed through any one hole in the aperture plate (see fig. 5.5). The screen is made up of a mosaic of the three colour phosphors aligned with the shadow mask such that the beam from the gun giving the red information can only illuminate red phosphor dots and similarly for the blue and green. The alignment is achieved by using the shadow mask as a processing mask in the deposition of the phosphor dots. Thus each screen corresponds to a particular mask and the two are kept together after laying the screen and incorporated in the final tube. The guns can be positioned either at the corners of a triangle as in fig. 5.5, the so-called delta gun arrangement, or mounted in line horizontally. The latter makes adjustment of the deflector coils, etc. to minimise distortion and colour aberration easier and supersedes the delta gun system. A modification of the system is seen in the 'Trinitron' from Sony whereby a single gun is used with the beam being split into three.

The main problem with the shadow mask tube for alphanumeric information is resolution. There is a mechanical limitation on the shadow mask aperture and phosphor dot resolution which is generally of the order of 0.75 mm pitch for the three-dot pattern. However, in order to ensure that at least one dot is fully activated, the beam diameter encompasses two to three dots of the same colour. This gives adequate resolution for the bandwidth of television but allows a maximum of 3000 characters for alphanumerics, even on a 26 inch diameter tube. However, the design of high resolution shadow mask tubes with a finer dot pitch are under

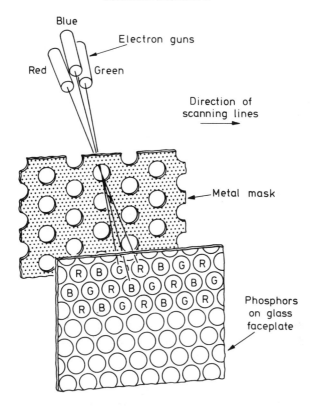

Fig. 5.5 Schematic diagram showing the principle of the shadow mask colour tube

investigation[5] and development samples with a dot pitch of 0.31 mm are available from one or two companies. The higher resolution, however, is achieved at the cost of brightness.

The alternative approach of using a voltage dependent phosphor in the 'penetron' tube does not have the same problem and offers potentially a higher resolution. It does, however, require a high voltage switch and a change of the scanning circuit for each colour and also the number of colours available is more limited. The possibility of current sensitive phosphors has also been reported where the colour changes with the current density.

The standard t.v. monochrome tube is suitable for alphanumeric application but requires better control of the deflector coils and circuits to ensure the required linearity. The normal 625-line resolution limits the character capacity to around 3000, but tubes are now available with higher resolution up to 1000 lines. This is mainly a matter of the electron gun design, but also a good quality screen is required without graininess or defects. For a full page of A4 typescript a resolution better than 1000 lines is required, especially if good 9 x 7 matrix characters are needed. At present the c.r.t. is used in half page editors for word processing, and the full page editor awaits the development of a suitable tube.

A design of tube which could fulfil the specification for a full page editor is the 'Charactron' designed for alphanumeric display. The charactron is a c.r.t. that has an internal stencil with an array of character shaped openings through which the electron beam passes to give it a character shaped cross-section. An electron optic lens then focuses the beam onto the phosphor screen so that the chosen character is displayed. Continued improvements to the tube have been made and the present design[6] uses magnetic deflection for selecting the character and for scanning the character positions on the screen. The tube will display thirty lines of 132 characters on a 38 cm (15 in) screen with a brightness of 300 cd/m^2. The font can be chosen to give superior character shapes than obtainable with dot-matrix formats.

The display on a cathode ray tube is not completely satisfactory. Fluctuations and instabilities in the voltages or circuit components will cause jitter (slight spatial movement) of the characters, whilst the scanning rate is often not fast enough to completely avoid flicker. It is difficult to obtain a linear scan which will prevent slight distortion at the corners and the sharpest focus cannot be maintained over the whole screen, which in any case is not 'flat'.

At this time it is not known to what extent these factors cause eye strain or fatigue, but because c.r.t. displays are coming into offices there is concern among trades unions and governments about their effects. In some countries, Sweden for example, legislation is being introduced to define conditions and restrict the hours that an operator should spend at a work station with a c.r.t. display, and no doubt other countries will follow. However, the shortcomings of the display are not the main criticism of the c.r.t. for alphanumeric application; it is the bulk of the tube or more correctly the depth required behind the screen which is its greatest disadvantage. It is particularly objectionable for small table-top equipment, but it also represents a limitation on the maximum screen size. It is not surprising, therefore, that in the quest for flat displays the c.r.t. has not been neglected, and considerable effort in research has been expended on the design of flat c.r.t.s.

5.2   Flat cathode ray tubes

The earliest attempts at a flat c.r.t. were made in the 1950s by Aiken[7] and Gabor[8], both using a conventional electron gun mounted with its axis parallel to the screen, and deflecting the beam onto the screen with electrostatic fields. The principle of the Aiken tube is illustrated in fig. 5.6. The beam emerging from the gun runs parallel to the bottom edge of the screen being deflected upwards by a series of horizontal deflection plates. Suitable variation of the voltages on these plates with time produced the line scan and a series of vertical deflection plates caused the ascending beam to deflect towards the phosphor screen to produce the field scan. Monochrome tubes with 15 in screens were demonstrated. The Gabor tube was similar but more complicated with a self-scanning system using secondary emitting electrodes. Neither of these early designs was commercially successful, but interest in the approach has recently been revived by the design of a small monochrome tube for pocket television. The tube has been developed by Sinclair Radionics Ltd[9] and measures about 15 cm x 5 cm x 2.5 cm with a picture diameter of about 7.5 cm.

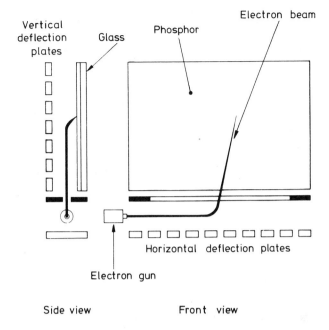

Fig. 5.6 Schematic diagram of the Aiken type flat cathode ray tube[7]. (Copyright © 1957 I.E.E.E.)

The tube is illustrated in fig. 5.7. The electron gun is located to one side of the screen with its axis parallel to the plane of the screen to produce a beam which can be deflected vertically by the first set of deflection plates. By producing a scanned height on the screen only one half of that required and magnifying the picture height optically using an external cylindrical Fresnel lens, deflection power is reduced and screen brightness increased at the expense of the viewing angle.

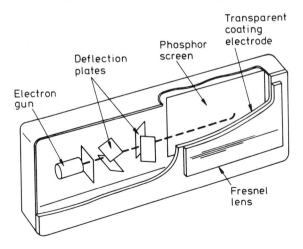

Fig. 5.7 Schematic diagram of the Sinclair flat c.r.t. for pocket television[9]

Horizontal deflection is also produced electrostatically by the second set of deflection plates and a final transverse field between the screen and a tin oxide conducting film on the viewing window. This arrangement helps to maintain the spot shape by keeping the beam landing angle approximately constant. Keystone distortion, due to the greater vertical deflection angle required nearer the gun, is reduced by superimposing a correction field on the main vertical scanning field. As the phosphor is viewed from the electron impact side, the required voltage can be much less than for a conventional c.r.t., i.e. around 5 kV, a factor that also reduces the power dissipation. It is claimed that the tube can be scaled up for larger displays and that it is possible to incorporate colour.

A completely different approach has been described by Goede[10] whereby an extended electron source is used and a gating system directs the electrons to the required position on the screen. The cathode consisted of an array of thermionic filament emitters, and the gating was achieved by a series of aperture plates, with holes corresponding to the number of display elements, and carrying electrode patterns. An exploded view of a simplified tube with sixty-four display elements is shown in fig. 5.8; each of the aperture plates, designated switching plates, has two separately connected electrode patterns which split the electron beam. Potentials are applied to the electrodes of each plate so that half the channels have an electron-accelerating potential and half have an electron-retarding potential. In this way each plate halves the number of channels through which the beam can pass until, at the last plate, a single beam emerges and impinges on the phosphor screen. By suitably addressing the plates, the emerging beam can be scanned through the sixty-four

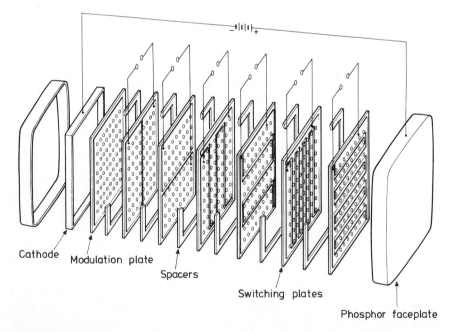

Fig. 5.8 Exploded view of the flat cathode ray tube described by Goede[10].
(Copyright © 1973 I.E.E.E.)

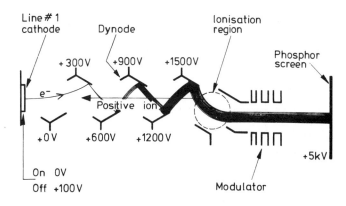

Fig. 5.9 Schematic diagram of c.r.t. design by Schulman and Schwartz[11] (Permission for reprint courtesy Society for Information Display)

positions and modulated by a further aperture plate. For a larger number of elements the plates carried several separately connected electrode patterns. A 512-character panel has been demonstrated and a 512 x 512 element panel has been described.

A similar idea of gating electrons from an extended source was suggested by Schulman and Schwartz in 1976.[11] In their arrangement, a small initial electron current was amplified by passing it down an electron multiplier consisting of a series of dynodes. The emerging beam was then accelerated to the phosphor screen. The tube was filled with helium to a pressure of 10^{-1} N/m^2 so that a small fraction of the electrons from the multiplier created positive ions by ionising collisions with gas molecules. The ions created in the output region could pass back down the multiplier to impinge on the cathode and produce secondary electrons. In this way, a closed-loop feedback system was obtained to self-maintain the electron current. The principle is shown schematically in fig. 5.9. The cathodes were metal strips mounted horizontally, defining the rows; electrons were emitted when the cathode voltage was zero and suppressed when biased to 100 V. The columns were defined by the modulators mounted at the output of the multipliers and consisted of vertical metal strips with apertures at each row. The potential on the modulator strips gave the line scan and grey scale with suitable voltage waveforms. A simplified version was proposed by R.C.A. in which the dynodes and modulating electrodes are bonded onto glass strips sealed at right angles to the cathode plate.[12] The advantage of this 'box' structure is that the envelope (front and back plates) is supported by the glass strips. This is an important factor since the larger and flatter the c.r.t. screen is made, the thicker must be the glass to withstand the atmospheric pressure. This makes a large flat c.r.t. heavy unless the glass can be supported internally and thereby reduced in thickness. This is a feature of further designs by R.C.A. published in 1980.[13,14] In these designs multiple beams are guided parallel to the front face and turned through 90° to impinge on the phosphor in a line dumped system. The beams are produced preferably by an array of electron guns and confined in a plane parallel to the screen by a system of periodic focussing electrodes. They are separated

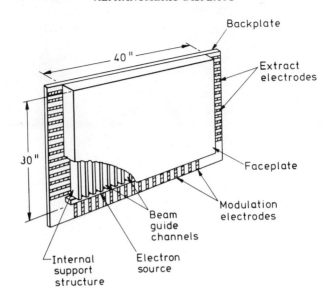

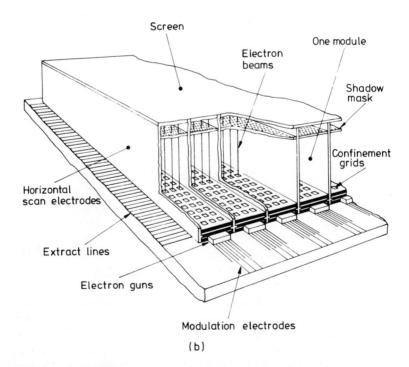

(b)

Fig. 5.10 Design principle of the R.C.A. flat t.v. tube described in 1980,[13],[14] (a) showing general layout, (b) showing detail of the channels. (Permission for reprint courtesy Society for Information Display)

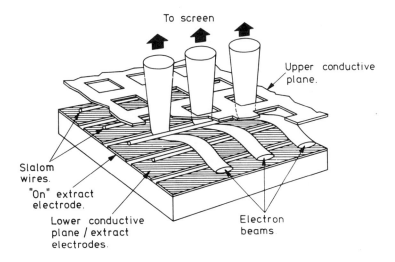

To screen

Upper conductive plane.

Slalom wires.

"On" extract electrode.

Lower conductive plane / extract electrodes.

Electron beams

Fig 5.11 Beam trajectory in the slalom type of R.C.A. tube. (Permission for reprint courtesy Society for Information Display)

by a channel structure which supports the front and back plates. The beams travel in a vertical direction and are extracted, focussed and accelerated to the phosphor screen by a series of horizontal electrodes deposited on the back plate combined with the periodic focussing electrodes. The basic structure is illustrated in fig. 5.10. Two periodic focussing electrode systems were described, one using two mesh grids and the other using a series of horizontal wires, designated the ladder and slalom guide systems respectively.[13] An illustration of the beam trajectory is shown in fig. 5.11 for the slalom system. A module 1 in wide and 12 in high has been success-fully addressed at t.v. rates giving a 340 cd/m^2 monochrome picture with acceptable contrast.

None of these flat c.r.t. tubes has reached commercial production at the time of writing, but future production of the Sinclair tube has been announced.

5.3 Projection systems

A flat display can be obtained by projecting an enlarged image of a c.r.t. picture by suitable optics onto a screen. The main interest here is large screen television but it could be applied to alphanumeric displays for announcement boards, etc. The problem with this type of display is in obtaining sufficient brightness. The luminance of the c.r.t. for a projection system needs to be several times higher than for a direct viewing tube owing to the magnification and the losses in the optics.

For economic reasons the optics must not be too great, and therefore they restrict the size of the c.r.t. to probably less than 5 in diameter. This implies a multiplication of at least 10, reducing the brightness by at least 100. Although the losses can be minimised by using suitable optics, nevertheless the amount of light reaching the screen is likely to be less than 30% of that emitted by the c.r.t. Thus in total the luminance must be at least 300 times that required for direct viewing. To obtain a high luminance a high accelerating voltage is required, 60–80 kV (see fig. 5.4), and this has problems of X-radiation which requires shielding. The maximum luminance then becomes a function of efficiency and power dissipation as discussed previously. The domestic projection sets which are available are restricted in screen size and need to be viewed in dimmed lighting. The normal phosphor used is the P45, and to obtain colour, three tubes are used with the appropriate colour filters. Often directional reflection screens are used to improve the luminance, but these must be curved to prevent specular reflections causing bright areas. A typical domestic projection t.v. is shown in fig. 5.12 and consists of the screen and the three-tube projection unit.

Alternative proposals have been made for large screen displays, in which an electron beam is used to address a light valve to form the picture and a powerful external light source is used to project the picture onto the screen. In this way a higher luminance can be obtained albeit at much lower efficiencies since the light source has to produce peak brightness continuously. Several systems have been suggested for the light valve but only one or two have reached commercial fruition. One of the earliest ideas, which was pioneered by Fischer in the 1940s[15] and

Fig. 5.12 Projection system for domestic television (courtesy of Philips Electrical Ltd.)

developed after his death by his team to eventual commercial exploitation, was the so-named 'Eidophor'.[16] Basically, the light valve consists of an oil film which is scanned by the electron beam. The beam charges up the film which is deformed by the electrostatic forces to form ripples. These ripples form a phase diffraction grating, which when placed in a dark field Schlieren system produces an intensity modulated image at the projection screen. The arrangement is shown diagrammatically in fig. 5.13. The xenon-lamp light source is imaged onto the mirror bar system, a series of thin strips with spaces between. This mirror system is situated at the radius of curvature of the concave mirror so that the image is reflected back onto the strips and no light passes through to the screen. When the oil layer on the concave mirror is deformed by the electron beam, the light rays are displaced by diffraction and pass between the mirror strips, and a picture of the charge pattern on the film is projected onto the screen. The viscosity of the oil is such that it takes a frame time for the deformation to decay. The oil film is continuously fed onto the mirror which slowly rotates, and the tube is continuously vacuum pumped. The system is used extensively for theatre t.v. and it is remarkable that what appears to be a rather crude arrangement in this electronic age, should produce such high definition pictures so successfully. A conceptually similar system has been developed by General Electric Corporation with a sealed-off tube capable of producing full colour t.v.;[17] the Eidophor uses three tubes for colour display.

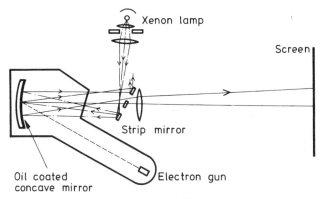

Fig. 5.13 Schematic diagram of the Eidophor[16]

Other similar systems of using a deformed surface in a Schlieren projection arrangement have been investigated, for example the use of an elastomer film instead of the oil film[17] which also has the merit of short term storage, and the use of a deformable metal foil mounted on a grid in close proximity to a glass substrate. One of the latest of this type of light valve has been described by Thomas et al.,[18] but differs in that the light valve is fabricated as a large array of small mirrors, 46μm across, each one mounted on a small post so that it can be deflected by electrostatic charges. The arrangement is illustrated in fig. 5.14.

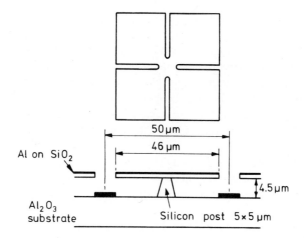

Fig. 5.14 Detail of the mirror in the mirror matrix light valve for projection display from Thomas *et al.*[18] (Copyright © 1975 I.E.E.E.)

An altogether different type of light valve uses the Pockel effect, birefringence induced by electrical polarisation in certain electro-optic crystals. Although one or two workers investigated the idea in the 1950s the main development has been made by Marie[19] and his co-workers in France. Named the 'Titus' tube, the device consists of a crystal plate of KD_2PO_4 (potassium-dideutero-orthophosphate), a ferroelectric material which crystallises in a uniaxial lattice, which is scanned by an electron beam. The crystal has its optical axis perpendicular to the plane of the plate, and when it becomes charged by the beam, birefringence is induced proportional to the electrical polarisation. A light beam from the projection lamp is passed through the crystal and is reflected from a coating on the back surface. If the light is plane polarised it will be reflected with a phase shift, which rotates the plane of polarisation. Using crossed polarisers a white-on-black data display is obtained, but since the effect depends on the field, the tube is capable of giving a grey scale.

5.4 Storage c.r.t.s

Because the information on a c.r.t. is continuously refreshed, it is necessary to hold the information for the complete display in a store. In the introductory period of alphanumeric display terminals, the digital store represented a major cost factor, and there was considerable interest in building the store into the tube itself. In the last few years the price of electronic digital stores has come tumbling down, and today there is little cost advantage in a direct view storage tube for data display. However, there is still an advantage in the stability of the display, eliminating, as it does, flicker and jitter.

Ideally we consider a storage display as one which, having been addressed, remains active until the information is erased or updated some time later, however long that time may be. In a cathode ray tube such indefinite storage has not been attained and we define a storage tube as one in which the image can be retained on the screen for the order of minutes: a high persistence phosphor would only retain the image for a second at most.

Several designs of storage tubes have been proposed, but they all depend on the same basic principle of utilising the secondary emitting properties of a dielectric to build up a charge pattern on a subsidiary mesh in front of the cathode. This pattern is then used to control the electron current to the phosphor screen from a 'flood' gun. A typical arrangement is shown schematically in fig. 5.15. The mesh or backing electrode is coated on the cathode side with a dielectric layer and the mechanism depends on the secondary emission coefficient, δ (δ is the number of secondary electrons emitted per incident electron), being less than one for electrons at the flood gun energy and greater than one for electrons at the write gun energy. When writing, the dielectric coating emits more electrons than it receives and charges up positively, with the value at any point being determined by the electron beam current at that point. After writing, the mesh is biased negatively and the flood gun switched on. Only where the mesh layer is positively charged will electrons pass through it to impinge on the screen; the more positive the charge the larger the electron current. Thus a pattern is seen on the screen corresponding to the charge pattern on the mesh. The electrons turned back by the mesh and the secondary electrons emitted during writing are collected by a second mesh, the collector. The picture remains on the screen so long as the charge pattern remains on the mesh. Unfortunately electrical leakage across the layer and electrons hitting the mesh limit this storage time and normally the information requires updating within a minute or so. Because of fabrication problems the screen size is limited and storage tubes are mainly used for oscilloscope applications. A more recent design, however, developed in the early 1960s offers full size screen potential up to 26 in diameter.

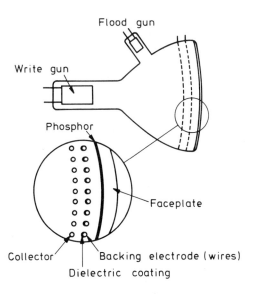

Fig. 5.15 Schematic diagram of a conventional storage c.r.t.

Called the bistable storage tube, the t.v. size design has been described by Curtin et al.[20] It differs from the other storage tubes in having the dielectric layer, phosphor screen and electron collecting electrode all laid on the tube front face. Indeed the phosphor itself acts as the secondary emitting dielectric. It is laid onto a tin oxide layer which has bumps protruding through the phosphor which acts as the collector. The screen structure is illustrated in fig. 5.16. The tube is much cheaper to construct than the conventional storage tube but has a limitation on luminance of the order of 25 cd/m^2.

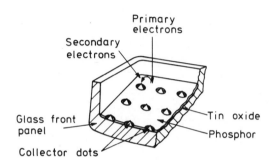

Fig. 5.16 Screen structure of the bistable storage tube according to Curtin et al.[20] (Permission for reprint courtesy Society for Information Display)

A different type of storage tube which should be mentioned is the cathodochromic storage display or 'dark trace' tube, which combines a storage capability with a passive display. In principle the phosphor in a c.r.t. is replaced by a crystallite layer in which colour centres can be induced by the electron beam. The colour centres absorb light, giving a dark character on a light background, which can be viewed by either transmitted or reflected light. Tubes of this type appeared in the 1940s using KCl as the cathodochromic material, but they gave poor contrast and life. A much better material was found in the 1960s, namely bromine doped sodalite[21] ($Na_6 Al_6 Si_6 O_{24} .2NaBr$), which has been studied extensively in the 1970s.[22] Sodalite is more stable than KCl and gives a much higher contrast, but it is more difficult to erase. At low contrast ratio (low beam current) the display can be erased by a high intensity light source, but at high contrast ratios it can only be erased completely by heating, i.e. the screen must be raised to around 250°C for the display to be bleached in a few seconds. This implies depositing the sodalite on a thin substrate rather than on the c.r.t. faceplate, to reduce the heat capacity, and this makes the tube rather fragile. The screen can be heated by a transparent resistive layer or by electron bombardment. The write times are rather slow, several microseconds per dot, and selective erasure is not possible. Recently, Todd et al.[23] have described a tube in which the characters can be erased by heat from the same electron beam used for writing and also the powder is deposited on the faceplate.

Todd has further developed his tube for a Schmidt lens projection system using an external light source.[24] The system is capable of displaying 66 rows of 140 characters on a 7 ft screen.

5.5 Scanned light beam displays

The idea of producing a display with a scanned light beam dates back to the early days of television before the invention of the c.r.t. when light from a modulated gas discharge lamp was scanned over a screen with rotating mirror drums. It came to the fore again in the late 1930s when the light from a high powered lamp was modulated by a liquid acousto-optic cell for a large screen display. The scanning was again obtained by rotating mirror drums, but in the case of the line scan, the rotational speed was matched to the speed of the acoustic wave across the cell so that the image of the acoustic wave carrying the correct modulation for a given picture point remained stationary on the screen for the time the wave took to travel across the cell. This is the so called Scophony technique[25] and effectively decreases the duty factor of the display and thus improves the luminance. Even so the luminance obtained would hardly match that achieved with modern television screens.

With the advent of the laser and the possibility of producing high energy narrow beams, renewed interest has been aroused in light scanned displays. The narrow divergence of the laser beam makes it possible to use much smaller mechanical mirror scanners, but more importantly it is now possible to use electro-optic or acousto-optic crystals for modulating and deflecting the beam.

There are several electro-optic effects covered by the general term electro-optic crystals, the main effects being the Pockel and Kerr effects. These effects arise essentially from small changes in the refractive index of the crystal with an applied electric field. The change in refractive index itself is very small and in practice the effect is used in an interference mode by splitting the beam into two components and recombining them after one or both components have been shifted in phase by the electro-optic effect. Most of the crystals are unisotropic (uniaxial or biaxial) and beam splitting into the ordinary and extraordinary rays, birefringence, occurs naturally. The resultant effect is the rotation of the plane of polarisation of an incident plane wave when the electric field is applied. Used between polarisers a high degree of modulation can be obtained. In the Pockel effect the angle of rotation is linearly dependent on the field whilst the Kerr effect depends on the square of the field. Basically electro-optic crystals are modulators but they can be combined with a birefringent plate or prism where the displacement or deflection angle is different for the ordinary or extraordinary rays, i.e. different for plane waves at right angles to each other. An array of crystals and prisms is required for a raster display, although it is possible to reduce the number with electro-optic prisms.

Acousto-optic crystals are of more interest since they can be used either as modulators or as deflectors. Sound waves are sent through the crystal causing density changes in the crystal. These density changes change the index of refraction, the so-called photoelastic effect. The variation in the index of refraction acts as a phase grating to the light, producing a diffraction pattern. If the beam is incident at a critical angle to the plane of the acoustic wave, known as the Bragg angle θ_B (analogous to the X-ray diffraction effect) most of the light is diffracted into the first-order refraction, the beam being diffracted through $2\theta_B$ where

$$\sin \theta_B = \frac{\lambda}{2\Lambda}. \tag{5.2}$$

λ is the wavelength of the light and Λ the wavelength of the sound wave, both measured in the crystal medium.

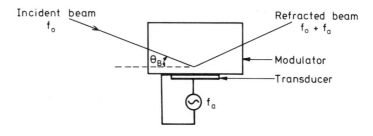

Fig. 5.17 Schematic diagram showing the principle of an acousto-optic modulator or deflector

The acoustic wave is produced by a piezoelectric transducer attached to the crystal. The arrangement is illustrated in fig. 5.17. Since the intensity of the refracted beam is proportional to the amplitude of the acoustic wave the beam can be modulated by varying the signal strength to the transducer. From equation 5.2 it is seen that varying the acoustic frequency will vary the angle of refraction, $2\theta_B$, and thus the crystal may be used as a deflector. The maximum deflection angle will depend on the bandwidth of the device, but it is not difficult to design a deflector to give over 500 discrete spots.

The main interest in laser displays has been for television applications and systems have been demonstrated giving acceptable pictures in both monochrome and colour. Usually modulation is carried out by acousto-optic or electro-optic crystals whilst rotating or vibrating mirrors have been used for the deflection. However, a head-up display using acousto-optic modulators and deflectors has been described by Green.[26] The systems have been too complex and expensive for commercial exploitation, and are limited to rather specialised application. A further obstacle to commercial exploitation of laser scanned displays is the low efficiency of the lasers; the most suitable ion lasers have efficiencies of less than 0.1%. Even for viewing in a dimly lit room, 1–2 watts output is required, implying an input of over 1 kW. For alphanumeric displays only about 5% of the screen will be illuminated at one time. Under these circumstances the laser power could be reduced by 95% if only those parts of the screen were scanned which required illuminating rather than the complete raster, effectively increasing the duty ratio. This requires a fast switching random scan which is possible with electro-optical or acousto-optical crystals. Such a scanning scheme has been described by Kruger et al.[27] using an array of electro-optic crystals and birefringent plates. The position of the light beam is defined by a digital code fed to the crystals of the deflecting system; n elements are required for 2^n display positions (i.e. eighteen elements for a t.v. size display).

In a similar way to the electron beam, a laser beam can also be used to address a light valve which is then used with a light source to project the display. A number of light valves have been suggested for such an application.[28] Either the light valve material itself can be thermally activated or it can be combined with a photoconductor. In particular, a liquid crystal can be thermally addressed and used as a light valve.[29] A liquid crystal cell filled with cholesteric or smectic liquid and with transparent electrodes is arranged in a Schlieren projection system. The optic axis is arranged normal to the electrodes and the liquid is transparent. When it is scanned by the infra-red beam from a Nd YAG laser, local heating occurs which produces a molecular disordered isotropic state. In this state light is strongly scattered. On cooling, the isotropic state remains, so that the panel possesses memory. Resolution up to 2000 lines on a 30 mm square cell has been obtained.

The main advantage of a light beam scanned display over the c.r.t. is that it does not require a large vacuum envelope. However, it has a long way to go before it becomes competitive.

References

1. Paszkowski, B. (1968) *Electron Optics*, London: Iliffe.
2. Zworykin, V. K. and Morton, G. A. (1954) *Television* 2nd edn. New York: Wiley.
3. Garlick, G. F. J. in Goldberd, P. *ed*. (1966) *Luminescence of Inorganic Solids*. N. York: Academic Press, 685.
4. Joint Electron Devices Engineering Council (1975) *Optical Characteristics of Cathode Ray Tube Screens*, J.E.D.E.C. Publication 16C, Washington D.C.: Electronic Industries Association.
5. Takata, M. and Hirai, R. (1980) 'Colour computer display tubes'. *Digest of Technical Papers, S.I.D. International Symposium*, 164–165.
6. Haflinger, D. J. (1976) 'A new CRT for alphanumeric computer terminals'. *Digest of Technical Papers, S.I.D. International Symposium*, 126–127.
7. Aiken, W. R. (1957) 'A thin cathode ray tube', *Proc. I.R.E.* **45**, 1599–1604.
8. Gabor, D., Stuart, P. R. and Kalman, P. G. (1958) 'A new cathode ray tube for monochrome and colour television', *Proc. I.E.E.* **105B**, 581–606.
9. Smith, K. (1979) 'CRT slims down for pocket and projection TVs'.*Electronics*, 19 July, 196–197.
10. Goede, W. F. 'A digitally addressed flat panel CRT'. *I.E.E.E. Trans.* **ED-20**, 1052–1061.
11. Schulman, R. and Schwartz, J. W. (1976) 'A novel cathodoluminescent flat panel TV display'. *Digest of Technical Papers, S.I.D. International Symposium* 134–135.
12. Endriz, J. G., Kememan, S. A. and Catanese, C. A. (1979) 'Feedback multiplier flat panel television. 1. System design', *I.E.E.E. Trans.* **ED-26**, 1324–1335.
13. Siekanowicz, W. W., Credelle, T. L., Vaccaro, F. E. and Anderson, C. H. (1980) 'Ladder mesh and slalom electron guides for flat cathodoluminescent displays', *Digest of Technical Papers, S.I.D. International Symposium*, 24–25.

14. Credelle, T. L., Anderson, C. H., Marlowe, F. J., Gange, R. A., Fields, J. R., Fischer, J. T., van Raalte, J. A. and Bloom, S. (1980) 'Cathodoluminescent flat panel TV using electron beam guides'. *Digest of Technical Papers, S.I.D. International Symposium*, 26–27.

15. Baumann, E. (1953) 'The Fischer large-screen projection system'. *J. Soc. Motion Pict. Telev. Eng.* **60**, 344–356.

16. Mol, J. C. (1962) 'The Eidophor system of large screen television projection'. *Photograph J.* **102**, 128–132.

17. Good, W. E. and True, T. T. (1973) 'Projection colour television displays'. *J. Vac. Sci. Technol.* **10**, 824–830.

18. Thomas, R. N., Guldberg, J., Nathanson, H. C., and Malmberg, P. R. (1975) 'The mirror matrix tube, a novel light valve for projection displays'. *I.E.E.E. Trans.* **ED-22**, 765–775.

19. Marie, G. (1969) 'Large screen projection of television pictures with an optical relay tube based on the Pockel's effect'. *Philips Tech. Rev.* **30**, 292–298.

20. Curtin, C., Hutcheon, J., Mason, W. and McTeague, J. (1973) 'A large screen display for bistable storage of up to 17,000 characters'. *Digest of Technical Papers, S.I.D. International Symposium.* 98–99.

21. Phillips, W. and Kiss, Z. J. (1968) 'Photo erasable dark trace cathode ray storage tube'. *Proc I.E.E.E.* **56**, 2072–2073.

22. Faughnan, B. W., Gorog, I., Heyman, P. M. and Shidlovsky, I. (1973) 'Cathodochromic materials and applications', *Proc. I.E.E.E.* **61**, 927–941.

23. Todd, L. T., Linz, A. and Farrell, E. F. (1975) 'Cathodochromic CRT employing faceplate-deposited sodalite and electron beam erase'. *I.E.E.E. Trans.* **ED-22**, 788–792.

24. Todd, L. T. and Starkey, C. J. (1980) '9,000 character projection CCRT terminal'. *Digest of Technical Papers, S.I.D. International Symposium*, 216–217.

25. Lee, H. W. (1939) 'Some factors involved in the optical design of a modern television receiver using moving scanners'. *Proc. I.R.E.* **27**, 496–500.

26. Green, H. (1974) 'Acoustooptic laser display system'. *Digest of Technical Papers, S.I.D. International Symposium*, 56–57.

27. Kruger, U., Pepperl, R., Schmidt, U. J. (1973) 'Electrooptic materials for digital light beam deflectors', *Proc. I.E.E.E.* **61**, 992–1007.

28. Flannery, J. B. (1973) 'Light controlled light valve', *I.E.E.E. Trans.* **ED-20**, 941–953.

29. Anderson, L. K. (1974) 'Projection images with liquid crystals', *Bell Lab Rec.* **52**, 223–229.

Chapter 6

Matrix displays

6.1 Introduction

As pointed out in chapter 4 there are several technologies exploited for matrix type alphanumeric displays, most of which are unrelated. There is, therefore, no logical sequence of presenting the sections of this chapter. Arbitrarily we have decided to deal first with those technologies depending on solid state phenomena, then those depending on the liquid state, and finally those which depend on vacuum or gas filled devices. Whilst we have tried to include all the known technologies that have been described for matrix displays, it would take a very much larger book to give adequate coverage of all the contenders. Therefore, to some extent the length of the sections generally reflects the importance of the technologies judged by their market share or their future potential. Even so only a fraction of the theoretical and technical information can be given and for a more detailed study the reader is referred to the appropriate literature on each technology.

6.2 Light emitting diodes

Light emitting diodes (l.e.d.s) for numerical display became available in the 1960s and built up rapidly to take a one-third share of the numeric display market within ten years. The initial impetus for the rapid technical development and mass production was provided by the pocket calculator market. The strength of the l.e.d.s lay in their reliability, low cost, high brightness and compatibility with low voltage integrated circuits. Although l.e.d.s now have a smaller share of the calculator market, owing to their power dissipation compared with liquid crystal displays, they still hold their own in the numeric display market with a range of sizes and colours to cover most applications.

L.E.D. devices depend on the phenomenon of electroluminescence, the emission of light in a solid as a result of passing an electric current through it. The basic process is the radiative recombination of electrons and holes generated in greater concentration than that pertaining to the equilibrium conditions.

Electroluminescent devices can be classified into two types, homojunction devices and heterojunction devices. The former refer to single-crystal p–n junctions, where the recombination takes place at the junction. Visible light is emitted if semiconductor diodes are made from materials with a suitable energy gap between the valence and conduction bands. It is this type from which the commercial l.e.d. displays have been developed. The heterojunction devices are more complex forms of p–n junctions across which the composition as well as electrical properties change. These represent the electroluminescent displays based on ZnS discussed in the next section.

The l.e.d. is essentially a forward biased p–n junction diode formed by minority carrier injection. The magnitude of the junction barrier is reduced under the forward bias, allowing conduction band electrons from the n-region and valence band holes from the p-region to diffuse across the junction and in so doing to increase considerably the minority carrier concentration above the thermal equilibrium value. This is illustrated in fig. 6.1. Recombination takes place between minority and majority carriers with the emission of light if the bandgap is greater than 1.7 eV. In some l.e.d.s recombination occurs only on one side of the junction or it is more efficient

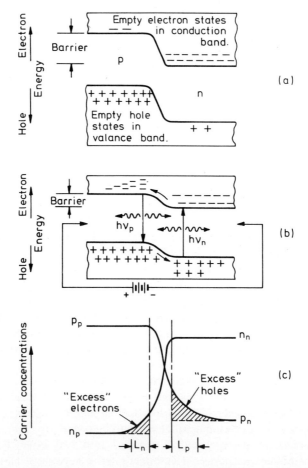

Fig. 6.1 Potential and minority carrier distribution in the p–n junction of an l.e.d.

on one side; red emitting GaP is an example where emission comes only from the p-region. Having produced the radiation there is then the problem of getting the light out from the junction, since the absorption in the surrounding material can be as high as 60% per micrometre.

The efficiency of an l.e.d. can be expressed in terms of the efficiency of producing and exciting the carriers, η_e, the quantum efficiency of radiation recombination η_{int} and the extraction efficiency η_x. The total efficiency η is then given by

$$\eta = \eta_e \eta_{int} \eta_x.$$

Sometimes the component efficiency is quoted rather than the total efficiency and the user should be aware of this.

There is a limited number of materials available which can form controllable p—n junctions with suitable bandgap energies and these are listed in table 6.1. There are some other III—V compounds, however, such as aluminium arsenide, which are under investigation, and also attempts have been made at fabricating l.e.d.s from wider bandgap materials such as ZnS or ZnSe using Schottky barrier type juntions to give blue emission. Some of the materials listed are direct bandgap semiconductors and some indirect. For a direct bandgap semiconductor the crystal momentum values of electrons and holes are equal and recombination can take place with conservation of momentum, the momentum of the photon being very small. The frequency of the light emitted, v, is proportional to the bandgap energy E_B according to Planck's formula

$$hv = E_B.$$

For indirect bandgap semiconductors there is a difference in momentum between electrons and holes and recombination can only take place in the presence of a third particle to provide conservation of momentum. Lattice vibration (phonons) can provide such a particle, but the probability of the three-body recombination is considerably less than for the two-body recombination in a direct bandgap semiconductor.

Initially it was considered that only direct bandgap semiconductors could produce l.e.d.s of adequate efficiency, but investigations in the 1960s showed that in fact higher efficiencies could be obtained in gallium phosphide than in gallium arsenide phosphide.[1] It was found that with suitable dopants the carriers could be trapped at neutral impurity centres to extend their crystal momentum to take up the momentum difference for recombination with the opposite carrier. In this way the third particle is not required and direct two-body recombination can take place in a similar way to that in direct bandgap semiconductors. As an example, zinc and oxygen impurity centres in gallium phosphide increase the efficiency giving red emission of about 0.4 lm/W compared with 0.15 lm/W for gallium arsenide phosphide.

The frequency of the light emission depends on the bandgap energy. If we consider the gallium arsenide phosphide system $GaAs_{1-x}P_x$, then as x is changed from 0 through to 1 the energy gap changes from 1.44 eV for pure GaAs giving emission in the near infra-red, through 1.91 eV for $x = 0.4$ which gives red emission with a peak at 6500Å, to 2.2 eV for GaP giving green emission at 5600Å close to the peak of the eye sensitivity. The presence of impurities will of course modify the

Table 6.1 L. E. D. materials and their characteristics

Material	Direct or indirect	Colour	Peak wavelength (μm)	p–n growth process		Approximate efficiency (lm/W)	
				n-layer	p-layer	Commercial	Best
GaP (Zn,O)	Ind.	Red	0.699	L.P.E.	L.P.E.	0.4	3.0
GaP (N)	Ind.	Green	0.570	L.P.E. (or V.P.E.)	L.P.E. (Zn-diff)	0.3	4.0
GaP (N)	Ind.	Yellow	0.590	V.P.E.	Zn diff	0.2	0.5
GaAs$_{0.35}$ P$_{0.65}$ (N)	Ind.	Orange	0.632	V.P.E.	Zn diff	0.4	0.9
GaAs$_{0.15}$ P$_{0.85}$ (N)	Ind.	Yellow	0.589	V.P.E.	Zn diff	0.2	0.9
GaAs$_{0.6}$ P$_{0.4}$	Dir.	Red	0.649	V.P.E.	Zn-diff	0.15	0.4
Ga$_{0.7}$ Al$_{0.3}$ As	Dir.	Red	0.675	L.P.E.	L.P.E.	—	0.4
In$_{0.42}$ Ga$_{0.58}$ P	Dir.	Orange	0.617	V.P.E.	Zn-diff	—	0.3
SiC	Ind.	Yellow	0.590	Direct crystal growth		—	0.01
GaN	Dir.	Green	0.515	Direct crystal growth		—	—

energy levels and thus also the wavelength of the emitted light. The choice of dopants for III–V compounds is usually made from group VI donors, Te, Se and S, and from group II acceptors, Zn, Cd and Mg. The concentration of the dopant is chosen as high as possible without causing crystal defects, since the recombination probability increases with concentration. A level of 10^{17} to 10^{19} atoms per cm^3 is required for high electroluminescent efficiency. Red emission can be obtained from GaP with Zn and O doping, because the oxygen provides a deep donor level, E_d = 0.80 eV. The resulting electron–hole recombination is around 1.79 eV.[2]

Gallium phosphide, gallium arsenide phosphide, and gallium aluminium phosphide are all currently used to produce commercial seven-bar displays with red emission. However, the market is dominated by gallium arsenide phosphide, mainly because of ease of fabrication and cost. The energy conversion efficiency of such devices is fairly high but because the emission wavelength is on the edge of the visible spectrum where the eye is insensitive, the total efficiency in terms of visibility i.e. lumens/watt, is not very high − less than 0.5 lm/W.

The major improvements that have been made in the 1970s have been brought about by the introduction of nitrogen doping. Substitution of phosphorus by nitrogen produces impurity centres which trap electrons. Because the centres have the same outer electron structure as the phosphorus they are electrically neutral and produce local deformation of the lattice. As a result the trapped electrons recombine with holes to emit photons with a wavelength only slightly less than expected from the bandgap energy, i.e. the dopant allows a direct recombination in indirect bandgap semiconductors. In particular it greatly increases the efficiency in the GaAs$_{1-x}$P$_x$ system for x greater than 0.5, i.e. for those compounds with radiation in the orange, yellow and green. As a result yellow and green emitting l.e.d.s can now be produced with output efficiencies of the same order as for red l.e.d.s; previously the efficiencies were down by a factor of thirty or more. Sample seven-bar devices with emission in the yellow, orange and green have been produced and are commercially available especially in the larger numeral displays. An efficient blue emitting l.e.d. is still being sought. Research is mainly concentrated on the II–VI compounds such as ZnS, ZnSe and CdS where bandgaps up to 3.6 eV are possible. Although such materials have been used successfully in electroluminescent displays (see section 6.3), it has been found extremely difficult to produce p- and n-type material suitable for p–n junctions. The approach has been rather to devise structures in which the carriers can be excited without forming a p–n junction. The Schottky diode offers an alternative but the minority carriers have a very low concentration. An improvement can be obtained by inserting an insulating layer between the metal and the semiconductor. With this so called m.i.s. structure higher injection efficiencies are obtained and thus higher values of η. However, the devices so far produced have some way to go before competing commercially with other l.e.d.s. Blue l.e.d.s have also been made with SiC where 6H–SiC has a bandgap of 3.0 eV. Such crystals are difficult to make and again the efficiencies are low. For a more detailed description of l.e.d. materials and their performance the reader is referred to the textbooks written on the subject.[3,4]

The successful application of l.e.d. material to numeric or alphanumeric display depends largely on fabrication techniques with consideration of cost being the dominant factor. L.E.D.s are normally made from epitaxially grown layers on single-crystal slices of GaAs or GaP depending on the lattice constant of the l.e.d. material required. Both GaAs and GaP single-crystal ingots are commercially available but because the growing technique for GaP is more difficult and ingots tend to have more defects the cost of GaP is three or four times greater than that of GaAs. On the other hand GaAsP grown on GaP has a higher output efficiency than that grown on GaAs owing to its higher light transmission. The layers are grown either by vapour phase epitaxy (v.p.e.) or by liquid phase epitaxy (l.p.e.). The p—n junction is formed by growing n- and p-layers or by Zn diffusion into an n-type layer (see table 6.1). The v.p.e. technology has been highly developed for GaAsP l.e.d.s whereby the dopants are controlled by precise flow of the chemical reactants in the gaseous phase. Further, the composition can be varied from GaAs to the required GaAsP composition as the layers are built up to give better lattice matching. L.P.E. is a less versatile and a more expensive technique, but recent improvements have allowed in situ growth of the p—n junction by introducing the dopants in vapour streams whilst the substrate is covered by a thin melt. Growth of GaN can be attained with a vapour transport technique using a sapphire substrate. It is important in the growth of the crystals and layers to avoid crystal defects from 'impurities' or deposition irregularities. Such defects can cause non-radiative recombination centres to be set up which will reduce the efficiency.

There are two general methods of fabricating an array of l.e.d.s for alphanumeric display. It is possible to take individual chips or lamps and to mount these on a suitable substrate akin to making a hybrid circuit. In this method the material is kept to a minimum but the assembly cost is significant. It has been used extensively for seven-bar displays and is particularly suitable for the larger numeric displays with character height above 5 mm. In this case each chip is mounted on a circuit board either within a reflecting cavity, with a suitable colour plastic overlay and a diffusing front plate as shown in fig. 6.2, or mounted with light pipes to the viewing face. For smaller character displays monolithic techniques are used to fabricate the complete array on a single substrate. For GaAsP the array can be fabricated by Zn diffusion through a SiO_2 mask into the n-type material. The metal connections are then made using standard photolithographic methods. To obtain adequate current spread over the segment from the electrical contacts the segments may be composed of several smaller segments. GaP cannot be fabricated in this way, and in any case because of the transparency of the material, it requires an optical barrier between segments. The solution is a mesa technology[5] whereby the p- and n-layers formed by l.p.e. are etched away to form the diodes as islands on the substrate, and connections are made with beam lead techniques. The etching also gives the necessary optical isolation between segments. Normally the small character on the chip is enlarged by using a magnifying lens encapsulation, which doubles the size at the expense of the viewing angle.

Monolithic technology is particularly suitable for the fabrication of a single numeral on one chip, using a seven-bar format. The substrate acts as the common negative lead and the seven segments are separately connected to the positive potential via the decoder. Several chips can be mounted on a circuit board to give a multi-digit display which can be multiplexed to share a single decoder. It is also

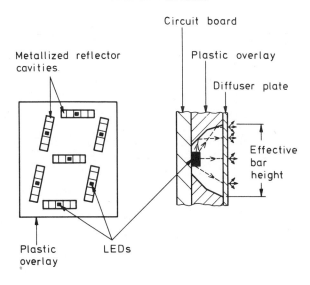

Fig. 6.2 Construction of large numeral l.e.d.s

possible to fabricate a monolithic array of several numerals on one chip, or a 5 x 7 dot-matrix array. The need for multiplexing then requires electrical isolation of the negative electrodes between segments or group of segments. This can be achieved by etching grooves through the n- and p-layers to the semi-insulating substrate in a manner similar to the mesa technique, or an isolation area can be introduced by diffusion or by ion implantation of suitable dopants. This, however, complicates the construction and adds to the cost.

The electrical characteristics of all l.e.d.s are similar. They have a reverse break-down of about 15 V and a low impedance in the forward direction. They operate in the 1.5 to 5 V region, but at rather high current, 1 to 20 mA per segment for a seven-bar device depending on size with a fast response time of 10–100 ns. The light output is variously quoted in the data sheets as a luminance of 350–850 cd/m² or expressed in candelas without reference to area as 100–300 μcd. A reasonable indication of their performance can be seen from the lumens efficiencies given in table 6.1. However, there is a spread on quoted values, with the best values reported being considerably higher than attained in commercial devices. The luminance increases with input power, but it tends to saturate at high currents so that there is a fall off in the attainable luminance at high duty factors. A 1980 review[6] discusses the reasons for the limitation of efficiency in present device technology and the possibility of improvements in terms of what is fundamentally achievable. Whereas we can expect to see better devices in the future it is unlikely that they will win back their position in the small battery operated display applications such as watches and pocket calculators, where an improvement of several orders would be required to compete with passive displays such as the liquid crystal. Typical examples of l.e.d. numerical indicators are shown in fig. 6.3.

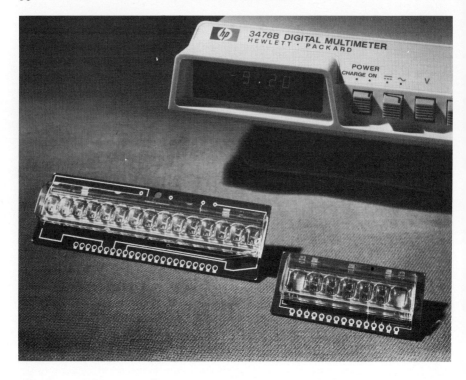

Fig. 6.3 HP 5082—7265 series l.e.d. displays from Hewlett—Packard (courtesy Hewlett—Packard Ltd.)

The high current characteristics mean that if say 100 segments in a dot-matrix array are to be addressed from a single cross-bar then the lead would have to carry one ampere or more. This coupled with the fact that cost is proportional to chip area makes l.e.d.s unsuitable for large alphanumeric displays. Nevertheless panels capable of displaying three rows of twenty-four characters have been demonstrated[7] and the drive circuits are discussed in chapter 7. Potentially larger arrays could be constructed, albeit at high cost, by incorporating integral drive circuits.

The main application of l.e.d.s has been for small registers of numerals, where seven-bar matrices suffice, and particularly where small numeral sizes, heights less than 0.5 inch, are acceptable. For the larger numerals modular packages of single digits are constructed allowing them to be mounted side by side as a register of a number of digits. The smaller numeral displays are mostly packaged as multi-digit arrays up to six digits in standard D.I.L. encapsulations. Special packages for clocks and other large market applications are often custom made. An example of a monolithic custom built l.e.d. display is shown in plate 1. Some of the latest seven-segment displays are supplied complete with drive and decoder circuit built into the same lead frame package. Dot-matrix 5 x 7 arrays are also commercially available for alphanumeric display, as are sixteen-bar star-burst pattern displays. A set of four alphanumeric characters in an integral package has been introduced by Hewlett—Packard Ltd which includes drive circuit and shift register (fig. 6.4).

Although l.e.d.s show some degradation of output during operation, especially at high currents, lives of several tens of thousands of hours can be expected before the luminance drops by 50%. Being solid state devices, l.e.d. displays are very rugged and compact and they are cost competitive with most other displays.

6.3 Electroluminescent displays

The use of heterojunction electroluminescence as a light source dates back to the study of electroluminescence in phosphors discovered in the early 1940s as a result of electrophotoluminescence (the modulation of photoluminescence in phosphors by electric fields). Some of the early work was carried out by Destriau and was reported in detail in 1947.[8] He obtained emission from sulphides, tungstates, silicates and other crystallite substances in a variety of cell designs. This work initiated considerable investigation of electroluminescent phosphors in the 1950s but with limited success. The phosphors were made by techniques already being employed for fluorescent lamps and c.r.t. screens and were activated by a.c. fields with insulation placed between the electrodes and the phosphor to prevent dielectric breakdown. Later designs embedded the phosphor particles in a dielectric plastic

Fig. 6.4 5 x 7 matrix l.e.d. alphanumeric display HDSP—2010 from Hewlett—Packard (courtesy Hewlett—Packard Ltd.)

layer. The phosphor system giving the best results at that time was zinc-sulphide/ zinc-selenide doped with a fairly high concentration of copper. The manufacture of the phosphors was very much an empirical art with the mechanism not completely understood. An optimistic future was forecast for these panels as extended area light sources, but the rather low luminance and the doubtful life limited their exploitation to fixed message signs in low light level environments.

With the interest in alphanumeric displays and the obvious attraction of a low cost large area solid state device, a second look has been taken at the electroluminescent phosphor. As a result of the investigations and perhaps a better understanding of the mechanism, new systems have emerged based on zinc sulphide activated with manganese which look promising for future display applications. Indeed matrix panels giving 300 or more characters had reached an advanced stage of development and were being commercially advertised at the end of 1981. The systems that have been developed fall into two categories having rather different mechanisms and characteristics; thin film layers which are mainly a.c. operated and powder layers which are either a.c. or d.c. operated.

Several mechanisms have been proposed to explain the electroluminescence effect in the various phosphor systems. In the case of manganese activated zinc sulphide, it is generally accepted that the characteristic yellow light emission is produced by excited manganese atoms returning to the ground state. It is assumed that the manganese atoms in the ZnS lattice are excited or ionised by electrons, but where the electrons originate and how they attain sufficient energy is more controversial. Zinc sulphide can only be made as an n-type low conductivity semiconductor and for practical purposes can be considered as an insulator. Therefore the electrons must be injected into the crystal via some form of heterojunction. For the d.c. powders which are copper doped, the particles are considered to be ZnS coated with a p-type layer of Cu_xS and the heterojunction formed between the ZnS and Cu_xS gives a region for injection and acceleration of the electrons. A feature of the d.c. electroluminescent panel is the forming process whereby the efficiency builds up with time during the initial running. During this process it is thought that, in the region close to the anode, the copper sulphide conducting coating diffuses away giving a high resistive layer with a high accelerating field across it. Most of the light emission seems to come from this region. For the a.c. operated thin film panel, the interface between the phosphor and the insulating film is thought to set up a heterojunction owing to surface states. Because of the smaller thickness of the phosphor layer the fields will be correspondingly higher than for the d.c. powder system. The actual mechanism of excitation by the electrons can be compared to the cathodoluminescence mechanism described in chapter 5.

The interest in d.c. electroluminescence of powder phosphors has developed from the extensive study by Vecht and his co-workers at Thames Polytechnic.[9,10] They found that the preparation of the phosphor was very important. The zinc sulphide particles needed to be small, $0.5-1$ μm, and of uniform size. The doping level had to be precise and the materials needed to be pure. To control the copper sulphide layer to the order of a monolayer on the particles, the copper layer was deposited by a separate chemical treatment. The phosphor layer around 50 μm thick with a suitable binder was screen printed or otherwise deposited onto a glass substrate on which a transparent tin oxide electrode pattern had been deposited. The tin oxide electrode was connected as anode. The cathodes were deposited on the top of the phosphor powder by evaporation, and covered with a protective layer.

Initial application of a direct voltage gives a high current with no light emission. At a critical power density the current falls and the light emission appears close to the positive electrode. This is termed the 'forming process' and is irreversible. The panel is usually operated at or slightly below the forming voltage, and typical $I-V$ characteristics are shown in fig. 6.5(a). Typical brightness—voltage characteristics are given in fig. 6.5(b). For a luminance of 170 cd/m² (50 ft L (foot-lambert)) a voltage of around 100 V is required with a current of 1 mA/cm² which implies an efficiency of around 0.5 lm/W. On life the impedance increases and the efficiency decreases, but lives of several thousand hours have been attained before the brightness falls to half level. Extension of life can be achieved by increasing the voltage to regain the luminance. Because both the $I-V$ and the light-output—V characteristics are non-linear, the display can be multiplexed with a good contrast ratio. Indeed it behaves well under short pulse conditions of approximately 15 μs when it can be pulsed above the forming voltage to give a higher peak brightness. Although the brightness saturates at high currents, it is still possible to obtain a mean luminance of 170 cd/m² even at a duty ratio of 1 in 20. This is partly due to the rather long decay time of ~1 ms. For this luminance the pulse current is around 200 mA/cm². Alphanumeric panels with a capability of displaying up to 480 characters are available and an example is shown in Plate 4.

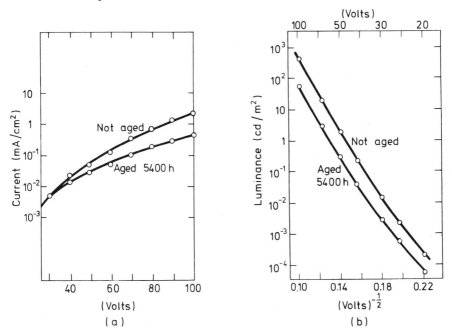

Fig. 6.5 Typical characteristics of a d.c. electroluminescent display according to Vecht et al.[10]: (a) $I-V$ characteristic, (b) luminance—voltage characteristic. (Copyright © 1973 I.E.E.E.)

The a.c. operated powder electroluminescent panel has been mainly exploited by Fischer[11] and stemmed from the discovery by Lehmann[12] that if the standard ZnS:Cu electroluminescent phosphor was fired and cooled in a vapour of sulphur, the output no longer decayed with the time even when operated at high frequencies. Fischer has obtained long life devices by immersing the phosphor powder in liquid sulphur under high pressure. The sulphur treatment is thought to suppress harmful diffusion of the copper activate from the particles. In the fabrication of his panel, Fischer uses a monograin layer which is held between thermoplastic layers. This electroluminescent layer is deposited on a glass substrate having the electrode pattern of tin/indium oxide covered by a 50 μm insulating layer of TiO_2 or Al_2O_3. The back electrode and encapsulating layer is black. An exploded view of the panel is shown in fig. 6.6. The layer can be driven with a 50 V 10 KHz signal but, unlike the d.c. powder layer,

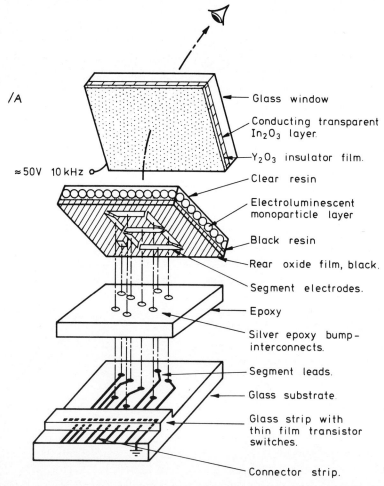

/A

≈50V 10 kHz

Glass window

Conducting transparent In_2O_3 layer.

Y_2O_3 insulator film.

Clear resin

Electroluminescent monoparticle layer

Black resin

Rear oxide film, black.

Segment electrodes.

Epoxy

Silver epoxy bump-interconnects.

Segment leads.

Glass substrate.

Glass strip with thin film transistor switches.

Connector strip.

Fig. 6.6 Exploded view of a.c. powder electroluminescent panel according to Fischer[11]

the a.c. electroluminescent layer does not possess adequate threshold to enable multiplexing without a separate drive element per cell. Methods of driving panels with thin film transistors have been examined by Fischer. The method is described in chapter 7 and allows storage to be incorporated to give a 100% duty ratio.

The a.c. thin film electroluminescence is at present receiving the more emphasis, especially in the U.S.A. and Japan. The investigation of electroluminescence from polycrystalline films vacuum deposited onto a glass substrate goes back twenty-five years, for example with the work of Thornton.[13] However, impetus for its further investigation arose from the developments at Sigmatron Inc. at the beginning of the 1970s[14] using manganese activated ZnS. Their structure was relatively complex and unsymmetrical. The transparent electrode pattern on the glass substrate was coated with a layer of GeO_2 to aid uniform nucleation of the evaporated ZnS layer. The ZnS was then coated with an As_2S_3 absorbing layer, then an insulating layer of $BaTiO_3$, followed by the rear electrode. The black absorbing layer gave good contrast since the ZnS and electrode pattern on the front surface were transparent. In this respect the thin film has advantage over the powder layer which diffusely scatters the incident light. Because of the good absorption of the black layer a lower luminance, $50-100$ cd/m^2, was considered acceptable. With this luminance the panels could be run at 1% duty cycle, but the voltage requirements were high, 600 V peak to peak. Lives of over 20 000 hr were reported. An improved symmetrical layer system was described by Inoguchi et al.[15] of Sharp Corporation in 1974 and most of the work since then has been based on their structure. In their panel the thin film ZnS layer, co-evaporated with Mn to give a 5% weight of Mn, was sandwiched between two insulating layers of either Y_2O_3 or Si_3N_4. If the latter was used it also acted as a protection against humidity, although later it was found necessary to seal the film in a glass enclosure with a silicon oil seal[16] to avoid life failure due to moisture. The panels ran at a lower potential than the Sigmatron panel with higher brightness. The luminance–voltage characteristic is shown in fig. 6.7, indicating a stabilising effect over the first eighty hours of life. The efficiency was of the order of 0.5 lm/W. With the high saturation brightness and the strong non-linear characteristic good discrimination was obtained on a 120 x 90 element panel multiplexed in a cross-bar addressed cyclic mode.

A feature of this type of panel is a memory or hysteresis effect, illustrated in fig. 6.8. With increasing voltage the luminance has a threshold voltage around 200 V where the emission increases very rapidly. With decreasing voltage, depending on the maximum applied voltage, the brightness follows a family of curves, maintaining the high luminance to voltages below the threshold. Thus with a bias of say 20 V the luminance can be increased from 10 to 100 cd/m^2 by a positive pulse, and returned by a negative pulse, thus giving the panel the property of storage with the added possibility of grey scale. Suzuki et al.[17] have exploited this storage phenomenon in a 240 x 320 element alphanumeric panel. To minimise the power load on the supply and output stages due to the high electrical capacity of the display, they used chokes in the drive circuit to give a resonant circuit element at a frequency of ~300 Hz. It has been found that the luminance level can be switched by an intense light pulse, and the possibility of operating the panel with a light pen has also been demonstrated by Suzuki and his co-workers.[18]

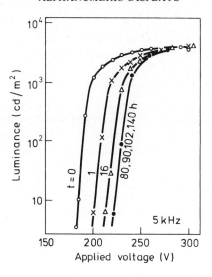

Fig. 6.7 Luminance–voltage characteristics of thin film a.c. electroluminescent panel on ageing according to Inoguchi *et al.*[15] (Permission for reprint courtesy Society for Information Display)

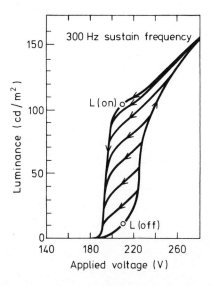

Fig. 6.8 Plot of light output against voltage showing the memory behaviour of a thin a.c. electroluminescent panel according to Suzuki *et al.*[17] (Permission for reprint courtesy Society for Information Display)

The efficiency of the thin film device is very dependent on the dielectric layer. A low capacity is required; on the other hand the dielectric layer must not break down under high field operating conditions. Because of the dielectric layers, the switching voltages are high, above the values that can be used with commercially available integrated circuits although special i.c.s have been fabricated to drive them.

A number of ideas have been proposed to reduce the voltage such as using a lower bandgap material and shallow ion implantation of the manganese. However, the most successful method has been found by Okamoto and his colleagues,[19] who used lead titanate (PT) and lead lanthanum titanate (PLT) thin films as the dielectric layers. PT and PLT have a dielectric constant of 190 and a breakdown strength of 500 kV/cm. Using layers of 0.5 μm thickness, which had a transparency of 80%, threshold voltages below 70 V could be achieved. This is about four times lower than found with Y_2O_3. Similar voltage thresholds have also been found with thin films of ZnS:Mn, Cu operated under d.c. conditions.[20]

Departure from the standard ZnS:Mn to produce other colours has been reported in both powder and thin film techniques. Vecht[21] has investigated other alkaline earth sulphides for his d.c. electroluminescent panels. Using CaS:Ce he obtained green emission with power efficiencies comparable to ZnS:Mn, Cu. Blue emission was obtained with SrS:Ce and red emission from CaS:Eu, but with lower output. Fischer[11] examined a range of phosphors to give different colours for the a.c. powder layers. In particular he prepared a white emitting phosphor by combining $ZnS_{0.5}Se_{0.5}$:CuBr (yellow) with ZnS:CuI (blue). Further colours could be obtained by dying the embedding resin with fluorescent pigments. White emission from thin film electroluminescent panels has also been reported by Yoshida et al.[22] By doping the ZnS matrix with rare earth elements, white light could be produced by a single luminous centre.

Summing up, both the d.c. powder and the thin film a.c. electroluminescent devices are emerging from the development stage for medium size display of alphanumerics. However, the a.c. thin film devices seem to offer a more promising future with higher brightness and better contrast. The commercial exploitation of electroluminescent panels has been slow to materialise. From the published papers it is not clear why this should be so, unless the performances reported for research or development samples are difficult to reproduce on a production basis.

6.4 Ferroelectric displays

In the early 1970s it was discovered that ceramic materials in the lead zirconate/titanate system could be made transparent, and further that such transparent ceramics exhibited strong electro-optic effects.[23] This led to an extensive study of such materials for display applications.[24,25] In spite of the phenomenon's promise for solid state passive display, devices based on it have never reached commercial development. Nevertheless they are worth a section in this book, representing as they do the only truly solid state devices which could challenge the liquid crystal display for low powered passive display applications.

The material of interest is the lanthanum doped lead zirconate titanate (PLZT) with a typical ratio La:Zr:Ti of 8:65:35. It is manufactured by normal ceramic techniques, for example by pressing mixed oxides and sintering at high temperatures. It can then be sliced and polished into transparent plates of up to a few inches in diameter. It has a high refractive index ($n = 2.5$) with a typical optical transmission of 65% for a slice of 100 μm thickness. Much of the loss, however, is due to reflec-

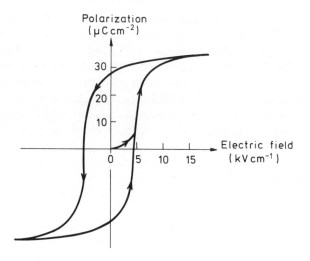

Fig. 6.9 Polarisation as a function of the field for PLZT

tions at the surfaces. Being a ferroelectric material it shows the classic polarisation/ electric field loop of fig. 6.9. If an electric field of the order of 6 kV/cm is applied to the PLZT, on removing and short circuiting the electrodes there remains a polarisation (remnant polarisation). This is known as poling and it is in this state that the PLZT is anisotropic and exhibits useful electro-optic effects. Basically the poling orientates the ferroelectric domains which are normally randomly orientated in the untreated material. The electro-optical properties depend on the way the field is applied and the exact composition of the PLZT. Two main effects have been exploited for display application: one is the change in birefringence with field, observed in fine grained samples, and the other is a scattering effect found in coarser grained samples. In the former, a transverse field is normally applied to the poled PLZT. As the field is increased, the birefringence and thus the path difference between orthogonally polarised components of the light increases. Placed between polarisers this has the effect of rotating the plane of polarisation, either increasing or decreasing the amount of transmitted light, I, depending on whether the polarisers are crossed or in line. Assuming no loss in the polarisers or PLZT,

$$I = I_0 \sin^2 \left(\frac{\Delta n \pi d}{\lambda} \right) \tag{6.1}$$

where I_0 is the incident intensity, Δn is the electrically induced birefringence and d is the thickness of the PLZT.

Thus grey scale can be incorporated and further since the birefringence follows a hysteresis loop (see fig. 6.9) the PLZT exhibits non-volatile memory. This means that the image remains on the PLZT when the applied potential is removed and can only be erased by applying a reverse field. In the scattering mode, a longitudinal field is applied. The light is multiply scattered as it is transmitted, the intensity of the scattered light being dependent on the remnant polarisation. It has the advantage over the birefringent effect in eliminating the need for polarisers. One of the early applications for PLZT using both effects was the Ferpic, whereby the PLZT was combined with a photoconducting layer to form an image storing device.[24,25]

Above a critical temperature, the PLZT material becomes 'paraelectric' showing zero remnant polarisation and little or no hysteresis. This critical temperature depends on composition but can be below room temperature; for a ratio of La:Zr:Ti of 9:65:35 the critical temperature is about 10°C. The PLZT then has no memory but driving is simplified since erase pulses are not required.

A practical numeric display can be made by placing a polished PLZT slice, with a diode electrode pattern deposited on one surface, between crossed polarisers with their axes at 45° to the electric field. Although a field of 1 kV/mm is required, by using interdigital electrodes seven-bar displays can be built with switching voltages of 40 V. The ceramic acts as a low loss capacitor so very little current passes. A typical capacitance value for a bar of a seven-bar device might be 500 pF, which would imply a dissipation of approximately 0.2 mW per digit when operated at 50 Hz. Unlike other passive displays discussed in the next sections the switching speed is less than 1 μs for the memory mode of operation. The main disadvantages of the PLZT are the reflections at the surfaces which degrade the contrast, the high field required and the lack of a threshold for multiplex operation. The first is a major problem and for a reflective mode of operation the display is poor, lacking contrast with a small angle of view. The high field makes it impracticable to use the PLZT in a longitudinal field operation and even with interdigital electrodes in the transverse field operation the voltage is too high for watch displays and similar applications. The fact that the PLZT is also piezoelectric can cause problems. If some of these disadvantages could be overcome, the PLZT could offer great promise for a low powered solid state display. Unfortunately there appears to be very little research being carried out on such devices.

Another phenomenon which is in some way akin to PLZT is the Faraday rotation in bismuth substituted iron garnets $Bi_x Y_{3-x} Fe_5 O_{12}$. This is the material used for bubble memories and in fact uses the production and propagation of magnetic bubbles to achieve a light valve pattern for a projection display.[26] Magnetic bubbles are small areas or domains set up in the garnet which are oppositely magnetised to the rest of the material. Normally they can be induced by high magnetic fields and are unstable, but they can be anchored and stabilised by permalloy elements in conjunction with a magnetic field. The crystal or crystal film is placed between polarisers arranged to block the light for one direction of magnetisation, which will then transmit light for the other, owing to the Faraday effect. In this way the bubbles can be used as light valves to display a message on a screen. A sequence of bubbles and spaces is fed into the panel from one corner and propagated around a folded shift register by standard bubble techniques using shaped permalloy patterns on the crystal. When the shift register is filled the bubbles form the required dot-matrix message. The bubble size is limited to about 20 μm and therefore the system is unsuitable for direct viewing. The speed of writing is also rather slow with an input bit rate of less than 15 kHz, which restricts it to a limited character capability. Its main advantages are that it can be serially addressed and it has a non-volatile memory. An example of such a display is shown in fig. 6.10.

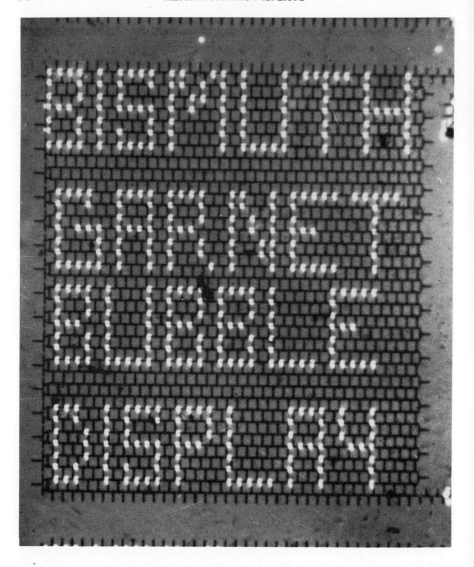

Fig. 6.10 Experimental magneto-optic bubble memory display from Lacklison *et al.*[26] Copyright © 1977 I.E.E.E.)

6.5 Liquid crystals

Like the ferroelectric display, liquid crystals form passive displays, where electric signals modulate the light passing through them. They can be used in either a transmissive or a reflective mode. Their main asset is their very low power consumption which makes them particularly useful for battery operation in small hand held equipment, such as watches and pocket calculators. They are also very competitive in cost.

Approximately 0.5% of organic substances because of their polar nature and the elongated shape of their molecules are able to preserve a high degree of long range orientational ordering of the molecules in a liquid condition (fig. 6.11). This intermediate state between solid and liquid, known as the mesomorphic or liquid crystalline state, exists between two temperature limits — at the lower end the melting point of the solid and at the upper end the isotropic transition point. Within this temperature range the liquid crystals are anisotropic, having dielectric constant, conductivity, viscosity and index of refraction which are characterised by two constants, one in the direction of the molecular axis and one perpendicular to it. As a result the liquid crystal exhibits optical properties, such as birefringence, which are sensitive to external stimuli, e.g. electric and magnetic fields, heat, etc. The anisotropic nature of the dielectric constant allows the molecules to be aligned in an electric field and is of prime importance to the display application. If the dielectric constant in the direction of the molecular axis $\epsilon_\parallel$ is greater than the perpendicular value $\epsilon_\perp$, i.e. $\epsilon_\parallel - \epsilon_\perp > 0$, then the liquid crystal is said to have a positive dielectic anisotrophy (p.d.a.). If $\epsilon_a = \epsilon_\parallel - \epsilon_\perp < 0$ the liquid crystal has a negative anisotrophy (n.d.a). When an electric field is applied the molecules will tend to orientate themselves into the direction giving the minimum electrostatic free energy. For p.d.a. material this minimum occurs when the axial direction or 'director' of the molecules is aligned parallel to the electric field, whereas for an n.d.a. material it occurs when the director is perpendicular to the field.

Three basic types of molecular ordering can be distinguished in the mesomorphic state, namely nematic, smectic, and cholesteric. The molecular alignments for these three types are shown schematically in fig. 6.12. In the nematic liquid crystal the rod like molecules try to line up parallel to one another and only molecules separated by several micrometres show any significant departure from parallel alignment of their mean axial direction (director). Smectic materials show alignment in all three directions in a layered structure. The axis of the molecules is not necessarily perpen-

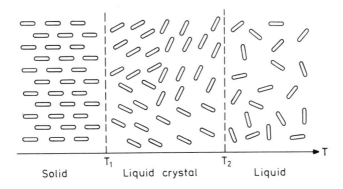

Fig. 6.11 Representation of molecule structure in solid, liquid crystal and liquid phases

dicular to the layer as in the figure. Smectic liquids are usually very viscous and have a slow response time to external fields. They have not yet found application in display. The cholesteric liquid crystal state, which incidentally is not confined to materials derived from cholesterol, is similar to the nematic state, but with the axis of the molecules twisted about the normal to the axis in a helical fashion; for convenience this is shown in planes in fig. 6.12.

Thin films of liquid of the order of 20–100 μm thick can be held in a uniform alignment over a large area to give an anisotropic single crystal analogous to an epitaxial single-crystal film. It is in this form that they can be exploited for display

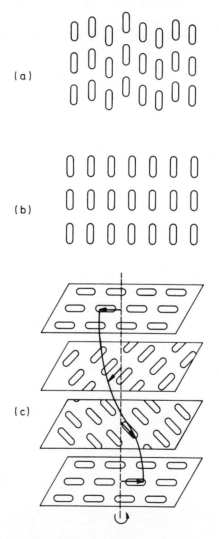

Fig. 6.12 Representation of liquid crystal structures, (a) nematic, (b) smectic, (c) cholesteric

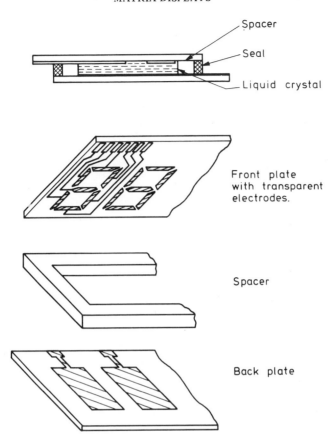

Fig. 6.13 Exploded view of typical liquid crystal display panel

applications. Basically the display device will consist of two glass plates with electrodes printed on them, one set at least being transparent. The plates are mounted parallel with a spacer frame between them. The hollow cell so formed is filled with the liquid crystal material and hermetically sealed round the edges (fig. 6.13). The alignment of the molecules is obtained by surface treatment of the glass. For lining up the molecules with their director parallel to the glass surface in a preferred direction the glass can be coated with a thin layer of SiO evaporated on to it at an oblique angle or by rubbing the surface. To obtain an alignment with the director at right angles to the glass surface, surfactants can be added to the liquid or applied to the surface, such as lecithin. The physical basis for these techniques is not completely understood. When the director is parallel to the glass surface the orientation is termed 'homogeneous' and when perpendicular to the surface it is termed 'homeotropic'.

The discovery of liquid crystals dates back to the nineteenth century but it was not until the 1960s that their potential use as display media was investigated. Much of the initial investigation was carried out at R.C.A. and was reported in 1968.[27] The investigations fall into two areas, studies of the electro-optic effects and their application to devices, and the study of liquid crystal materials. The latter is very much the province of the organic chemist.

There are several possible electro-optic effects which can be exhibited by liquid crystals, the main ones of interest for display being termed dynamic scattering, twisted nematic, phase change and memory effects. These are listed in table 6.2 with some of the parameters pertaining to them.

Dynamic scattering was the earliest display technique to be exploited and requires a nematic material with a relatively low impedance of about 10^{11} ohm/cm. The alignment can be either homogeneous or homeotropic. The homogeneous alignment is now more commonly used with a material having a positive dielectric anisotropy. At zero field the liquid is transparent. When a field is applied the molecules rotate with their director parallel to the field. However, the presence of the current will cause the liquid to flow. Owing to the conductivity anistropy there will be a displacement sideways of the molecules which will tend to distort the alignment giving rise to instabilities. As a result, forced convection currents are set up which become turbulent above a critical voltage. This turbulence contains a large number of refracting boundaries in motion and causes the incident light to be strongly scattered giving the liquid a 'frosted' appearance. The effect depends on the field, but also on the current. A voltage of 15–30 V is normally required across the cell, with a current of 3–10 $\mu A/cm^2$. This means that for say a watch display only 100 μW would be needed. To avoid electrolysis in the liquid, a.c. signals are normally employed at frequencies in the range of 25–500 Hz. At higher frequencies above a critical value dynamic scattering does not occur because of the liquid's viscosity. Since the light is mainly scattered in a forward direction the cell must be backed by a reflecting layer, unless used in a transmissive mode. The contrast is not very high especially if there is specular reflection of a strong light source from the front surface.

The twisted nematic effect requires a liquid crystal with a positive dielectric anisotropy and a high impedance. The alignment of the molecules is arranged parallel to the glass plates in a preferred direction. On assembly the plates are mounted with the preferred directions orthogonal. As a result the molecules line up with a 90° molecular twist across the cell illustrated in fig. 6.14. This twisted nematic structure has the effect of rotating the plane of plane polarised light through 90°. Since the liquid has a positive dielectric anisotropy a small voltage, 1.5 to 3 V, applied to the cell aligns the molecules in the direction of the field, the 90° twist is eliminated and plane polarised light passes straight through. By placing the cell between polarisers a light display on a dark background or vice-versa can be obtained depending on whether the polarisers are parallel or crossed. The effect is due entirely to the field and the only current passing is leakage current, so that the total power can be a fraction of a microwatt per character. The display can be used in a reflective mode by placing a diffuse reflector behind the cell plus polarisers. In general the contrast is greater than for the dynamic scattering mode, but the display appears dimmer owing to transmission losses in the polarisers. The angle of view is poor, but can be improved by increasing the voltage. Dynamic scattering and the twisted nematic are

Table 6.2 Characteristics of liquid crystal displays

Type	Dielectric anisotropy	Drive effect	Voltage	Current	Impedance	Switching On time	Switching Off time	Appearance change
Dynamic scattering	Either	Current	15–30 V threshold	3–10 $\mu A/cm^2$	$10^9-10^{12}\ \Omega/cm$	20 ms	100–200 ms	Clear to cloudy
Twisted nematic	Pos.	Field	<5 V threshold	1 $\mu A/cm^2$	$>10^{12}\ \Omega/cm$	10 ms	200 ms	Transmitting to absorbing with polarisers
Phase change	Pos.	Field	100 V threshold	1 $\mu A/cm^2$	$>10^{12}\ \Omega/cm$	30 μs	100 μs	Cloudy to clear
Cholesteric memory	Neg.	Current and field	20 V threshold (50 V to turn off)	1 $\mu A/cm^2$	$10^{10}\ \Omega/cm$	30 ms	–	Cloudy to clear Both states stable
Guest host (cholesteric)	Pos.	Field	20 V	2 $\mu A/cm^2$	$>10^{12}\ \Omega/cm$	–	100 ms	Colour change

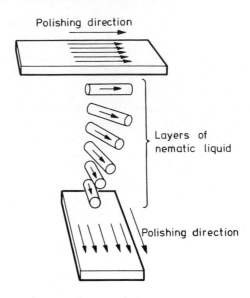

Fig. 6.14 Arrangement of molecules in a twisted nematic display

the two modes exploited for seven-bar numeric displays although because of the lower voltage and power the twisted nematic has more or less superseded the dynamic scattering displays for small battery operated equipment. The switching speed is poor, 10–20 ms 'on' time, 100–200 ms 'off' time, but adequate for multiplexing up to say eight characters, the high persistence allowing them to be addressed at a field rate of less than 50 Hz.

For the phase change effect a cholesteric material is required of high resistivity and with a positive dielectric anisotropy. The cholesteric planes are arranged to be approximately perpendicular to the cell walls. The molecules are then randomly orientated with respect to the walls and in this state the liquid is strongly scattering (fig. 6.15). Unfortunately this state is not stable at zero field and will revert to a

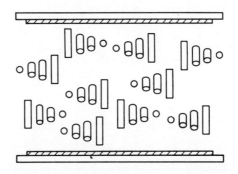

Fig. 6.15 Arrangement of molecules for the phase change effect

transparent state with the helix axis perpendicular to the cell walls. It can, however, be maintained by a bias field. Further increase of the field causes the helices to unwind until, at a critical value, all the molecules are aligned in the field and the liquid is effectively nematic in character and transparent. The critical field is rather high, 100 V across the cell, but the effect switches fairly rapidly in less than 50 μs. It is therefore of interest for multiplexing an array such as an alphanumeric panel.

The memory effect also requires a cholesteric material but with a negative anisotropy and lower resistance. It is basically the same effect as the dynamic scattering, but the scattering state reverts only very slowly back to the transparent structure with the helix axis perpendicular to the cell walls. It can be returned to the clear state by an a.c. signal above a critical frequency, i.e. 500–1000 Hz.

The efficiency and reliability of these electro-optical effects and particularly the temperature range over which they function are dependent on the liquid crystal material and how it is handled. Although there are many organic compounds exhibiting liquid crystalline properties many of them are solid at room temperature and those that are not often have a very limited temperature range. The further requirements on chemical stability, and also electrochemical and photochemical stability and the need for the right dielectric anisotropy and resistivity add up to a formidable specification. Much of the improvement that has taken place during the last few years has been due to the extensive studies of liquid crystal materials. The compounds of the most interest for the nematic phase have two aromatic (benzene) rings linked with a central group comprising a double or triple bond:

The central group may be —N=N— (azo compounds) —N=N (azoxy compounds) or
$$\underset{O}{}$$

—CH=N— (Schiff's bases). The last named is of particular interest and is used for the dynamic scattering mode. The terminal groups (R and R′) are usually alkyl or alkyloxy groups. The first example of a single Schiff's base compound to exhibit nematic behaviour at room temperature (actually 22–48°C) was prepared by Kelker and Scheurle[28] and was MBBA (p- methoxybenzylidene -p′-butylaniline).

If this is mixed with a similar Schiff's base material EBBA which on its own has a temperature range of 35–77°C, a liquid crystal is derived with a temperature range of 0–60°C:

These and similar materials have a negative dielectric anisotropy and are suitable for dynamic scattering applications. By substituting the alkyl terminal group by a cyano group (C≡N) a positive dielectric anisotropy material is obtained, for example:

$$C_6H_{13} - \left\langle \bigcirc \right\rangle - CH = N - \left\langle \bigcirc \right\rangle - CN$$

Schiff's base materials are liable to oxidation and hydrolysis and are difficult to obtain pure. They must be handled in clean conditions and hermetic sealing of the devices must be good. Impurities are required in the crystal for the n.d.a. dynamic scattering material, but lack of control of the dopant often results in irreproducibility of characteristic and life. A range of more stable nematic compounds has been developed at Hull University[29] for p.d.a. twisted nematic applications. They are based on biphenyl and terphenyl compounds,

$$R-C_6H_4-C_6H_4-CN \qquad \text{or} \qquad R-C_6H_4-C_6H_4-C_6H_4-CN$$

where R is an alkyl group.

The common type of compound exhibiting cholesteric phase is the group of cholesteryl esters with a steroid structure. About 5 to 10% of cholesteric compound is dissolved in a nematic liquid for the phase change and memory electro-optic effects. The mixing of liquid crystal materials to give the best characteristics is important and the proprietary brands now available have been made in this way. A more detailed discussion of the chemistry of liquid crystals can be found in Gray's book on the subject.[30]

The problems of life and limited temperature range in early liquid crystal displays have now been largely overcome. The main criticism of the liquid crystal display is the grey rather poor contrast and in some cases the limited viewing angle. The lack of contrast is mainly due to the fact that not all the liquid crystal is reorientated by the electric field. There will always be regions near the glass surfaces where the molecules are 'anchored' and retain the zero field orientation. Although increasing the field reduces this boundary layer thickness and thus improves the contrast, the voltage required for a significant improvement could make the liquid crystal unattractive commercially. Present research and developments therefore are aimed at improving the visual characteristics but also at attaining faster switching times for multiplex applications.

Improved contrast and viewing angle have been attained for direct drive twisted nematic displays by arranging the molecules to have a tilt with respect to the electrode planes.[31] This has the effect of providing a bias and reduces the boundary effects. Unfortunately the tilt also reduces the threshold and makes it unsuitable for multiplexing. Improvements have also been made by paying attention to the reflecting layer behind the liquid crystal. These have been greatly improved over the years to give high reflectivity without any specular reflection. An interesting approach to improve the display has been made by Baur and Greubel[32] by mounting the liquid crystal on a plastic plate doped with fluorescent molecules. The ambient light is collected by the plate which is larger in area than the liquid crystal cell. It is converted to fluorescent light, guided by internal reflection and emitted at the digit segments by suitably cut facets in the plate. The l.c.d. is used in the transmission mode and light amplification is obtained proportional to the ratio of incident surface area to display area.

The main advance made toward the end of the 1970s was the incorporation of colour. A colour display can be obtained by incorporating a 'guest' pleochroic dye in a p.d.a. nematic 'host' material. The pleochroic dyes have different absorption coefficients parallel and perpendicular to their optic axis and can be orientated by the liquid crystal molecules. Switching the liquid crystal from parallel to perpendicular with respect to the electrodes gave a colour display when used with a single polariser. More recently White and Taylor[33] used the 'guest–host' interaction of a dye in a liquid crystal operating in the phase change mode. In this system unpolarised light is used where the absorption is more efficient and therefore the contrast ratio higher in the reflective mode. Unfortunately the system is unsuitable for multiplexing and does not offer colour contrast, since display and background are of the same colour shade. A further improvement is claimed by Uchida et al.[34] by using a double-layered cell. Basically this consists of two guest–host displays one behind the other but with the orientation of the molecules in one cell being perpendicular to that of the other as shown in fig. 6.16. In the off state both compounds are absorbed by

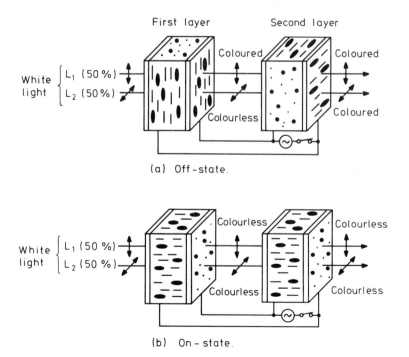

(a) Off-state.

(b) On-state.

Fig 6.16 Double-cell arrangement for guest–host l.c.d. according to Uchida et al.[34] (a) off state. (b) on state. (Permission for reprint courtesy Society for Information Display)

either the first or second layer, and in the on state neither are absorbed. Attempts have also been made to improve the contrast by using a fluorescent 'guest' material, europium chelate, which gives enhanced light output at low ambient light levels.[35]

Commercial liquid crystal displays are normally limited to arrays of a few numerals as shown in fig. 6.17. Their slow speed and threshold problems make them unsuitable for multiplexing in larger arrays. In the reflective mode there are also contrast ratio problems for larger arrays as discussed in chapter 3, necessitating the incorporation of memory. Nevertheless, because of its low power and the ease of fabricating cells of any size, the possibility of large dot-matrix arrays is being actively investigated. There are two main approaches, one to use the decay time or memory of the liquid crystal, and the other to attach a separate memory element to

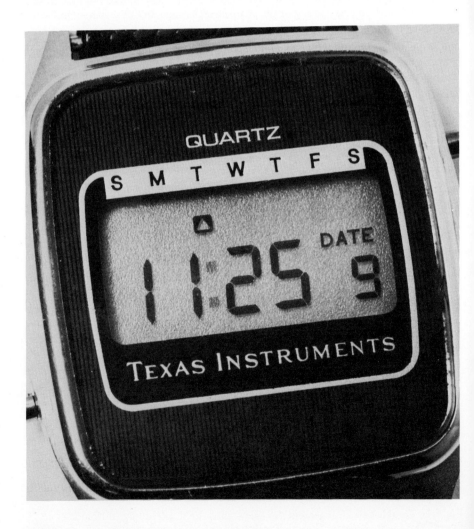

Fig. 6.17 Example of a twisted nematic display

each pixel. Several workers have used the first method and panels with up to 260 x 260 elements have been reported[36] using a cholesteric memory mode mechanism. Investigation of bistable effects in liquid crystals has also shown memory possibilities in nematic and smectic materials.[37] However, the slow switching time of the memory effect means that several seconds are required to address such a panel. More modest arrays of up to fifty rows have been successfully demonstrated with other types of liquid crystal, particularly the faster phase change mode. It has been found that if the display is cycled at a field rate faster than the decay time then successive pulses will switch it on even if the duration is less than the switch-on time, e.g. it may take several cycles to switch on. The problem then is that the off cells receive half pulses at a faster rate than the on cells receive full pulses and the contrast is poor owing to background light. Dargent and Robert[38] have used a liquid crystal for which the dielectric anisotropy changes sign at higher frequencies. By use of two frequencies the background has been considerably reduced.

The other approach, that of using a separate memory switch, was initially investigated by Brody et al.[39] They used a matrix of thin film transistors distributed over a 6 x 6 inch panel giving a thin film circuit with 14 000 transistors which was in direct contact with a twisted nematic liquid crystal. The display has a 20 lines/in resolution and could be operated at t.v. rates. A contrast ratio of 25:1 was measured. Alternative switching elements have been examined such as varistors fabricated on a ZnO substrate in contact with the liquid crystal[40] and metal–insulator–metal non-linear elements.[41] A silicon substrate has also been used with m.o.s.f.e.t. circuits.[42]

Panels giving two or three lines of alphanumeric characters are available commercially, but larger panels giving satisfactory displays for commercial exploitation are yet to be achieved. Methods of scanning a liquid crystal array with an electron beam or thermally scanning it with a laser beam have also been investigated (see chapter 5).

6.6 Electrochromic displays

Electrochromic displays offer the main challenge to the liquid crystal for low powered passive seven-bar numeric displays. They normally operate at low voltage of the order of a few volts and most have non-volatile memory so that their maintenance power is low. Their main asset is their appearance; they have a better colour contrast and a wider viewing angle than the liquid crystal, more nearly approaching the printed page. Their main disadvantage is lack of threshold and narrow range of switching voltage making matrix addressing difficult. The phenomenon of electrochromism can be broadly defined as the changing of the light absorption properties of certain solid state materials by an externally applied electric field. The colour change usually remains after the field is removed and can only be bleached by reversing the polarity. Although first observed in the 1930s in alkali halides in connection with the production of colour centres in ionic crystals, electrochromism has not been extensively investigated and is still not well understood. In general it only occurs in solids with gross defects such as occur in amorphous materials, or in non-stoichiometric thin films of the transition metal oxides. However, a number of different physical mechanisms may be involved under the broad title of electrochromism, for example, the formation of colour centres in ionic crystals, charge exchange between impurity centres, and electro-chemical redox reactions in which non-coloured species are reduced or oxidised to coloured species. The latter are often referred to as electrochemical displays. One parameter which seems to be essential for the phenomenon is the presence of both electronic and ionic conduction. The materials that have been investigated for electrochromic displays are listed in table 6.3 together with some of their properties.

The formation of a blue colouration of WO_3 by an electric field was first demonstrated by Deb.[43] He deposited a film of WO_3 about 1 μm thick on a tin oxide coated glass substrate, and subsequently deposited a second electrode of gold. With the gold electrode as cathode, the layer developed a deep blue colouration in a few seconds, with 2 V across it. The colour centres were considered to be produced by charge injection from the negative electrode. It is now considered that the presence of water in the film was responsible for the effect. The H_2O dissociated and the protons migrate in the field to the cathode compensating the injected electrons and forming a hydrogen tungsten bronze H_xWO_3 (where $0 < x < 1$), i.e. a redox type process. The system was not reversible, but could be made so by intro-ducing an insulating layer between one electrode and the WO_3 film. Molybdenum trioxide exhibits a similar effect, and both materials have been further examined by other workers. The contrast and response time, however, are not particularly suitable for a practical display. If, however, the tungsten oxide film is combined with an electrolyte so that protons or other ions can be injected into the film the bronze can be more easily formed with faster switching speeds and the effect is reversible. The process can be expressed by the reversible reaction:

$$xM^+ + xe^- + [WO_3] \rightleftharpoons M_x^+ [WO_3] \ e_x^-.$$
$$\text{clear} \qquad\qquad \text{coloured}$$

The colouration is due to the trapped electrons, the injected ions acting merely to compensate the charge. The theory of the processes is described by Faughnan $et\ al.$[44] Early studies used sulphuric acid[45] to give the H_xWO_3 bronze, but also $LiClO_4$ was used to give a $LiWO_3$ bronze which is similarly blue coloured.[46] Display devices based on this system are similar to liquid crystal cells, consisting of two glass plates carrying the electrode patterns sealed together with a spacer frame between. The WO_3 is deposited on the front transparent electrode pattern and the electrolyte fills the cell which is typically around 1 mm deep. The electrolyte is often loaded with a white pigment to give good contrast. Early devices had serious life problems and improvements in technology have lessened these problems.[47] Attempts have also been made to replace the liquid electrolyte by a solid. In some an insulating layer is used and the process depends on the presence of absorbed water as for the Deb device. Using Cr_2O_3, Inoue $et\ al.$[48] claims the water is tightly bound and unaffected by the environment even working in a vacuum. Another idea is to use solid electro-lytes; for example, a device has been fabricated with phosphotungstic acid $(H_3PO_4(WO_3)_{12} . nH_2O)$ compressed as a powder between electrodes.[49] A similar inorganic system based on IrO_2 has been studied at the Bell Laboratories. In this

Table 6.3 Electrochromic materials for display

Material	Reaction	Colour	Characteristics		
			Switching volts or field	Charge density for 10:1 contrast	Switching time*
Tungsten trioxide (WO_3)	Formation of $H_2|$-tungstate bronze	Blue	10^4 V/cm	–	1–3 s
Molybdenum trioxide (MoO_3)	Formation of molybdenate bronze	Blue	10^4 V/cm	–	1–3 s
WO_3 + electrolyte	Redox + solid film	Blue	2 V	15 mC/cm^2	0.2–1 s
Diheptylviologendibromide	Redox + chemical reaction	Purple	1.5 V	2 mC/cm^2	10–50 ms
Luteteum diphthalocynine		Multicolour			
Sodium tungstate + acid	Redox polytungsten anion	Blue	2 V	25 mC/cm^2	–
Iridium oxide (IrO_2)	Redox	Blue-black	1.5 V		40 ms

* The switching time is the required charge divided by current density and depends on the conductivity of the cell and applied voltage.

system the colouration occurs at the anode and appears to have better life characteristics.[50] Combining the device with tantalum oxide cathode has introduced a voltage threshold, sufficient to allow in principle large matrix multiplexing.[51] An excellent review of such electrochromic displays has been given by Faughnan and Crandall.[52]

Various organic systems have been investigated, but probably the most promising depended on the use of the organic compounds known as viologens investigated by Schoot and his co-workers.[53] The specific compound used is diheptyl viologen dibromide dissolved in water:

$$C_7H_{15}Br \text{———} N \langle\bigcirc\rangle\langle\bigcirc\rangle N \text{———} C_7H_{15}\,Br$$

The compound is reduced at the cathode by a single electron step to form a radical ion which reacts with the bromine to give an insoluble purple solid, $[(C_7H_{15})_2 (NC_5H_4)_2\ Br]$, which precipitates onto the cathode. Thus, if the front electrode is made transparent and segmented to form a character, then when it is made negative the character will appear purple on a light background. An example of an experimental viologen electrochromic display is shown in Plate 2.

A newer and more interesting system is that using the rare earth diphthalocyanines especially lutetium diphthalocyanine.[54] The organic film is deposited on the tin oxide electrode pattern and the cell filled with a liquid electrolyte, usually potassium chloride, with a counter electrode of silver. The interesting property of the diphthalocyanines is that the colour of the film, normally green, changes from deep blue and violet at negative potential through various shades of green to orange and red at positive potential, thus giving the possibility of a multi-colour display.

The behaviour of all electrochromic displays is very similar. There is usually a threshold field for commencement of colouration, but this is low, requiring only one or two volts across a millimetre gap. The gap is not critical, since the degree of colouration is not dependent on field but on the total charge passed, $\int i\,dt$. As a result, response time depends on the electrical conductivity of the material, and as soon as sufficient contrast has been built up, the current source should be switched off. The colour layer then remains on the electrodes. Current is only taken during switching; thus the displays only consume power during the switching time and life is a function of the number of switchings, not necessarily operational hours. The information is erased by reversing the current through the cell. However, in some systems this results in colouration occurring on the counter electrodes. This not only degrades the contrast, but if allowed to go too far will make the next write—erase cycle slow. Since the coloured layer charges up, its presence can be detected by comparing the electrode potential with that of a reference. The problem of over-erasure, therefore, can be reduced by introducing a reference electrode, held at the so-called saturated calomel potential. When the cathode potential is equal to the reference potential, the erasure pulse is removed. The contrast on a reflective display can be enhanced by introducing an opaque white filler material such as TiO_2 into the liquid or by using a white porous membrane.

The main problem with electrochromic displays has been the life or number of switching cycles. Although up to 10^7 switching cycles have been achieved, the life would still be unacceptable for some applications, for example indicating seconds on a watch. The limitation is due to deterioration of the contrast and/or deterioration of the switching speed. The effects may be due to electrolysis, but often the fatigue mechanism is not understood. Basically it can be ascribed to a materials problem which hopefully can be overcome in the future. In the meantime life performance is inferior to that of liquid crystals and this has been a major barrier to their commercial exploitation.

6.7 Electrophoretic displays

In electrophoretic displays, charged pigment particles suspended in a liquid are attracted and deposited at the cathode under an electric field. If the particles are say black suspended in a milky liquid and the cathode is in the form of transparent segments disposed on the front surface of a cell, then the appearance of the display will be very similar to that obtained by electrochromism, a dark character on a white background with wide viewing angle and good contrast.

The phenomenon of electrophoresis dates back to the early nineteenth century and is used in many industrial processes for coating purposes. The main problem in applying the system to display is to hold the particles indefinitely in suspension, i.e. avoid precipitation, but at the same time to obtain fast deposition on the electrodes under low field conditions, which is reversible and repeatable. The rate of precipitation of particles in suspension is given by Stokes's law:

$$\frac{dx}{dt} = \frac{2ga(\rho - \rho')}{9\eta} \tag{6.2}$$

where g is gravitational acceleration, a is the particle diameter, ρ is the density of the particle, ρ' is the density of the liquid and η is the viscosity of the liquid. Unfortunately, however, most of the parameters in equation 6.2 have limitations. If the particle size is too small, of the order of the wavelength of light, it will not act as a good scatterer of light and will reduce the contrast. If the viscosity is too high then the time taken for the particles to deposit on the cathode, i.e. switching time, will be too great. Ideally ρ is chosen as close to ρ' as possible but it is difficult to match the densities over a reasonable temperature range and in any case the best reflecting particles have a higher density than can be attained in a liquid. The development of electrophoretic displays therefore depends very much on the choice of suitable materials.

The first electrophoretic display was described by Ota et al.[55] They used layers 25–100 μm thick in cells similar to liquid crystal cells. The coloured suspending liquid was prepared by dissolving dyes in insulating organic solvents such as tetrachloroethylene. The particles were chosen to give densities equal to the liquid and were from 0.5 to 3 μm diameter. The organic pigment, hansa yellow, could be used freely suspended, but higher density TiO_2 could also be used by encapsulating it in a resin of lower density. Control agents were used to improve the dispersion and charging of the particles. Ota et al. gave preliminary data on experimental numeric cells and several laboratories have now taken up the idea. To obtain good contrast, the counter electrode at the back of the cell can be segmented, and reverse polarity applied to the unrequired display segments so that the particles in their area are drawn to the back plate. Typically, 50 to 100 V are required across the cell to give good contrast with a current during the switching pulse of the order of 1 $\mu A/cm^2$. As with the electrochromic display the particles remain attached to the electrodes when the potential is removed and erasure is obtained by reversing polarity. The response time is of the order of 10 ms.

The main effort over the last few years has been devoted to obtaining stable colloidal suspensions with suitable characteristics for display. One of the major problems has been the agglomeration of particles either in the liquid or when deposited. It results in a granular appearance of the display and increases the rate of precipitation. There are also problems of migration of the particles from the display area and the particles not sticking to the cathode sufficiently. The choice of dye is also important; it must give a good contrast with the particles but not dye them. These problems are discussed in a review article by Dalisa.[56]

The appearance and life of electrophoretic displays have been greatly improved since the early samples, but further development is still required before a successful product is available. Initially the work was aimed at numeric applications with seven-bar devices. They offered a display with good colour contrast and wide viewing angle with non-volatile memory but unfortunately their switching voltages were rather high. The present emphasis is on larger cross-bar addressed alphanumeric panels. For this, a threshold characteristic is required. This can be achieved by suitable choice of materials and Chiang[57] outlines three techniques which can give such thresholds. Singer and Dalisa,[58] however, introduced an external threshold by incorporating a third control electrode and operating in a triode mode. They considered the system to be more reliable than those depending on choice of material and with the added advantage of a reduced addressing time. The construction of their panel is shown diagrammatically in fig. 6.18. Assuming the pigment to be negatively charged, then it can be loaded into the potential 'well' around the column electrodes by applying a positive potential to all the column electrodes (~30 V) and keeping the row control electrodes at 15 V and the anode at 0 V. The anode is then reset to +50 V. To address the display the potential on the appropriate column is reduced and the potential of the required row is made equal to or greater than the potential on the column. As a result the pigment at the crosspoint will be transported by the field to the anode. The potentials are chosen such that the half pulse on either control electrode or column electrode will not allow the pigment to escape. The display is viewed from the column electrode side but an alternative arrangement can be used to view from the anode side. By making the insulator black a good contrast is obtained. A 512-character panel based on this principle has been described[59] with a dot pitch of 0.5 mm. As with electrochromic devices the life is dictated by the number of switching cycles rather than hours, and is determined by a deterioration in the contrast. Precipitation on 'shelf life' can also be a problem. The technology is relatively young compared with that of liquid crystals and improvements can be expected in the future. Whether they will compete with the liquid crystal display, however, can only be a matter of conjecture.

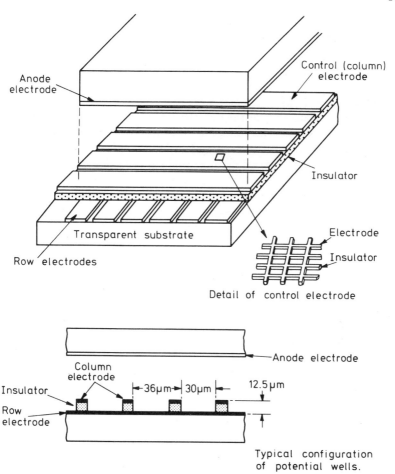

Fig. 6.18 Schematic of a three-electrode electrophoretic panel according to Singer and Dalisa.[58] (Permission for reprint courtesy Society for Information Display)

6.8 Gas discharge displays

Gas discharge display, one of the oldest display technologies, still remains competitive for numeric application in spite of its relatively high operating voltages. For large alphanumeric application it represents the main challenge to the c.r.t.

Gas discharge display devices utilise the light output of a cold cathode discharge. There are two processes for the emission of photons in a gas, excitation of the atoms or molecules by electron bombardment giving radiation when they return to the ground state, and radiative recombination of ions and electrons; both represent efficient methods of producing light. The luminous efficiency is especially high for low voltage plasmas, such as the positive column of an arc discharge, where 50 to

60 lm/W are attainable in, for example, sodium and mercury vapour lamps. For cold cathode glow discharges, extensively used for electronic display applications, where the glow emanates from a region known as the negative glow close to the cathode surface, the efficiency of the discharge is lower, 0.5 lm/W. Nevertheless it compares favourably with alternative devices, and gives useful light output for most applications.

However, the main asset of the gas discharge for display devices is its threshold electrical characteristics. The voltage–current relationship of a discharge between parallel plates in a gas at reduced pressure is shown in fig. 6.19 as a semi-logarithmic plot. As the voltage is increased the current builds up, at first slowly and then more rapidly until the ignition threshold is reached at V_s. This build-up of current is due to ionisation in the gas characterised by η, the ionisation coefficient, and by secondary emission processes at the cathode characterised by a coefficient γ. However, up to this ignition stage the current is very small, typically less than 1 μA/cm^2, and no visible glow is apparent. At the ignition threshold there is a large increase in current producing space charge which results in an actual reduction in the potential drop across the electrodes until a minimum is reached. At the minimum the potential remains substantially constant over a wide current range and the physical characteristics of a glow discharge are observed. In this region the discharge can be considered essentially as a constant voltage device requiring an external impedance to control the current. Lowering the voltage below the minimum extinguishes the discharge giving a second threshold, the extinction voltage V_e. If the discharge display device is held at a potential between V_s and V_e the discharge can be switched on by applying a pulse which will temporarily raise the potential above V_s, and switched

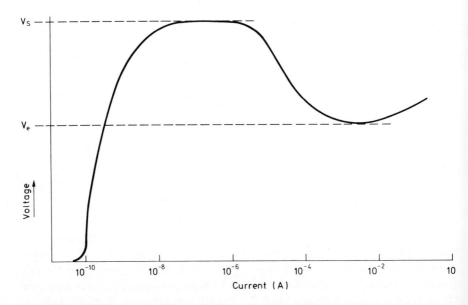

Fig. 6.19 Voltage–current characteristics of a glow discharge

off by a pulse lowering the potential below V_e. Thus the display has the potentiality of 'storage' or memory of information. The values of V_s, V_e and the running voltage V_m are functions of the coefficients γ and η which in turn are dependent on geometry, the gas composition and pressure, and cathode material. This means that the voltages can be controlled to some extent by the selection of these parameters. On the other hand, in segmented displays where there are several cathodes, differences in geometry and cathode surface conditions will mean that although V_s, V_e and V_m will be similar for all segments there will be spreads in their values. The magnitudes of the spreads are important to the drive circuit design.

When operated under pulsed or a.c. conditions a further factor has to be taken into account and that is the temporal growth and decay of the discharge, i.e. the ionisation and deionisation times. They not only limit the rate at which the discharge can be addressed but they also affect the voltage requirements. In general, the shorter the pulse the higher the amplitude required to initiate the discharge; typically to switch a cell in less than 10 μs requires a voltage 25% higher than the direct voltage ignition value. On the other hand, the cell can be 'primed' by the presence of charged particles in the vicinity, in which case the required pulse amplitude and/or width will be reduced. The priming may be provided by an adjacent discharge or as a result of incomplete deionisation, resulting from a previous discharge in the same region. Thus not only is the ignition voltage higher for pulsed operation, but also the spread may be increased if priming conditions are varied.

One of the characteristics of the glow discharge is that negative glow follows faithfully the cathode contours, surrounding it in a glowing sheath. This property was exploited in the first type of gas discharge character display device, the numerical indicator.[60] In this tube thin cathodes shaped as the characters were stacked one behind the other, and surrounded by a common anode structure, the front and part of the sides of which were in the form of a mesh with good optical transmission. The glowing sheath was much wider than the cathode and could be clearly seen even from the backmost character. Commonly the tube contained the numerals 0–9. To operate the tube the anode is held above the ignition voltage and the cathodes positively biased so that little or no current passes to them. The required character is selected by switching the appropriate cathode to earth. A bias, and thus a switching voltage, of 40 to 60 V is required, which is within the capabilities of integrated circuits, and no pattern encoder is needed. The numerical indicator tube represents therefore a very cheap easy to drive device for numeric display.

The stacked cathode array has disadvantages from the subjective point of view. The viewing angle is restricted, the digits in a register are not on the same plane and the non-selected electrodes give it a 'cluttered' appearance. The modern trend is to seven-bar matrix displays for numerals, and fortunately the gas discharge technology can be adapted to this format, with seven cathode bars and a common anode. It offers the same flat package as other technologies, and the threshold characteristics make it particularly suitable for multiplexing, so that multiples of up to sixteen numerals can be packaged in one envelope. Such a multiple display can be constructed with metal electrodes mounted on a lead frame with mica insulation, as shown in the example of a two-digit tube shown in fig. 6.20(a). Alternatively the electrodes and connections may be deposited on the glass envelope by a silk screen

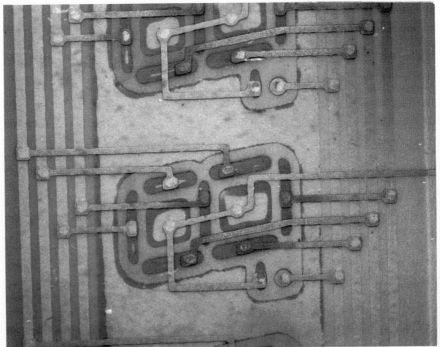

Fig. 6.20 Examples of multi-digit glow discharge numerical displays (a) two-digit glow discharge numerical indicator ZM1150 from Philips, (courtesy Mullard Ltd) (b) silk screen printed electrode pattern for numerical indicator

Plate 1 A 40 × 40 monolithic l.e.d. matrix on a 1 in. slice. (Courtesy G.E.C. Research Laboratories.)

Plate 2 An experimental viologen electrochromic display. (Courtesy Philips Research Laboratories.)

Plate 3 Cathodoluminescent character display tubes. (Courtesy English Electric Valve Company Ltd.)

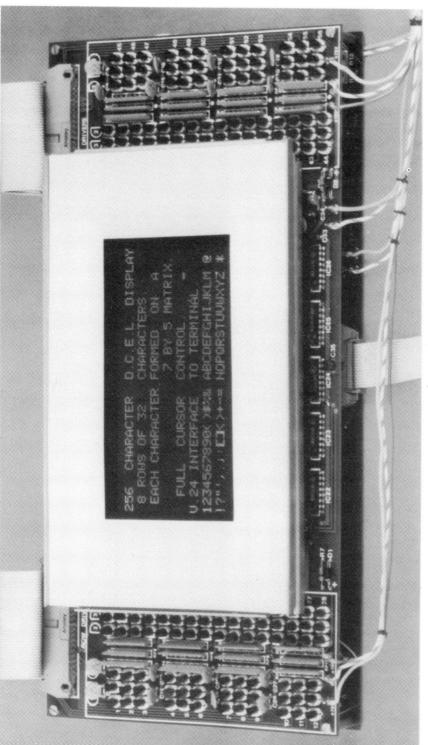

Plate 4 256-character d.c. electroluminescent panel. (Courtesy Phosphor Products Company Ltd.)

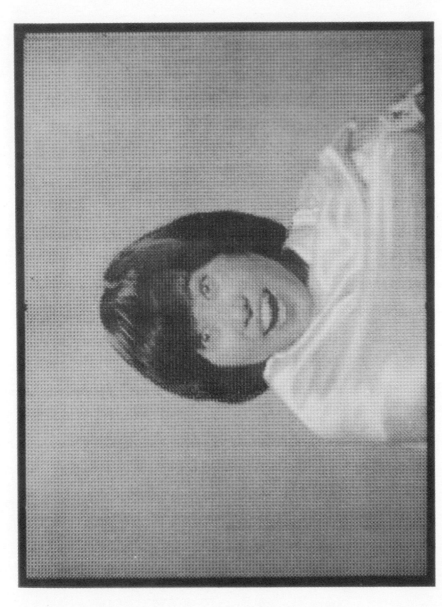

Plate 5 T.V. picture on a 16 in. gas discharge colour panel. (Courtesy N.H.K. Technical Research Laboratory.)

printing technique developed for hybrid circuits. By printing four or five layers of alternate conductor and insulating patterns, the complete electrode pattern with cross-over points, etc. can be printed on one plate. An example of the design is illustrated in fig. 6.20(b).

Although fifteen-bar star-burst pattern arrays have been made in gas discharge technology for alphanumeric displays on a similar basis, the gas discharge lends itself to a dot-matrix array which can be cross-bar addressed. The main development in gas discharge displays over the past decade has been the exploitation of such dot-matrix arrays for displaying up to 3000 characters or graphics, the so-called plasma panels.

Basically the plasma panel consists of a two-dimensional array of discrete gas discharges which can be selectively addressed by cross-bar electrodes. In many designs the discharges are confined in separate cells formed by apertures in an insulating plate which is placed between two glass plates on which the orthogonal system of electrodes is mounted. An exploded view of such a panel is shown in fig. 6.21. The three plates are sealed together round the edges and filled with a gas mixture which is predominantly neon at a reduced pressure, $1 \times 10^4 - 4 \times 10^4$ N/m^2.

The panels may be operated under a.c. conditions in which each set of electrodes acts alternately as anodes or cathodes, or under d.c. conditions in which one set of electrodes acts always as cathodes and the other as anodes. Both methods of operation are exploited in commercial designs. In the a.c. operation the electrodes need not be in contact with the gas but may be isolated from it by an insulating

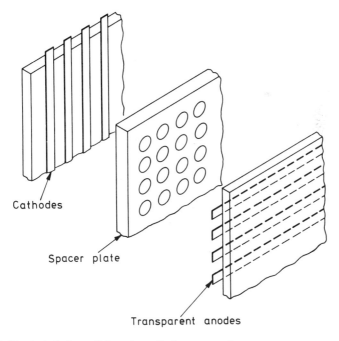

Cathodes

Spacer plate

Transparent anodes

Fig. 6.21 Exploded view of d.c. glow discharge panel

layer. Two drive modes may be distinguished: cyclic, in which each cell is illuminated only during the address pulse; and storage, in which a cell once addressed remains on until it is erased some time later. The bias and pulse conditions (relative to the spreads in ignition and extinction voltage) for the two modes of operation are illustrated for the case of the d.c. panel in fig. 6.22. In the cyclic mode the cells are biased below the extinction voltage. A single pulse must not take it up above the minimum ignition voltage, whereas two pulses must take it above the maximum ignition voltage. For minimum pulse amplitude a narrow gap is required between V_s and V_e and narrow spreads. For the storage mode where the bias is between V_s and V_e, the sum of the spreads of V_s and V_e must be less than the gap between $V_{e\ max}$ and $V_{s\ min}$. For this mode a wider voltage gap between ignition and extinction potential is required. Once the discharge is on, the current through the cell must be limited by a series impedance. In the cyclic mode, the impedances can be placed

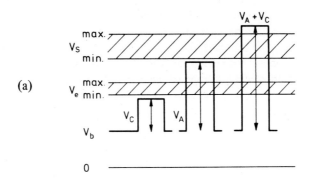

(a)

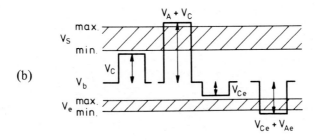

(b)

Fig. 6.22 Drive pulse and bias conditions for addressing d.c. plasma panels, (a) for cyclic mode operation, (b) for storage mode operation. V_C and V_A are the cathode and anode pulse amplitude respectively

outside the panel in series with one set of electrodes, and time shared between the cells on the electrodes to which they are connected. In the storage mode time sharing of the impedances is not possible and a series impedance is required for each cell. For the a.c. panel, which has similar characteristics, the insulating layer provides a capacitive impedance to each cell. Incorporating an impedance for storage mode in a d.c. panel is more difficult. Thin film and thick film techniques have been used to produce a resistor of the order of 1 MΩ at each cell position, but although the feasibility of both these techniques has been demonstrated, problems of resolution and tolerances on resistor and circuit make it unlikely that large panels could be constructed economically. Smith[61] showed that an inherent storage d.c. panel could be designed, without series resistors in each cell. By using graphite cathodes, which give a low secondary emission coefficient γ, and pure neon gas at a pressure of 1.3 x 10^4 N/m^2, a glow discharge could be obtained with a steep positive V–I characteristic so that the current in the ignited state was virtually limited by the impedance of the discharge itself. Unfortunately the dissipation of the panel was too high for large panels to be used without forced air cooling.

The d.c. panel has been more satisfactory as a cyclic operated panel, and various designs have been proposed. Because the light output increases with current and fairly high pulsed currents can be taken, duty cycles up to 1:200 can be employed with adequate mean brightness for applications used in a normally lit room. This allows up to 1000 characters to be displayed with a line dumping system. An experimental display panel of this type is illustrated in fig. 6.23. Since the circuit cost of a matrix display increases more or less proportionally to the number of cross-bar connections, they cannot compete with the c.r.t. for large capacity displays. However, panels with a limited character capability, less than 500 characters, become very cost competitive with the c.r.t. and offer a more compact package. Especially successful for these limited size displays has been the Self-Scan® panels marketed by Burroughs Corporation in which the number of leads is significantly reduced in one direction, to decrease circuit costs.[62] An exploded view of their first design of panel is shown in fig. 6.24. The panel can be considered as having two sections, (1) the glow scan section, which consists of the scan anodes and the rear side of the cathode conductors, and (2) the display section, consisting of the display anodes and the front side of the cathodes with an insulating aperture plate in between, similar to the conventional d.c. panel (cf. fig. 6.21). The two sections are linked via the small glow priming apertures in the cathodes.

In operation, a glow is transferred down the length of the panel at the rear of each cathode at a field rate of approximately 60 Hz. It is hardly visible from the front as the cathode apertures are very small, but it primes the display cells in front of the glow, reducing significantly their ignition voltage. If, therefore, an anode pulse is applied at the appropriate time of such an amplitude that it will ignite a primed cell but not an unprimed cell, then a visible glow will occur at the designated crosspoint. Thus by parallel addressing the anodes in synchronism with the glow transfer, the desired data can be displayed. The transfer of the glow along the back of the cathodes is effected by connecting every third cathode in parallel and applying voltage pulses of the order of 100 V in sequence to the three bus-bars so formed. The amplitude of the pulses is such that they will only ignite the heavily primed cathode adjacent to the lit cathode. The extra current taken through a common anode load resistor lowers the anode voltage to extinguish the glow on the previous cathode. The fact that the adjacent cathodes are heavily primed and have a lower ignition voltage than the rest of the cathodes ensures that the glow progresses a step at a time in one direction with the application of sequential pulses. For larger panels a six or twelve clock pulse system is employed with six or twelve bus-bars,

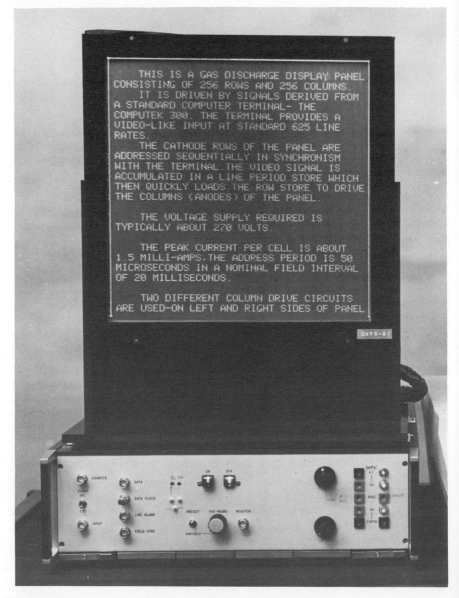

Fig. 6.23 Data display on an experimental d.c. plasma panel

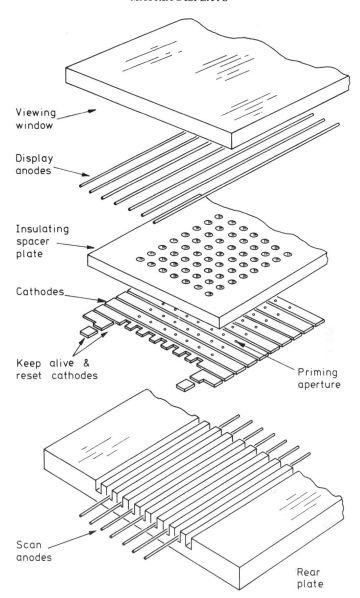

Viewing window

Display anodes

Insulating spacer plate

Cathodes

Keep alive & reset cathodes

Priming aperture

Scan anodes

Rear plate

Fig. 6.24 Exploded view of the Burroughs Self-Scan® panel

but the principle is the same. The same company introduced a second design aimed at reducing the panel cost. In this design the glow is transferred along the front of the panel between the display cells hidden from view by a wide transfer anode strip. Being coplanar the cathodes and insulating barriers can be silk screen printed on one plate and the glow transfer and display anodes on the other with an aperture plate between. A larger dot pitch has to be used, however, to accommodate the glow transfer sections.

For 1000 or more character capability storage in the panel is required because of the switching time and also to improve the brightness. It is in this area that the a.c. panel comes into its own. The first a.c. panels were similar in structure to the d.c. panel (fig. 6.21) except that the electrodes were placed on the outer surfaces of the two electrode carrying plates.[63]

Consider an a.c. signal applied across the electrodes, of such an amplitude V_f that a gas discharge breakdown can occur on each half cycle. The establishment of the discharge on say the positive half cycle will result in the build-up of charge on the glass surfaces in front of the cathode, which will set up a voltage V_{we} in opposition to the applied voltage. These wall charges have two effects. First, they can reduce the voltage during the half cycle to a value below the extinction voltage and extinguish the discharge (which can happen in less than a microsecond), and second, on reversal of the polarity the wall charge voltage V_{we} adds to the applied voltage to allow breakdown at a lower applied potential (i.e. $V_f - V_{we}$). At any voltage between V_f and $V_f - V_{we}$ the cell has a bistable characteristic; a cell initially ignited will reignite each half cycle, but an off cell will never be ignited. Thus, one can consider the a.c. panel as having breakdown and extinction potential analogous to the d.c. case, with, incidentally, the same problems of voltage spreads. The operation of the panel is illustrated in fig. 6.25 which shows the sustainer voltage waveform

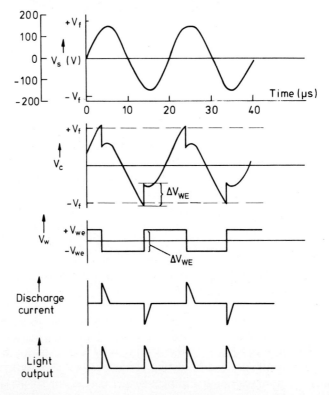

Fig. 6.25 Sustainer voltage V_s, tube voltage V_c and wall voltage V_w for a typical a.c. plasma panel together with current and light output waveforms

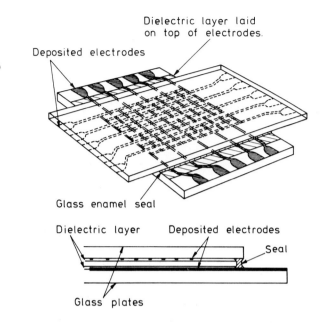

Dielectric layer laid
on top of electrodes.

Deposited electrodes

Glass enamel seal

Dielectric layer   Deposited electrodes

Seal

Glass plates

Fig. 6.26 Schematic diagram of the Owen–Illinois Digivue panel

V_s and voltage across cell V_c and wall voltage V_w for a typical panel. In general, the wall charge is greater when the discharge is short and of high intensity, and this to some extent depends on the gas pressure and composition.

Since the current pulse, also shown in fig. 6.25, is only on for a microsecond or so, the brightness will depend on frequency as well as the pulse amplitude. There is, however, a maximum frequency of about 100 kHZ above which the panel will not function owing mainly to cancellation of the wall charge by residual ions when the field is reversed. At this frequency the duty cycle is about one in one hundred. The amplitude of the current pulses will be determined by the signal voltage, and the capacitive impedance of the glass wall which acts as the individual impedance for each cell. For maximum current at the lowest signal voltage the impedance should be as low as possible, inferring a thin glass wall. The fabrication of large panels with thin glass walls, however, would be extremely difficult, and therefore alternative structures have to be considered.

One of the most successful early designs was that developed by Owen–Illinois Inc.[64] Essentially the electrodes are deposited on the inside surface of relatively thick glass plates (i.e. 6 mm thick) forming the panel walls, and subsequently coated by a thin glass dielectric film. In their design it was also found possible to eliminate the centre aperture plate by placing the outer plates close together. Thus the panel consists of two plates placed parallel so that the electrodes form a cross grid, the narrow space between being sealed round the edges with glass enamel and filled with gas. A schematic diagram of the panel is shown in fig. 6.26. Because of the simplicity of the structure, having no geometrical registration restrictions, a resolution up to sixty lines per inch is obtainable. Panels having up to 512 x 512 lines were

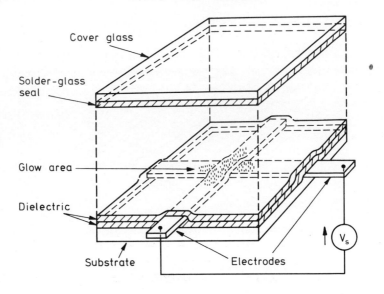

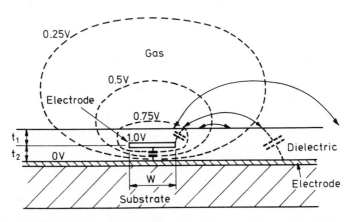

Fig. 6.27 Schematic diagram of the single-substrate plasma panel according to Dick and Biazzo.[65] (Copyright © 1976 I.E.E.E.)

commercially available, and although Owen–Illinois have ceased production similar designs are available from other manufacturers. A further simplification of the structure has since been suggested by Dick and Biazzo[65] whereby both sets of electrodes are deposited on one substrate, thus obviating the need to maintain accurate spacing between the two plates, a serious problem for large displays. The principle of this approach is illustrated in fig. 6.27 which also shows the field and some electron paths.

To change the state of an a.c. cell it is necessary to alter its wall voltage, i.e. from zero for the off cell to a finite value V_w for an on cell. This is normally achieved by superimposing addressing pulses of the order of 2 μs duration on the sustainer voltage suitably timed relative to the sustainer waveform. As for the d.c. panel, ignition of a particular cell is obtained by applying coincident pulses to the appropriate electrodes, the sum of which takes the voltage above the ignition value, whereas a single pulse is insufficient to ignite any cell. The principle can be seen in fig. 6.28 where the address pulses are shown for a square wave sustainer waveform, together with the wall voltage values. The square wave sustainer is preferred and has now superseded the sine wave drive for a.c. panels. It has the advantage of being simpler to generate and allows a greater tolerance on voltages and the timing of the address pulses.

Panels are filled with a neon—argon mixture to give low voltages and a recent development has been to coat the dielectric layer with MgO[66] to reduce the values further. Typical driving pulses are 100 V sustaining (200 V peak to peak) with switching voltages less than 150 V. The inherent memory of the panel allows random write, random erase, but it is more complex to drive than the d.c. cyclic panel. In particular it needs a driver for each electrode. Investigations of schemes to reduce the number of electrodes have been reported. They mainly consider a self-shifting system whereby the information is fed into the panel at one corner and transferred to other parts by applying successive pulses to two transfer electrodes interposed between each display cell.[67,68] Because of the extra electrodes these systems reduce the resolution by a factor of three. Fujitsu described a self-shift system in the horizontal direction only, whereby one of the transfer electrodes was between the anodes and the other between the cathodes which were interdigitally connected in the anode direction.[69] A cell pitch of 0.5 mm was attained by this technique. Perhaps the most interesting approach, however, is the latest Burroughs panel which combines a d.c. Self-Scan with an a.c. display area.[70] Like the d.c. Self-Scan panel it has a scanning section and display section with interconnecting priming holes. The display section, however, has dielectric coated electrodes to give a memory display. A cut-

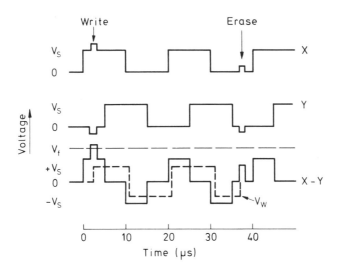

Fig. 6.28 Address pulses and sustainer waveform for an a.c. plasma panel

away view of the design is shown in fig. 6.29. The panel has the advantage of the a.c. panel in giving a non-flicker display, whose luminance of ~135 cd/m² is independent of panel size, with the Self-Scan economy of drive circuit. The structure, however, is more complicated than either d.c. or a.c. panels alone. An alternative approach to reduce the number of connectors and drivers is to designate each pixel by three electrodes which require three coincident signals to operate the output. In theory n pixels can be operated by $3 \times n^{1/3}$ drivers compared to $2 \times n^{1/2}$ for a two-electrode system. Such systems have been proposed for both a.c.[71,72] and d.c.[73] panels.

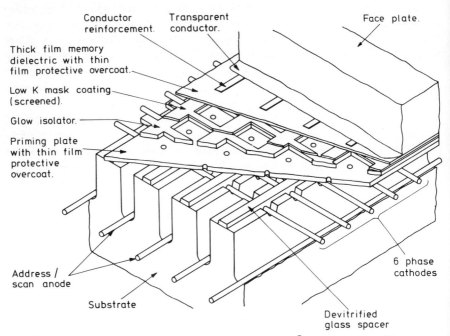

Fig 6.29 Cut-away diagram of the Burroughs Self-Scan® memory panel.[70] (Permission for reprint courtesy Society for Information Display)

A section dealing with plasma panels would not be complete without mentioning their application to television. The television engineers dream has always been the large picture-on-the-wall display and the plasma panel probably represents the strongest contender. The two main requirements for television over and above the requirements for alphanumerics are variations in brightness, i.e. half tones, and the production of full colour. Work on both these subjects is being carried out in the United States and Japan using a.c. and d.c. operated panels.

Since it would be difficult, if not impossible, to consider cells containing different gases in the same panel to produce different colours, and in any case there are no gases which give efficient output in the green or blue, the achievement of colour depends on combining the discharge with phosphors. The phosphor can either be activated by the electrons (cathodoluminescence) or ultraviolet stimulated (photoluminescence). Most of the experiments, however, have been carried out with photoluminescent phosphors. The gas mixture is selected to give the maximum emission in the ultraviolet region with a minimum emission in the visible; xenon, krypton or mercury are used, often admixed with other inert gases. The early experiments were carried out with standard panels and t.v. tube phosphors, the phosphor dots being deposited on the window in front of the cells or, in the case of the d.c. panels, on the walls of the individual cells. The luminous efficiencies were rather low with losses occurring in the phosphor layers. In the a.c. panels there were problems of optical cross-coupling and the phosphor affecting the electrical characteristics. Better application of the phosphor and use of ultraviolet absorbing barriers has considerably reduced the latter problems. This is particularly so for the single-substrate type of panel.[74] Improvements in efficiency were also obtained by the choice of gas and by better matching of the phosphor to the ultraviolet radiation. A further improvement was obtained by using the positive column of the discharge[75] as in fluorescent lamps. To make best use of this enhancement the discharge should be turned through a right angle so that the column is viewed side on.[76] Even so, the efficiencies obtained are still about an order too low for television application.

Half tones present a special problem for storage panels, where a common sustainer voltage is applied to all the elements. However, because the a.c. panel is more advanced, several techniques have been proposed for incorporating grey scale in such panels. In one system described by de Jule and Chodil[77] a complex waveform is applied by which the cell is ignited twice, four times or six times in a given time period, depending on when the address pulse is applied. Four intensity levels were obtained including 'off'. Alternatively, the panel can be scanned several times in each frame period, the brightest spots being turned on in the first scan, the next level in the second scan and so on. Systems have also been proposed in which the grey scale is attained by the spatial distribution of the lighted cells.[78] In one case spatial distribution using four cells per picture element was combined with the complex waveform technique[79] to give sixteen grey scale levels. All these grey scale techniques are complex and would probably be uneconomic even if sufficient intensity levels could be achieved.

For a d.c. cyclic panel where the cells are sequentially addressed the problem is greatly simplified. In a line dumped system each cell can be either current or time modulated or both during the line period. The principle was first demonstrated in 1968 using a time modulation system with an experimental d.c. panel having 100 x 100 cells.[75] Several others have built systems since then, for example Chodil et al. who used the Burroughs Self-Scan 256-character panel to show part of a television picture.[80]

In the late 1970s several Japanese firms demonstrated full colour television pictures using d.c. panels with coloured phosphors albeit with low resolution and with low light output. The largest of these was a 16 in diagonal display with an array of 240 x 320 elements on a 1 mm pitch demonstrated by N.H.K. Laboratories.[81] The luminance, however, was limited to around 25 cd/m^2. A photograph of the resulting display is shown in Plate 5. To improve the luminance, incorporating storage in the d.c. panels and displaying the picture for a frame time have been suggested.[82,83] However, without a considerable improvement in efficiency, tube dissipation would still be a problem.

6.9   Vacuum fluorescent displays

Vacuum fluorescent display was the name given to the seven-bar numerical tube based on low voltage cathodoluminescence developed in Japan in the late 1960s, and it has become accepted in spite of its poor description. The simple numeric devices consist of an oxide coated thermionic emitter in the form of a filament, and seven anodes in a figure-of-eight configuration mounted in a vacuum envelope. The anodes are coated with a low voltage phosphor, ZnO, which gives a bluish-green luminance when bombarded with electrons of energy around 20 eV (see fig. 5.4), with an efficiency of from 5 to 10 lm/W. The filament is located in front of the anodes, but is run at a low temperature so that it is barely visible. By raising the potential on the selected anode segments to say +12 V relative to the cathode the required numeral can be displayed. Typically for a 15 mm high character about 100 μA is required by each segment to give 700 cd/m^2 luminance.

The first tubes available were single-digit devices mounted in standard electron tube envelopes.[84] By inserting a grid between the cathodes and anodes it was found that a threshold characteristic could be introduced allowing several numerals to be multiplexed. The corresponding anode segments were interconnected and the digit position selected by the grid potential. Only the digit which receives both anode and grid signals will be illuminated; signals to the grid or anode segments alone produce no light.

This grid controlled arrangement resulted in the development of flat multi-digit packages which were to make a significant impact on the small hand held calculator market in Japan.[85] The construction of the electrodes was built up on the back plate of the panel. First the anode segments with interconnections were silk screen printed onto the plate. Next the grids were mounted above the anode patterns onto connection pads and finally a fine cathode filament was stretched along and in front of the row of grids. A front boat-shaped viewing window sealed to the back plate completed the tube which was then evacuated to a high vacuum. The luminance depends on the applied potentials to the grid and anode segments. Normally the same potential is applied to both and in fig. 6.30 the characteristics are shown for a panel with 3.7 mm high characters. For a nine-digit tube giving 600 cd/m^2 the total dissipation including the filament power is about 50 mW.

Further development has inevitably led to the production of dot-matrix panels for alphanumeric displays.[86] Such panels normally have fixed character positions with the thirty-five anode dots interconnected and with separate grids for each character position. For more than one line of characters each grid may address a vertical column of characters. The arrangement is illustrated in fig. 6.31; typically a dot pitch of 0.75 mm is used giving a character height of 5 mm.

The above arrangement is resorted to because it is difficult to construct and mount separate grids for each column or row of dots and there are problems with field penetration between grids if they are mounted too close. Nevertheless the possibility of a dot-matrix display with every dot addressable for graphic application has been described.[87] The arrangement is more complex than a simple cross-bar system, and is illustrated in fig. 6.32. Each grid covers three dot columns and to overcome the field penetration problem the grids each side of the designated grid

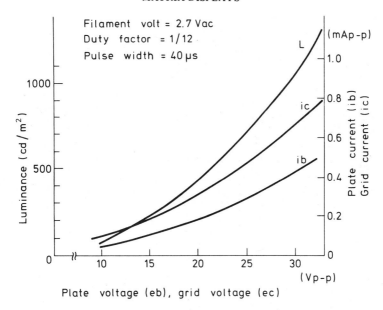

Fig. 6.30 $I-V$ and $L-V$ curves for a vacuum fluorescent tube. Filament voltage, 2.7 V (a.c.); duty factor, 1/12, pulse width 40 μs. (Permission for reprint courtesy Society for Information Display)

are held also at the positive potential. This necessitates six connections for each row of anode dots as the figure shows so that the three dots either side of the designated grid do not receive any anode signal. The resolution and size of panel is rather restricted in this configuration and it is suggested that further expansion to say television pictures would require a circuit element for each dot.[88]

Vacuum fluorescent displays are manufactured mainly in Japan and most of the range use the ZnO:Zn phosphor, P15, giving a bluish-green display. There has been considerable interest, however, in low voltage phosphors, not only for vacuum fluorescent display but also for colour c.r.t.s which could be operated in low voltages. Low voltage cathodoluminescence is accomplished by lowering the resistivity of the phosphor, low enough to avoid the build-up of negative potential on the phosphor surface by the bombarding electrons. The problem is to find phosphors in which the resistivity can be reduced without diminishing the number of luminescent centres. One obvious way to reduce the resistivity is to mix the phosphor with a conductive material. Hiraki et al.[89] mixed various phosphors with conductive but not luminescent ZnO or In_2O_3, to give red ($Y_2O_2S:Eu + In_2O_3$) and blue (ZnS:Ag + ZnO) emission at voltage thresholds below 20 V. They also mixed Zn or MgO with Ga_2O_3 to produce single type gallate phosphors which gave green emission. Matsuoka et al.[90] produced a low voltage red phosphor $SnO_2:Eu$ without any conductive material and Kukimoto et al.[91] reduced the resistivity of ZnS phosphors by incorporating a coactivator of Al. Thus they obtained ZnS:Ag Al (blue), ZnS:CuAl (green) and ZnCdS:AgAl (red) with threshold voltages around 15 V. Although luminance values of the order of 300 cd/m^2 can be obtained with these phosphors the efficiencies are much lower than for ZnO:Zn. Nevertheless vacuum fluorescent

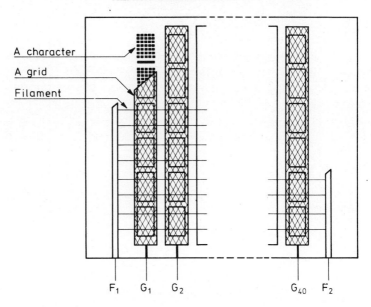

A character

A grid

Filament

F_1 G_1 G_2 G_{40} F_2

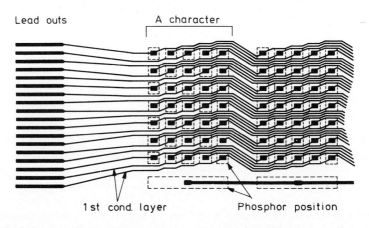

Lead outs   A character

1st cond. layer   Phosphor position

Fig. 6.31 Schematic diagram showing the construction of a dot-matrix alphanumeric vacuum fluorescent display panel(Kasano *et al.*[86])(Permission for reprint courtesy Society for Information Display)

tubes with blue, yellow and orange emission are available with red available in the near future.

A tube which is not unrelated to the vacuum fluorescent device is the c.r.t. introduced by English Electric aimed at large character applications such as sports arena score boards. A separate tube is required for each character but the packaging allows the tubes to be mounted close together. The tube consists of a thermionic cathode producing a flood beam which passes through a stencil onto the fluorescent screen which is in close proximity to the stencil. The tube can be used for fixed messages or signs but the main application is for seven-bar numeric or thirty-five-dot alphanumerics. For these applications the stencil is divided into segments which can be separately addressed, the switching voltage requirements being compatible with integrated circuits. The tube is available with 4 in or 8 in character heights giving an output of several thousand cd/m^2, and can be obtained with red, blue, white, yellow or green emission. The close proximity of the stencil and screen gives good definition to the characters, and recent improvements have produced flatter displays with the possibility of introducing a second screen so that the tube can be viewed from both sides. Examples of Character Display Tubes made by English Electric are shown in Plate 3.

6.10 Incandescent filaments

Since filament lamps are used extensively for lighting, one obvious choice for a light emitting display technology must be the heated tungsten filament. Indeed there were several ideas for numeric displays employing small filament lamps in the early days, when numeric readouts started to appear in the market-place. In one arrange-

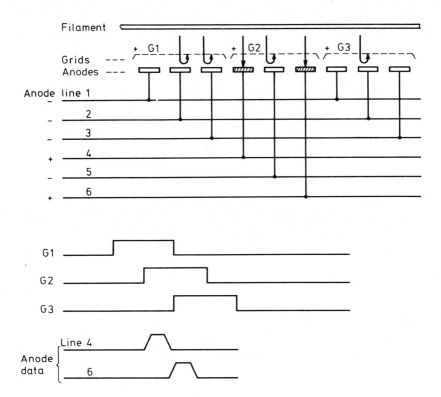

Fig. 6.32 Electrical connections and drive waveforms for the dot-matrix vacuum fluorescent panel according to Kasano et al.[87] (Permission for reprint courtesy Society for Information Display)

ment, ten lamps, one for each numeral, were mounted in a module with a stencil and lens in front of each one. The numeral was projected on to a small screen which formed the front face of the module. In another arrangement the lamps were used to edge light a stacked array of plastic plates with the numerals, as dotted outlines, cut into them. These displays were relatively expensive and had a rather poor luminance. Lamps frequently had to be replaced, although no decoder was required. Later designs used seven lamps to illuminate a seven-bar matrix of windows in a figure-of-eight arrangement. Small compact modules were available, but also large numerals were possible for signboard application. Of course lamps were also used in dot-matrix signboards for sports stadiums etc.

Incandescent filament displays, however, took a leap forward in the early 1970s when tubes were introduced with the seven-bars made up from actual glowing filaments. Initially the life and ruggedness of the principle were suspect, but improvements have now made the filament seven-bar display for numerals a very competitive device.[92] For long lives of over 10 000 hours the filaments are considerably under-run compared with a normal light bulb. Nevertheless the luminance is normally around $6000 \, \text{cd/m}^2$, well above that of any competitive device. Also the processing schedule is more stringent than for a light bulb, carried out under better vacuum conditions to reduce contamination which is often the cause of burnout.

The power requirement for a 12 mm high character is around 75 mW per segment at a filament voltage of 5 V. They can be run at a higher power for greater brightness but usually at the expense of life. The modern designs illustrated in fig. 6.33 are single-digit tubes constructed in a flat pack execution for mounting on circuit boards and with a matt black background for maximum contrast. One end of every filament is connected to a common terminal. Since the brightness varies almost logarithmically with voltage a limited number of digits can be multiplexed by interconnecting the corresponding segments and selecting the digit position with the voltage on the common terminal. The response time under d.c. conditions is around 10 ms but by overvolting the filament from 5 V to 15 V they can be addressed with 0.1 ms pulses.

These incandescent filament displays are particularly suitable for applications where the ambient light level is high, for example in cock-pits and on petrol pumps. They probably are the only active displays which are still readable in direct sunlight. The main criticism is the rather thin outline given by the filament and the difficulties of multiplexing.

6.11   Other displays

Practically every phenomenon capable of producing or modulating light has been investigated at some time or another in the quest for better displays. Some have received brief mention in the literature whilst others have been the subject of several papers. In the previous sections the technologies which have reached production or are in development have been described in some detail. Some of the more promising research type technologies have also been dealt with. One or two others are worth mentioning although their future exploitation is rather more doubtful.

The ideas for active displays which come in this category are electrochemi-

Fig. 6.33 Incandescent filament numerical indicator KW515 from Oshino (courtesy FR Electronics)

luminescence and the fluorescent dyes. Electrochemiluminescence can be defined as the raising of molecules capable of luminescing to the excited state by electrochemical energy. It has been observed in certain luminescent organic substances and has been considered as a possible display technology.[93] The use of fluorescent dyes has been proposed by Hamblen and Clarke.[94] Europium chelate solution provides a bright red fluorescence when illuminated by ultraviolet radiation. However, if a d.c. field is applied across the liquid the fluorescence is quenched at the cathode electrode as a result of electron ejection. The quenching is a charge conduction effect, and requires only a low field, 1–3 V across a 50 μm cell. The current required is around 5 mA/cm^2 for a quenching time of a few milliseconds. The quenching time can be reduced with higher fields and currents. The principle has been applied to a small experimental cross-bar matrix display.

For passive displays several ideas have been proposed for moving particles or segments in either electrostatic or magnetic fields. In the first category are the electroscopic displays based on the idea of an electroscope, i.e. the movement of a foil in an electrostatic field. In one arrangement described by Bruneel *et al*.[95] thin foils were deflected when charged up to open and close ports arranged in a matrix in front of a light source. Since then passive reflective displays have been described in several arrangements,[96,97] one being very similar to the EPID in that a plate or grid is moved in a fluid to the front surface of a cell. The grid, attached by springs to the back surface, is coated with silver to give a white surface appearance and is immersed in a non-conducting black solvent. On application of about 40 V it is attracted to the front surface and becomes clearly visible, the dyed solvent passing through the holes.

Another device depending on electrostatic forces is the gyricon, proposed by Sheridon and Berkovitz.[98] Insulating spherical particles are coated on the two opposite hemispherical surfaces with material having different contact potential as well as colour. In contact with a dielectric liquid in spherical cavities in an elastomer sheet, ionic double layers are set up with different charge densities associated with the two different hemispherical surfaces. Application of an external electrostatic field orientated the balls so that either the dark or light side of the spheres faces the observer. The ball diameters were around 50 μm. The principle is illustrated in fig. 6.34. A similar idea but using magnetic particles in a magnetic field has been worked on by Lee.[99] In his initial experiments he used 0.8 mm diameter magnetised particles, each individually encapsulated in a cavity. He has since fabricated particles around 80 μm diameter. The particles are black and are half silvered to give the contrast when rotated. In a dot-matrix display many particles would be involved at each pixel so that alignment of individual particles is not critical.

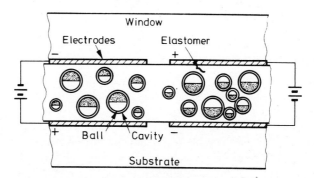

Fig 6.34 Principle of the gyricon display (Sheridon and Berkovitz[88]). (Permission for reprint courtesy Society for Information Display)

These ideas are very much in the research area, and little is known about their characteristics or performance. The use of the magnetic field to address a segmented signboard display is very much a commercial proposition. Following the flap-board used at many airports the large size dot-matrix character display has been introduced. One such display has been developed by Telefonbau and Normalzeit in which the dots are formed by magnetic discs that can be rotated in a magnetic field.[100] Each

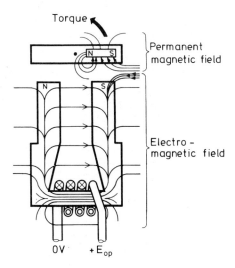

Torque

Permanent magnetic field

Electro - magnetic field

0V + E_{op}

Fig. 6.35 Schematic of the rotating disc module for announcement board display[100]

dot is a separate module with its own magnetic circuit. The disc rotates through 180° and is painted white on one side and black on the other. The principle of the module is illustrated in fig. 6.35. Similar systems are commercially available from other firms. A rather novel approach by Nihon Advanced Products uses cubes with different coloured faces which can be rotated by a magnetic field. The panel may be made up of 100 000 cubes and is addressed by a row of magnetic coils which are mechanically scanned down the panel to give a colour display.

References

1. Grimmeiss, H. G. and Scholz, H. (1964) 'Efficiency of recombination radiation in GaP'. *Phys. Lett.* **8**, 233–235.
2. Morgan, T. N., Welber, B. and Bhargava, R. N. (1968) 'Optical properties of Cd–O and Zn–O complexes in GaP'. *Phys. Rev.* **166**, 751–753.
3. Berg, A. A. and Dean, P. J. (1976) 'Light emitting diodes'. Oxford: Clarendon Press.
4. Williams, E. W. and Hall, R. (1978) 'Luminescence and the light emitting diode'. Pergamon Press.
5. Schumaker, N. E., Kuhn, M. and Furnanage, R. A. (1971) 'Gallium phosphide beam lead electroluminescent devices'. *I.E.E.E. Trans.* **ED-18**, 627–633.
6. Peaker, A. R. (1980) 'Light-emitting diodes'. *Proc. I.E.E.* **127**, part A, 202–210.
7. Frescura, B. L., Luechinger, H. and Bittmann, C. A. (1977) 'Large high density monolithic *XY*-addressable arrays for flat panel l.e.d. displays'. *I.E.E.E. Trans.* **ED-24**, 891–897.
8. Destriau, G. (1947) 'New phenomenon of electro-photoluminescence and its possibility for investigation of crystal lattice'. *Phil. Mag.* **38**, 700.

9. Vecht, A., Werring, N. S. and Smith, P. J. F. (1968) 'High efficiency d.c. electroluminescence in ZnS(MnCu)'. *J. Phys. D. Appl. Phys.* **1**, 134–135.
10. Vecht, A., Werring, N. S., Ellis, R. and Smith, P. J. F. (1973) 'Direct current electroluminescence in zinc sulphide. State of the art'. *Proc. I.E.E.E.* **61**, 902–907.
11. Fischer, A. G. (1976) 'Flat TV panels with polycrystalline layers'. *Microelectronics J.* **7.4**, 5–15.
12. Lehmann, W. (1966) 'Hyper-maintenance of electroluminescence'. *J. Electrochem. Soc.* **113**, 40–42.
13. Thornton, W. A. (1962) 'D.C. electroluminescence in zinc sulphide films'. *J. Appl. Phys.* **33**, 3045–3048.
14. Soxman, E. J. and Ketchpel, R. D. (1972) 'Electroluminescent thin films research'. JAINAIR report 720903.
15. Inoguchi, T., Takeda, M., Kakihara, Y., Nakata, Y. and Yoschida, M. (1974) 'Stable high brightness thin film electroluminescent panels'. *Digest of Technical Papers, S.I.D. International Symposium*, 84–85.
16. Takeda, M., Kanatani, Y., Kishishita, H., Inoguchi, T. and Okano, K. (1980) 'Practical application technologies of thin film electroluminescent panels'. *Digest of Technical Papers, S.I.D. International Symposium*, 66–67.
17. Suzuki, C., Kanatani, Y., Ise, M., Misukami, E., Inazaki, K. and Mito, S. (1976) 'Character display using thin film e.l. panel with inherent memory'. *Digest of Technical Papers, S.I.D. International Symposium*, 50–51.
18. Suzuki, C., Ise, M., Inazaki, K. and Mito, S (1977) 'Optical writing and erasing on e.l. graphic displays'. *Digest of Technical Papers S.I.D. International Symposium*, 90–91.
19. Okamoto, K., Nasu, Y. and Hamakawa, Y. (1980) 'Low threshold-voltage thin film electroluminescent device'. *Record I.E.E.E. Biennial Display Research Conference*, 143–147.
20. Abdalla, M. I., Thomas, J. A., Brenac, A. and Noblanc, J. P. (1980) 'Performance of d.c. EL co-evaporated ZnS:Mn, Cu low voltage devices'. *Record I.E.E.E. Biennial Display Research Conference*, 165–167.
21. Vecht, A., Higton, M., Mayo, J. and Blackmore, J. (1980) 'DCEL dot matrix displays in a range of colours'. *Digest of Technical Papers, S.I.D. International Symposium*, 110–111.
22. Yoshida, M., Tanaka, K., Taniguchi, K., Yamashita, T., Kakihara, Y. and Inoguchi, T. (1980) 'AC thin-film E.L. device that emits white light'. *Digest of Technical Papers, S.I.D. International Symposium*, 106–107.
23. Haertling, G. H. and Land, C. E. (1972) 'Recent improvements in the optical and electrooptical properties of PLZT ceramic'. *Ferroelectricity* **3**, 269–280.
24. Smith, W. D. and Land, C. E. (1972) 'Scattering mode ferroelectric photoconductor image storage and display devices'. *Appl. Phys. Lett.* **20**, 169–171.
25. Maldonado, J. R. and Meitzler, A. H. (1971) 'Strain biased ferroelectric-photo conductor image storage and display devices'. *Proc. I.E.E.E.* **59**, 368–382.
26. Lacklison, D. E., Scott, G. B., Giles, A. D., Clarke, J. A., Pearson, R. F. and Page, J. L. (1977) 'The magneto-optic bubble display'. *I.E.E.E. Trans.* **MAG-13**, 973–981.
27. Heilmeier, G. H., Zanoni, L. A. and Barton, L. A. (1968) 'Dynamic scattering: a new electro-optic effect in certain classes of nematic liquid crystals'. *Proc. I.E.E.E.* **56**, 1162–1171.

28. von Kelker, H. and Scheurle, B. (1969) 'Ein flussig – kristalline (nematische) phase mit besonders niedrigem erstarrungs punkt'. *Angew. Chem.* **81**, 903–904.
29. Gray, G. W., Harrison, K. J. and Nash, J. A. (1974) 'Wide range nematic mixtures incorporating 4 n-alkyl-4 cyno-p-terphenyls'. *J. Chem. Soc. D. Chem. Commun.*, 431–432.
30. Gray, G. W. (1967) *Molecular structure and properties of liquid crystals*. New York: Academic Press.
31. Meyerhofer, D. (1975) 'Field induced distortion of liquid crystals with various surface alignments'. *Phys. Lett.* **51A**, 407–408.
32. Baur, G. and Greubel, W. (1977) 'Fluorescence-activated liquid crystal display'. *App. Phys. Lett.* **31**, 4–6.
33. White, D. L. and Taylor, G. N. (1974) 'New absorptive mode reflective liquid crystal display device'. *J. Appl. Phys.* **45**, 4718–4723.
34. Uchida, T., Seki, H., Shishido, C. and Wada, M. (1980) 'Bright dichoic guest-host LCDs without polarizer'. *Digest of Technical Papers, S.I.D. International Symposium*, 192–193.
35. Yu, L. J. and Labes, M. M. (1977) 'Fluorescent liquid crystal display utilizing an electric-field-induced cholesteric-nematic transition'. *Appl. Phys. Lett.* **31**, 719–720.
36. Takata, H., Kogure, O. and Murase, K. (1973) 'Matrix addressed liquid crystal display'. *I.E.E.E. Trans.* **ED-20**, 990–994.
37. Boyd, G. D., Cheng, J. and Ngo, P. D. T. (1980) 'Liquid crystal orientational bistability and nematic storage effects'. *Appl. Phys. Lett.* **36**, 556–558.
38. Dargent, B. and Robert, J. (1977) 'Twisted nematic flat panel display'. *Digest of Technical Papers, S.I.D. International Symposium*, 60–61.
39. Brody, J. P., Asars, J. A. and Dixon, G. D. (1973) 'A 6 x 6 inch 20 lines per inch liquid crystal display panel'. *I.E.E.E. Trans.* **ED-20**, 995–1001.
40. Castleberry, D. E. and Levinson, L. M. (1980) '2 inch x 5 inch. Varistor controlled liquid crystal matrix display'. *Digest of Technical Papers, S.I.D. International Symposium*, 198–199.
41. Baraff, D. R., Boynton, R., Gribbon, B., Long, J. R., Mclaurin, B. K., Miner, C. J., Serinken, N. M., Streater, R. W. and Westwood, W. D. (1980) 'The application of metal-insulator-metal non linear devices in multiplexed liquid crystal displays'. *Digest of Technical Papers, S.I.D. International Symposium*, 200–201.
42. Crossland, W. A. and Ayliffe, P. J. (1981) 'A dyed phase-change liquid crystal display over a MOSFET switching array'. *Digest of Technical Papers, S.I.D. International Symposium*, 112–113.
43. Deb, S. K. (1969) 'A novel electrophotographic system'. *Appl. Opt.* **8**, 192–195.
44. Faughnan, B. W., Crandall, R. S. and Heyman, P. M. (1975) 'Electrochromism in WO_3 amorphous films'. *R.C.A. Rev.* **36**, 177–197.
45. Chang, I. F. and Howard, W. E. (1975) 'Performance characteristics of electrochromic displays'. *I.E.E.E. Trans.* **ED-22**, 749–758.
46. McGee, J. H., Kramer, W. E. and Hersh, H. N. (1975) 'A tungsten bronze electrochemical character display'. *Digest of Technical Papers, S.I.D. International Symposium*, 50–51.
47. Migoshi, T. and Iwasa, K. (1980) 'Electrochromic displays for watches'. *Digest of Technical Papers, S.I.D. International Symposium*, 126–127.

48. Inoue, E., Kawaziri, K. and Izawa, A. (1977) 'Deposited Cr_2O_3 as a barrier in a solid state WO_3 electrochromic cell'. *Japan J. Appl. Phys.* **16**, 2065–2066.
49. Tell, B. and Wagner, S. (1978) 'Electrochromic cells based on phosphotungstic acid'. *Appl. Phys. Lett.* **33**, 837–838.
50. Shay, J. L. and Beni, G. (1979) 'Anodic iridium oxide films a new electrochromic'. *I.E.E.E. Trans.* **ED-26**, 1138–1142.
51. Beni, G. and Schiavone, L. M. (1981) 'Matrix addressable electrochromic display cell'. *Appl. Phys. Lett.* **38**, 593–595.
52. Faughnan, B. W. and Crandall, R. S. (1980) 'Electromic displays based on WO_3' in Pankove, J. ed. *Topics in Applied Physics.* Vol. 40. New York: Springer.
53. Schoot, C. J., Ponjee, J. J., van Dam, H. T., van Doorn, R. A. and Bolwijn, P. T. (1973) 'New electrochromic memory display'. *Appl. Phys. Lett.* **23**, 64–65.
54. Nicholson, M. M. and Galiardi, R. V. (1978) 'A multicolour electrochromic display'. *Digest of Technical Papers, S.I.D. International Symposium*, 24–25.
55. Ota, I., Ohnishi, J. and Yoshiyama, M. (1973) 'Electrophoretic image display (EPID) panel'. *Proc. I.E.E.E.* **61**, 832–836.
56. Dalisa, A. L. (1977) 'Electrophoretic display technology'. *I.E.E.E. Trans.* **ED-24**, 827–834.
57. Chiang, A. (1980) 'Electrophoretic displays: the state of the art'. *Record I.E.E.E. Joint Biennial Display Conference*, 10–12.
58. Singer, B. and Dalisa, A. L. (1977) 'An $X-Y$ addressable electrophoretic display'. *Proc. S.I.D.* **18**, 255–266.
59. Liebert, R., Lalak, J. and Wittig, K. (1980) 'A 512-character electrophoretic display'. *Record I.E.E.E. Joint Biennial Display Conference*, 26–30.
60. McLoughlin, N., Reaney, D. and Turner, A. W. (1960) 'The digitron: a cold cathode display tube'. *Electronic Eng.* **32**, 140–143.
61. Smith, J. (1975) 'Experimental storage display panel using d.c. gas discharges without resistors'. *I.E.E.E. Trans.* **ED-22**, 642–649.
62. Cola, R., Gaur, J., Holtz, G., Ogle, J., Siegel, J. and Somlyody, A. (1977) 'Gas discharge panels with internal line sequencing (Self-Scan displays)' in *Advances in Image Pickup Devices.* Vol. 3. New York: Academic Press, 84–170.
63. Bitzer, D. L. and Slottow, H. G. (1966) 'The plasma panel – a digitally addressable display with inherent memory'. Joint Computer Conference. *A.F.I.P.S. Conference Proceedings* (Spartan, Washington) **29**, 541–547.
64. Nolan, J. F. (1969) 'Gas discharge display panel'. *Record I.E.E.E. Electron Device Meeting*, 54.
65. Dick, G. W. and Biazzo, M. R. (1976) 'A planar single substrate a.c. plasma display'. *I.E.E.E. Trans.* **ED-23**, 429–437.
66. Urade, T., Iemori, T., Nakayama, N. and Morita, I. (1974) 'Consideration of protecting layer in a.c. plasma panels'. *Record I.E.E.E. Joint Conference on Display Devices and Systems*, 30–33.
67. Umeda, S. and Hirose, T. (1972) 'Self shift plasma display'. *Digest of Technical Papers, S.I.D. International Symposium*, 38–39.
68. Weikart, G. S. (1975) 'Independent subsection shift and a new simplified write technique for self-shift a.c. plasma panels'. *I.E.E.E. Trans.* **ED-22**, 663–668.

69. Andoh, S., Oki, K., Yoshikawa, K., Miyashita, Y., Shindoda, T., Sato, S. and Sugimoto, V. (1978) 'Self-shift plasma display panels with meander electrodes or meander channels'. *I.E.E.E. Trans.* **ED-25**, 1145–1151.

70. Holz, G., Ogle, J., Andreadakis, N., Siegel, J. and Maloney, T. (1981) 'A self-scan memory plasma display panel'. *Digest Papers, S.I.D. International Symposium*, 168–169.

71. Schermerhorn, J. D. and Miller, J. W. V. (1975) 'Discharge logic drive schemes'. *I.E.E.E. Trans.* **ED-22**, 669–673.

72. Dick, G. W. (1980) 'Single substrate AC plasma display structure with Kth order internal decoding'. *Record I.E.E.E. Biennial Display Research Conference*, 40–45.

73. Smith, J.(1980)'A gas discharge display for compact desk-top word processors'. *Record I.E.E.E. Biennial Display Research Conference*, 79–82.

74. Shinoda, T., Miyashita, Y., Sugimoto, Y. and Yoshikawa, K. (1981) 'Characteristics of surface-discharge colour a.c. plasma display panels'. *Digest of Technical Papers, S.I.D. International Symposium*, 164–165.

75. van Houten, S., Jackson, R. N. and Weston, G. F. (1972) 'D.C. gas discharge panels'. *Proc. S.I.D.* **13**, 43–51.

76. de Jule, M. C. and Chodil, G. J. (1975) 'High efficiency, high luminance gas discharge cells for T.V. displays'. *Digest of Technical Papers, S.I.D. International Symposium*, 56–57.

77. de Jule, M. C. and Chodil, G. J. (1971) 'A grey scale technique for plasma display panel and similar 'on'–'off' devices'. *Digest of Technical Papers, S.I.D. International Symposium*, 102–103.

78. Judice, C. N., Jarvis, J. F. and Ninke, W. H. (1974) 'Bi-level rendition of continuous-tone pictures on an a.c. plasma panel'. *Record I.E.E.E. Joint Conference on Display Devices and Systems*, 89–98.

79. Umeda, S., Murase, K., Ishizaki, H. and Jurahashi, K. (1973) 'Picture display with grey scale in the plasma panel'. *Digest of Technical Papers, S.I.D. International Symposium*, 70–71.

80. Chodil, G. J., de Jule, M. C. and Markin, J. (1972) 'Good quality T.V. pictures using a gas discharge panel'. *Record I.E.E.E. Joint Conference on Display Devices*, 77–81.

81. Kojima, T., Toyonaga, R., Sakai, T., Tajima, T., Sega, S., Kuriyama, T., Koike, J. and Murakami, H. (1979) 'Sixteen-inch gas-discharge display panel with two lines at a time driving'. *Proc. S.I.D.* **20**, 153–158.

82. Murakami, H., Sega, S. and Tajima, T. (1980) 'An experimental TV display using a gas discharge panel with internal memory'. *Proc. S.I.D.* **21**, 327–332.

83. Okamoto, Y. and Mizushima, M. (1980) 'A positive column discharge memory panel without current limiting resistors for colour T.V. display'. *I.E.E.E. Trans.* **ED-27**, 1778–1783.

84. Raago, R. T. (1969) 'A low cost general purpose alphanumeric readout device'. *Inf. Disp.* **6** (May), 33–36.

85. Kiyozumi, K., Masuda, M. and Nakamura, T. (1976) 'Flat panel multi-digit display'. *Digest of Technical Papers, S.I.D. International Symposium*, 130–131.

86. Kasano, K., Masuda, M., Shimojo, T. and Kiyozumi, K. (1980) 'A 240 character vacuum fluorescent display and its drive circuitry'. *Proc. S.I.D.* **21**, 107–111.

87. Kasano, K., Masuda, M. and Nakamura, T. (1980) 'A random access memory 26 x 258 dot flat panel vacuum fluorescent display'. *Digest of Technical Papers, S.I.D. International Symposium*, 74–75.

88. Iwade, M., Kasano, K., Masuda, M. and Nakamura, T. (1981) 'Vacuum fluorescent display for TV video images'. *Digest of Technical Papers, S.I.D. International Symposium*, 136–137.
89. Hiraki, M., Kagami, A., Hase, T., Narita, K. and Mimura, Y. (1976) 'Properties of ZnO-containing phosphors under low voltage cathode ray excitation'. *J. Luminescence* **12/13**, 941–946.
90. Matsouka, T., Nitta, T. and Hayakawa, S. (1980) UK patent application GB 2026530A.
91. Kukimoto, H., Oda, S. and Nakayama, T. (1979) 'Preparation and characterization of low-voltage cathodoluminescent ZnS'. *J. Luminescence* **18/19**, 365–368.
92. Cartwright, D. L., Guennewig, J. T. and Hemming, A. G. (1976) 'Incandescent readouts in military applications'. *S.P.I.E.*, vol. 99. *Proceedings 3rd European Electro-Optics Conference*, 209–214.
93. Schwartz, P. M., Blakeley, R. A. and Robinson, B. B. (1972) 'Efficiency of the electro-chemiluminescent process'. *J. Phys. Chem.* **76**, 1868–1871.
94. Hamblen, D. P. and Clarke, J. R. (1973) 'An experimental fluorescent dye panel'. *I.E.E.E. Trans.* **ED-20**, 1028–1032.
95. Bruneel, J. L., Crosnier, J. J. and Micheron, F. (1976) 'A bistable electret display device'. *Digest of Technical Papers, S.I.D. International Symposium*, 140–141.
96. Goodrich, G. W. and O'Connor, J. M. (1980) 'Dye-foil digital display'. *Digest of Technical Papers, S.I.D. International Symposium*, 130–131.
97. te Velde, T. S. (1980) 'A family of electroscopic displays'. *Digest of Technical Papers, S.I.D. International Symposium*, 116–117.
98. Sheridon, N. K. and Berkovitz, M. A. (1977) 'The gyricon – a twisting ball display'. *Digest of Technical Papers, S.I.D. International Symposium*, 144–145.
99. Lee, L. L. (1975) 'A magnetic particle display'. *I.E.E.E. Trans.* **ED-22**, 758–765.
100. Ludes, R. and Rudel, P. (1976) 'A display system on the modular principle with bistable and indicator elements'. *Proceedings Conference Electron Displays*, Session 2, 2–12.

Chapter 7

Drive circuits

7.1 Classification of drive circuits

Two factors have contributed to the recent rapid progress in the world of displays. The first, discussed in chapter 6, is the improvement of the technologies themselves and the consequent identification of new markets especially in the realms of smaller alphanumeric systems where low power consumption and/or size have been the controlling factors. The second factor is much more universal and that is in the development of support circuitry making use of the latest integration processes. Without the reduction in both cost and size of these components it is unlikely that any of the driver intensive displays (which includes all the matrix displays) could compete with the ever dominant cathode ray tube.

Many of the longer established display technologies owe a great deal to discrete circuit designs. This is especially true of the high voltage devices where it has only just become possible to integrate the output drive stages at a reasonable cost. For this reason we will be making several references to such circuits if only to understand more fully the detailed requirements of any particular display configuration.

The cathode ray tube drive circuits are not discussed in detail, because of their extensive coverage elsewhere. However, the research into high resolution c.r.t.s has led to several developments in the way that they are addressed as well as suggesting ways forward to the elusive flat c.r.t. In this chapter we will be looking at the techniques of raster and vector display as well as providing some idea as to the prospects of further improvements due to advances in 'intelligent' display drive. The subsystem electronics to support these displays is rather more general and is the subject of a separate chapter (chapter 8).

The drive circuitry for any given display must not only provide the correct drive waveforms but also incorporate mechanisms to cope with device to device variations and changes throughout the life of the display once it has been installed. The more advanced systems are generally only in the pilot production phase and hence less than fully characterised. The engineer is usually required to build in large operating margins which increase the drive complexity. Such interim solutions are rarely candidates for integration and it has become important to achieve rationalised designs at the earliest possible stage in product development.

The organisation of this chapter broadly follows that of chapter 6. Many of the electrical characteristics have been examined in that chapter and it is generally assumed that the reader is familiar with the material presented there. The circuits themselves make use of most of the available integrated and discrete semiconductor devices and some prior knowledge of the broadest functionality of these is also expected.

7.2   Light emitting diodes

Light emitting diodes (l.e.d.s) have several electrical properties common to the silicon diode. The forward voltage conduction characteristic is given in fig. 7.1 The two important features of this curve are a threshold of about 1.8 V and a relatively low slope impedance. The reverse voltage breakdown is not particularly high (in terms of typical diode behaviour) and breakdown may be as low as 5 V. Reverse conduction can cause device failure if more than a few milliamperes is allowed to flow.

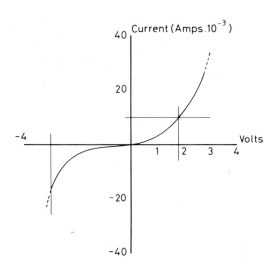

Fig. 7.1 Typical l.e.d. characteristic

The threshold voltage varies slightly from device to device as well as with temperature and this makes it unwise to drive the devices directly from a low impedance voltage source. The usual practice is to limit the current flow. The trivial but common solution is to place a resistor in series with the voltage source to set the current to a few milliamperes. If tolerance to power supply variation is required then a constant current source or sink can be used. There are several ways of achieving this and a standard discrete solution with the related equations is given in fig. 7.2. Many i.c.s exist which provide this form of drive and are used in digital clock circuits or other systems where a crude power supply is anticipated.

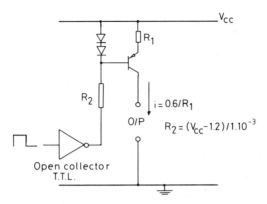

Fig. 7.2 Constant current drive

7.2.1 Multiplexing l.e.d.s

The sharp threshold and low voltage operation is ideal for multplexing l.e.d. arrays and multi-segment digits. The two integrated technologies applicable to smaller systems are bipolar and n-m.o.s./p-m.o.s. C.M.O.S. cannot sink or source sufficient current for array addressing unless several output stages are joined together to boost its output capability. Bipolar i.c.s (for example the 74 series family) will provide up to 40 mA which is enough to multiplex about four digits at adequate brightness. n-p-n devices are preferred in these i.c.s as they have a better current capability.

Bi-polar circuits with much higher operating currents are fairly easy to make and the latest generation of display drivers provides several drivers capable of switching in excess of 1A in a single package. This level of current is soon reached in the l.e.d. multiplexed display. Table 7.1 gives the approximate current requirements for a range of arrays from 5 x 5 to 50 x 50. The sharp increase in power consumption is due to the drop in dot duty ratio and increasing line length. A relatively new technology which has been employed in l.e.d. drive is the vertical f.e.t. (v.f.e.t.). This device has high current capability, but its f.e.t. gate structure is directly compatible with the logic drive circuits. V.F.E.T.s have been fabricated to give 20 A output currents which is required in the larger arrays.

Table 7.1 Matrix drive. Current requirements for l.e.d. arrays

Array size	Pulse current/element	Pulse current/line
5 x 5	30 mA	150 mA
10 x 10	50 mA	500 mA
20 x 20	75 mA	1.5 A
30 x 30	113 mA	3.4 A
40 x 40	163 mA	6.5 A
50 x 50	180 mA	9 A

The driver output stage for a multiplexed array must be a low impedance switch with a fast rise time. The l.e.d. itself has a submicrosecond response so that high frequency scanning is possible. There are a few complications as the technology is basically low voltage so that factors such as elemental capacitance and line inductance do not play a significant role in increasing the power dissipation. Line resistance in monolithic arrays is more important. This arises from bond lead contact resistances and the maximum diameter of the bond wire itself. The effect of these impedances is to cause a loss of uniformity in light output owing to the progressive drop in voltage along the display electrodes. It is not generally possible to rectify this effect by modifying the drive conditions.

Crosstalk is surprisingly common in l.e.d. displays. The column and line select timing is at fault if this occurs, as there is little charge storage within the display which would be the other principal cause. Chapter 3 discusses the timing required to avoid crosstalk.

7.2.2   Output stages

Two output drivers are required in the multiplexed array, a source driver for one axis and a current sinking driver for the orthogonal axis. These drivers need only be single ended. Figure 7.3 gives the general schematic. The transistors should have a low 'on' saturation voltage and the minimum rise time if dissipation is to be minimised.

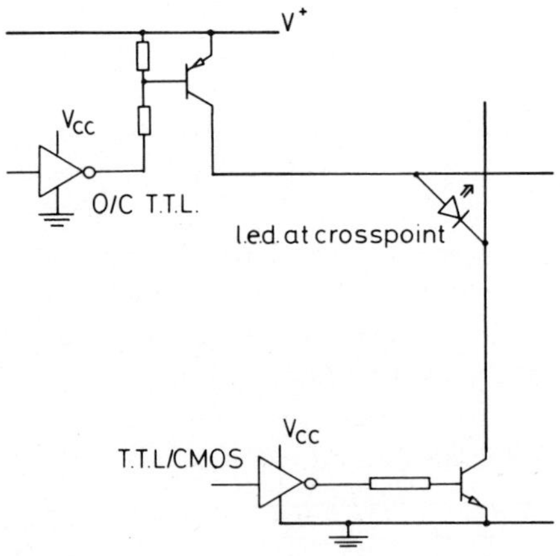

Fig. 7.3 Crosspoint drive

The translation of levels between the logic of the subsystem and the output stage is simple enough as any level shifting is of the order of a few volts at the most. The conventional level shift interface is also shown in fig. 7.3. The drive pulse width can be microseconds to milliseconds. The lower limit is dictated mainly by the driver and is rarely less than ten microseconds as the driver rise/fall time starts to become significant at this width. The duty factor for these displays can be very low (0.25% will still give a good brightness) as l.e.d.s can be overrun at high currents without significant lifetime problems.

7.2.3   Grey scale

Grey scale is achieved by pulse width modulation in l.e.d. systems. Non-multiplexed displays can use the direct modulation of current but this is an exception. The operation of pulse width modulation is shown in fig. 7.4. where four levels of brightness are achieved by applying four different pulse widths to several elements. The output stages are identical as this function is managed in the logic of the display system. Because of the inherent stability of the l.e.d. with time, several levels of grey scale can be achieved.

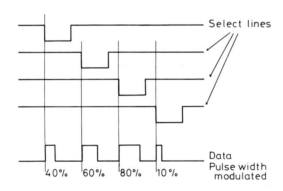

Fig. 7.4 Pulse width modulation for grey scale

7.3   Electroluminescent displays

As we saw in chapter 6 there are four different types of electroluminescent display to consider — a.c. powder, a.c. thin film, d.c. powder and d.c. thin film. Each operates in a quite different way and requires different drive circuitry. In every case the drive is critical to the performance and maintenance of the display. The renewed interest in a.c. thin film has brought about several important developments in the drive technology for these displays, most significantly by producing high voltage drivers in integrated form. None of the electroluminescent displays can be described as easy to drive as there are several factors which lead to a compromise in the design of a realistic output stage.

7.3.1   A.C. powder

A.C. powder is now almost exclusively used in simple backlighting for other displays such as liquid crystal. The drive for such a device is an alternating sine (or square) wave of between 100 and 400 V (peak to peak) at frequencies between 50 and 2000 Hz. The output driver is usually a transformer with a current limiting resistor. The levels of luminance are so low (3 to 30 cd/m^2) that more complex displays are not considered realistic. The a.c. thin film drivers (section 7.9.2) could be pressed into service if the need to address several elements ever arose.

7.3.2   A.C. thin film

Unlike a.c. powder, a.c. thin film has found almost all its applications in the more complex matrix displays of which there are a few commercially available examples. Considerable effort has been put into the design of optimised integrated drivers for these displays.

The a.c. thin film panel is capacitively coupled. There is an insulator between the display electrodes (one or both electrodes can be isolated). The simple display is excited with a square wave of a few hundred hertz at up to 600 V (peak to peak) depending on the display construction.

In the multiplexed array, the axis selection is superimposed upon this a.c. waveform although the latest displays use somewhat lower voltages. There are two methods by which the matrix array may be addressed, the conventional line-at-a-time technique discussed in chapter 3 and a storage mode made possible by using the hysteresis effect described in section 6.3. Line-at-a-time addressing thin film a.c. electroluminescent (a.c.e.l.) display is much more complex than for l.e.d.s. Firstly, we are dealing with a high voltage technology which has made the development of i.c.s difficult. Secondly, the display elements have a high capacitance and these have to be charged and discharged at a high frequency. Thirdly, the duty ratio and frequency of display refresh lie within tight limits, restricting the design options. The question of power dissipation within the display itself must be considered and several approaches have been taken to bring these within reasonable limits.

The first consideration must be the interaction of high capacitance and high voltage. The display driver (in a multiplexed system) is expected to operate under short pulse conditions. In the case of the panel the pulse width for any select pulse is in the range 10 to 100 μs. Fig. 7.5 gives the plot of current versus time for short pulse excitation. The initial surge of current is associated with charging the display capacitance. The plateau region which may be very short lived reflects the actual current drawn by the luminescing junction and the reverse current flow is the discharging spike as the applied voltage is reversed. A great deal of this energy is wasted. Actually it is dissipated in the display and the output stage which is why we have to consider the power losses. The ratio of useful energy (which activates the luminescing region) to wasted energy can be as low as 1:10. The technique by which this energy may be reclaimed is generally termed power scavenging. In thin

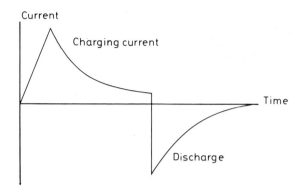

Fig. 7.5 Current waveform in electroluminescent display

film a.c. panels inductors have been used to resonate with the display lines to act as a storage element. The frequency of resonance is narrow (a high Q resonator) but this does not cause problems in most designs where the system clock is usually crystal controlled anyway.

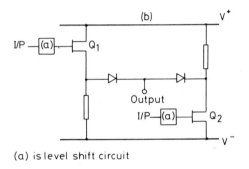

(a) is level shift circuit

Fig. 7.6 A.C. drive using m.o.s.

Leaving aside the complications of a resonant system, a typical driver for a thin film a.c. array will take the form of fig. 7.6. Stage (a) of this driver is a level shifter required to interface between the logic of the subsystem and the output stage. Stage (b) forms the driver. There are several types possible, this being the bare bones of most designs. The switch is formed with two transistors Q_1 and Q_2 each operating on opposite half cycles. The diodes act to protect the 'off' device. Such circuits can cope with the heavy inrush currents but occasionally a series resistor is used to limit the current flow to a safe level. This cannot be used where the time delays introduced by charge and discharge would become too great. The use of inductors to scavenge power is shown in fig. 7.7. The diode configuration serves to route the power to the appropriate line in conjunction with the switching devices. The hysteresis of thin film a.c. panels is used to provide storage by the introduction

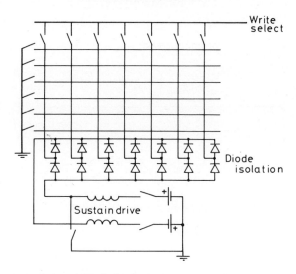

Fig. 7.7 Power scavenging using inductors

of a three-level drive. The operation is not dissimilar to that used in a.c. gas discharge displays (section 7.5.2). The action follows the principles shown in fig. 7.8 where the three levels of drive are shown with the corresponding effect on the light output. A three-level driver may take several forms but the 'diode-or' configuration of fig. 7.9 is a typical solution.

The integrated circuits which support a.c. thin film display systems are commercially available and up to thirty-two stages have been incorporated onto one substrate. Some are available with grey scale capability and many include the shift register logic required to pass dot information to the display.

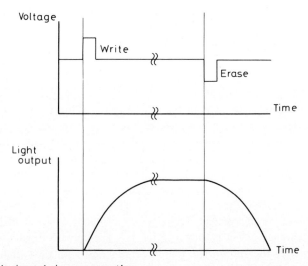

Fig. 7.8 Write/sustain/erase operation

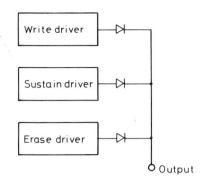

Fig. 7.9 Three-level drive

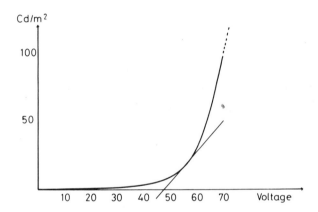

Fig. 7.10 D.C. electroluminescent forward voltage characteristic

7.3.3   D.C. electroluminescent systems

The d.c. electroluminescent (d.c.e.l.) display is addressed directly (fixed legend displays) or line-at-a-time. The $L-V$ characteristic applicable to fixed legend displays is given in fig. 7.10. The slope resistance at the threshold (which is about 70 V) is sufficiently high to permit the direct application of a voltage. However, the characteristic drifts with time and a compensation network is preferred. The practice of incorporating a series resistor or a constant current source is quite common. The best networks approximate a constant power source and one example is given in fig. 7.11. A drawback to these circuits is that a substantially greater voltage source is required to allow for the voltage drop across the network. Power is therefore wasted. The more complex matrix displays make use of the pulsed $L-V$ characteristic of fig. 7.12. This is a good characteristic for multiplexed operation because it shows the required sharp threshold with a good margin for overdrive. The operating area for multiplexed d.c.e.l. systems is restricted as limits are imposed to prevent

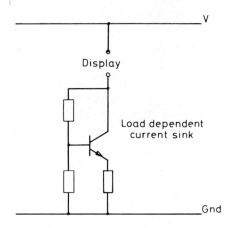

Fig. 7.11 Compensation drive for fixed legend display

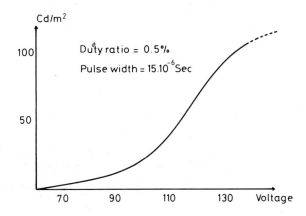

Fig. 7.12 D.C. electroluminescent pulse characteristic. Duty ratio 0.5%, pulse width 15 μs

excessive ageing. The pulse operating conditions are given in fig. 7.13. As can be seen from this, the panel behaves best with a short pulse, low duty ratio, drive. The operating voltages of ± 60 V for d.c. powder down to ± 15 V for thin film are considerably lower than used in a.c.e.l. systems but they have to be increased during life to maintain brightness. A margin of 50% on these voltages is expedient. The drivers will also have to be designed with such a margin. D.C. thin film and d.c. powder displays are similar enough in terms of drive requirements to be treated as one. The main (and important) difference is the operating voltage which is considerably lower in the case of d.c. thin film. This is an advantage as capacitance and voltage drive complicate the operation of these displays.

The electrical model for a d.c.e.l. element is shown in fig. 7.14. The element is capacitive (3000 pF/cm²). The series resistance R is mainly the lead and contact resistance and the parallel voltage dependent resistor is the luminescing junction. The display driver and timing must allow for the time constants introduced by such a network and handle the charging currents. Fig. 7.15 gives a discrete version of a typical output driver. The two axes use different drivers but their operation is similar. The driver has to switch in about 500 ns if dissipation is to be kept to a reasonable level. Scavenging power in these systems has not been successfully

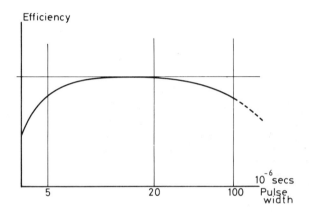

Fig. 7.13 D.C. electroluminescence: efficiency versus pulse width. Duty ratio 0.5%

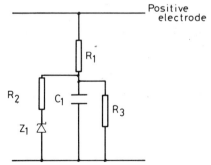

R_1 – Electrode contact
$R_2.Z_1$–Non–linear current sink
C_1–Elemental capacitance
R – Bulk material leakage

Fig. 7.14 Equivalent model of e.l. element. C_1 is elemental capacitance, plus the layer capacitance, R_2 and Z_1 form non-linear elemental equivalent

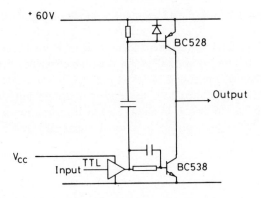

Fig. 7.15 Output stage for positive axis of d.c.e.l. panel

demonstrated. The complete list of requirements for a driver supplying a 120 × 120 array is given in Table 7.2.

Table 7.2 System characteristics of d.c.e.l. panel

Typical power consumption	6.5 W
Line pulse current	150 mA peak
Elemental current	3 mA peak
Optical fall time	2 ms
Frame refresh	300 Hz
Drive pulse width	15 μs
Supply voltages	±60 V
Duty ratio	0.5%
Luminance	90 cd/m^2

Integration is possible. The difficulties of high voltage totem pole drive are not easily solved. Some m.o.s. devices are available to drive smaller displays but it is probable that a bipolar solution will be needed to meet the rise time requirements. Thin film d.c. panels have not been developed sufficiently to enable comment on the applicability of existing integrated circuits.

7.4   Liquid crystal displays

The liquid crystal display is a low voltage, low current technology. There are several varieties but the circuitry of each is similar. The electrical properties of these devices are such that we have to look at their optoelectrical response in some detail to understand the various limitations and how novel drive techniques can be used to overcome these.

The twisted nematic liquid crystal has become commonplace in wrist watches and calculators. In both these examples the response time is not particularly important and multiplexing is confined to a handful of digits. Twisted nematic l.c.d.s are field effect devices, that is they respond to the presence of a potential rather than the flow of current. They have to be driven with an alternating voltage as a unidirectional field ages them rapidly. The display driver should not impose a voltage offset for this reason and must therefore provide a truly symmetrical a.c. waveform. Fortunately the complementary metal oxide semiconductor technology (c.m.o.s.) provides a nearly ideal output voltage swing with the added bonus that it too is a very low power technology. A standard output stage is shown in fig. 7.16. It comprises an exclusive-or gate which is used as a conditional inverter, one input term being a square wave which inverts the input data each half cycle. A voltage swing of 3 V (peak to peak) is sufficient to drive most small l.c.d.s. Dynamic scattering is another effect made use of in some l.c.d.s. These require a slightly higher drive voltage (up to 15 V if the display area is large or needs switching quickly). C.M.O.S. drivers can provide this requirement quite easily and circuits for both technologies are quite similar. The dynamic scattering effect is not used a great deal in small displays any more.

7.4.1   Multiplexing liquid crystal displays

This is more complicated. The factors we have to consider are related to the electromechanical response of the device and the effect of temperature on its behaviour. Many of the shortcomings of these devices can be surmounted using complex circuitry. This is not a great problem as c.m.o.s. being an integrated technology, can offer this complexity at a low cost.

We talk about an electromechanical response in l.c.d.s because their operation is just that; the movement of molecular material under the influence of an electric field. This is clearly considerably slower than non-mechanical systems and leads to several limitations when multiplexing.

Multiplexed displays (dynamically addressed) require regular refreshing at low duty factors. The liquid crystal material responds to the r.m.s. value of any field applied to it. The observed effect when multiplexing l.c.d. arrays is a loss of contrast

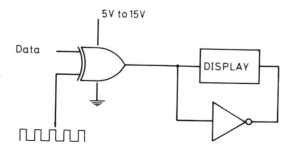

Fig. 7.16 A.C. drive using c.m.o.s. exclusive-or gate

owing to elements not switching fully from the 'on' to the 'off' state. It is not difficult to see that the r.m.s. voltage applied to an 'on' element is a function of the duty factor and the pulse voltages at each axis. Thus

$$V_{on}^{2} = \frac{1}{N}(V_x + V_y)^2 + \frac{N-1}{N}(V_y)^2 \qquad (7.1)$$

where V_x is the x axis voltage, V_y the y axis voltage and N the number of scanned lines in the matrix. The r.m.s. voltage for an off element is given by

$$V_{off}^{2} = \frac{1}{N}(V_x - V_y)^2 + \frac{N-1}{N}(V_y)^2. \qquad (7.2)$$

Optimum contrast is achieved when the 'on' to 'off' voltage ratio is at its greatest. Thus increasing the number of lines will inevitably lead to a reduction in on/off contrast. Alt and Pleshco[1] showed that for an N-row matrix the r.m.s. voltage ratio could be as high as

$$\{[\sqrt{(N)} + 1] \, / \, [\sqrt{(N)} - 1]\}^{\frac{1}{2}} \qquad (7.3)$$

when using conventional addressing techniques. The limit on array size is about fifty lines along the scanned axis (less if a high contrast ratio is required). Displays of eighty characters have been produced commercially. The temperature dependence of these devices usually means that even this size of display makes use of temperature compensation which is achieved by monitoring the display temperature and adjusting the applied pulse drive waveforms.

The electromechanical response times of these devices imposes other restrictions in performance when rapid update of display information is required. Alphanumeric displays do not normally require high rates of update although word processing applications often make use of flashing markers which could become a problem.

However, much larger l.c.d. displays have been produced, including a 512-character display produced by Seiko. These displays make use of a more complicated addressing mode known as two-frequency addressing.

Certain nematic materials exhibit the property of low frequency dielectric relaxation. To understand this effect we need to look at the operation of a conventional nematic material first. Fig. 7.17(a) shows the basic response of a twisted nematic l.c.d. The rise time of the device is fairly rapid as it is being actively driven from its relaxed state to an active mode. The turn-off time is slower because the device has to revert to its inactive state without a field drive. The requirement is to be able to increase the response by actively driving the display both on and off. This can be achieved in some twisted nematic materials because their action is governed by the frequency of the a.c. drive applied. Fig. 7.17(b) shows this effect and gives some idea of the improvement in response obtained. Unfortunately, it is a very temperature dependent effect and compensation is essential in all the examples demonstrated to date. The two-frequency drive is shown in fig. 7.18. The total drive voltages are somewhat higher than in earlier examples at about 40 V peak to peak. The off frequency is 150 Hz and the on frequency 50 kHz. With this set of conditions responses of 200 ms are achieved in medium size panels. Special high voltage c.m.o.s. devices (capable of 70 V operation) have been developed to drive this and future displays addressed using this method.

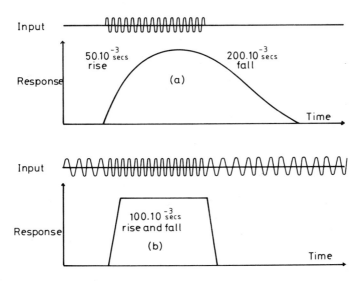

Fig. 7.17 Conventional versus two-frequency drive for l.c.d.s

7.4.2   Active crosspoint drive

To obtain rapid update of information on an l.c.d. display (flicker free) the use of active crosspoint drive has been suggested. This can take many forms. The two systems demonstrated so far are based upon a silicon-on-sapphire substrate and a thin film transistor substrate. Commercial production of such devices is some way in the future as yield is very low (owing to the need to produce large fault free semiconductor devices).

Both examples make use of the intrinsic capacitance of the l.c.d. (in conjunction with the substrate capacitance) to provide storage cells at each crosspoint which are, in turn, used to determine the state of a switching transistor in close proximity to the liquid crystal material. Each crosspoint is therefore of the type shown in fig.

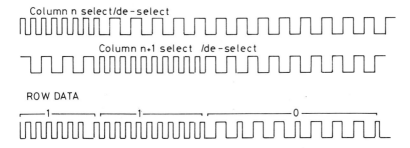

Fig. 7.18 Two-frequency drive waveforms

7.19. The eventual goal of such a design must be to produce a video display, and this will involve the proof of a reasonable number of grey scale levels (probably best achieved using pulse width modulation). Large displays will be difficult. End stacking several substrates has been demonstrated although the cost of such a project has yet to be revealed.

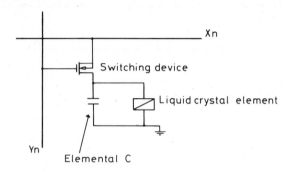

Fig. 7.19 Crosspoint memory on silicon

7.4.3   Laser addressing

Some liquid crystal materials will become opaque when heated. This effect has been used to demonstrate projection systems where a liquid crystal substrate replaces the slide. The writing beam is a solid state laser which raster scans the l.c.d. Elements are written to by rapidly heating selected areas with the coherent light from the laser. The deflection electronics are electromechanical (mirrors/servo-motors) and so the writing speed is limited to about twenty characters per second. Once written the page only requires updating very occasionally to maintain the contrast. Erasing is achieved electrically by applying an a.c. field to the whole liquid crystal substrate.

7.5   Gas discharge displays

Gas discharge displays have come the nearest to competing directly with the cathode ray tube in large area alphanumeric systems. This is mainly because their properties are conducive to array addressing. The d.c. and a.c. versions behave quite differently and consequently the drive circuits for each will be dealt with separately.

7.5.1   D.C. gas discharge

The operation of the various devices using d.c. gas discharge phenomena has been explored in detail in chapter 6. The three classes of display drive that we should consider are small digit displays, multiplexed displays and the large dot-matrix

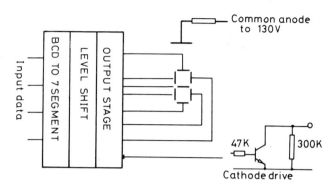

Fig. 7.20 Gas discharge driver

arrays. The directly addressed gas discharge digit (seven-segment being the common format) can be addressed using any of the high voltage driver i.c.s which have been purpose designed. In many cases an external limiting resistor is required. A typical arrangement is given in fig. 7.20. The information is supplied in encoded form (binary coded decimal – chapter 8) and can be continually applied to the display. The common anode is connected to a positive rail. The step to multiplexing several digits is a simple one and the addition of an anode driver is required of the type shown in fig. 7.21. This is also available in integrated form. The switch must be capable of supplying current for all the segments of the digit, and because the duty ratio will be lowered in proportion to the number of digits being multiplexed, the current limiting resistors are smaller in value. There is no great difficulty in address-ing twenty digits in this manner.

The supply voltage for these circuits is in the region of 200 V. When several devices are multiplexed this has to increase to offset driver losses and increase peak levels of luminance. The multiplexing frequency is bounded by the recovery time between pulses which is of the order of 2ms. Flicker will not occur in smaller systems.

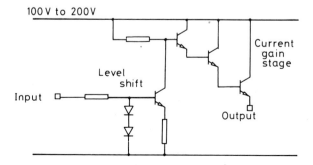

Fig. 7.21 Anode driver with low current impedance

Digit drive current is in the microampere range for a directly addressed digit rising to a few milliamperes for a twenty-digit line. As the number of elements increases so the maximum elemental duty ratio decreases. When this ratio falls below about 2% the maximum output luminance starts to fall off owing to a saturation in the pulse $I-V$ characteristic (chapter 3). A technique for reducing the driving circuit called Self-Scan® has been developed by Burroughs Corporation. The construction and operation of this type of panel has already been discussed (chapter 6). The duty cycles of the scan pulses range from 12.5 to 30% depending on the number of common cathodes. Fig. 7.22 shows the drive arrangement. In this system the drivers operate at higher duty ratios and the additional dissipation combined with high voltage drive means that discrete circuitry is generally used in the larger displays, if not on both axes then at least on the cathode lines. The level conversion from the subsystem to the output stages is similar to that used in other high voltage displays (e.g. electroluminescence). The capacitance of these high voltage panels cannot be neglected and apart from allowing for increased charging currents some discharge mechanism (often a clamping resistor) is required to avoid crosstalk. This resistor does increase panel dissipation slightly.

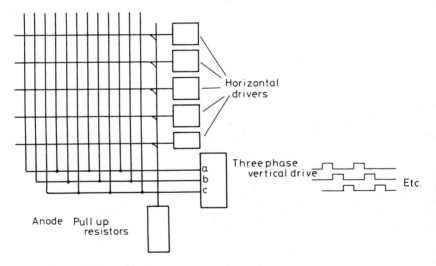

Fig. 7.22 Phase drive in Self-Scan panels

Conventional array addressing is feasible if a simple panel construction is desirable. Although inherent storage is possible using limiting resistors it is not exploited commercially. Line-at-a-time addressing is limited to arrays of less than about 1000 characters as duty ratios below 0.5% lead to a dim panel. The arguments applied to d.c. electroluminescence hold in the main for this type of display. The output drivers are based on discrete circuitry which has caused the interest in refreshed d.c. arrays to decline over the last few years.

7.5.2   A.C. gas discharge

A.C. gas discharge was one of the first technologies to demonstrate reasonably large alphanumeric panels (greater than 500 x 500 elements). There are several different constructions and in most cases the drive circuitry is unique to the particular device. In this section we will examine the principles of addressing used in the more successful systems. Because the emphasis must always be on circuitry which can ultimately be integrated we shall concentrate on the saturated square wave drive techniques as employed in the more recent systems.

A.C. gas discharge is not really suitable for small displays mainly because of the high voltage requirements and the ready availability of l.c.d. and l.e.d. displays. As a direct competitor to the c.r.t., the matrix addressed a.c. array offers high resolution and acceptable levels of brightness. These panels are driven in a memory mode (not dissimilar to that for a.c. electroluminescent panels (section 7.3.2) although the drive requirements are somewhat different). The large number of lines in these displays makes the use of one driver per line highly undesirable (about 5000 components would be required for a 500 x 500 display) so diode routing logic is generally employed to reduce the number of active output drivers. Although sine wave drive has been used in earlier panels the square wave drive shows several advantages. Firstly, it leads to a more stable panel performance as the high slew rates intrinsic to square wave drive mean that there is a rapid excursion through the threshold voltages. Secondly, the output drivers are either 'on' or 'off' which keeps dissipation to a minimum. The waveforms required to drive an a.c. matrix were given in fig. 6.28(a). The x and y co-ordinate drive pulses are shown and the difference $(x - y)$ depicts the waveform that will appear across the driven element. The three conditions of write, sustain and erase are all shown, and it can be seen that in order to turn on an element a narrow pulse is applied to both co-ordinates such that the discharge threshold is reached and the element fires, thereafter sustained by the sustain drive which is the a.c. drive upon which the write pulse is superimposed. Erasing is achieved by a short pulse which cancels out the wall charge voltage (chapter 6), hence inhibiting further discharges. The drive shown here is time critical and other more complex systems of phase shift drive have been described by Johnson and Jackson.[2] The output stage itself is shown in fig. 7.23. The output driver is of the 'clamped follower' construction which provides an active source and sink of current. It is very common to see inductors used in these drivers but as these are not integratable, we have chosen to show a directly coupled driver which has similar characteristics, i.e. fast rise time and reasonably efficient switching performance. The output voltage swing is large (>180 V) and this leads to quite high losses in the output stages when charging display capacitances. This is not a problem with discrete transistors, but fairly large areas of silicon are required when these drivers are reproduced in i.c. form which obviously increases the cost. The sustain drive waveform can be derived separately and routed onto the output stage via diodes. This can decrease the load on the write/erase drivers at the expense of extra packages.

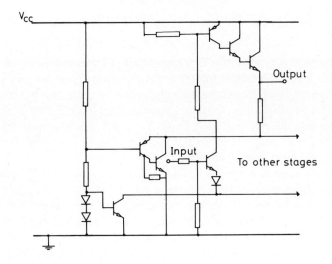

Fig. 7.23 Typical output stage for a.c. driver

7.6   Vacuum fluorescent displays

This technology made its impact in calculators and other hand held equipment where high efficiency and medium light output were required. Since then matrix displays of 240 characters have become commercially available. The fact that this technology is in the intermediate voltage range (20 V or so) has meant that integrated circuits have been easy to design and virtually all displays are driven with custom devices. The function of this section is to briefly examine the drive requirements from a user's point of view.

In all v.f.d.s there is a source of hot electrons, the filament. It is driven with an a.c. waveform of between two and ten volts. The easiest way of deriving this is with a transformer/invertor which follows the design of fig. 7.24. These are efficient

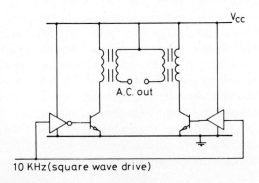

10 KHz(square wave drive)

Fig. 7.24 Transformer for v.f.d. filament drive

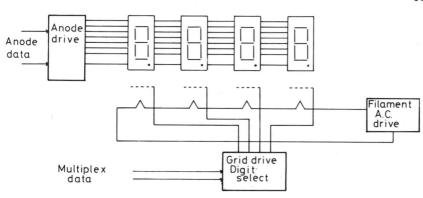

Fig. 7.25 Multiplexing v.f.d.s

(about 70% when loaded) and can be physically small. The drive of small displays (seven-segment) is usually multiplexed, the arrangement being given in fig. 7.25. The segment drive and digit drive are usually the anode and grid respectively, and when both of these are switched sufficiently positive with respect to the cathode (the filament) the appropriate digit and segments are energised. The driver in this example could easily be replaced by any 30 V i.c. buffer capable of sourcing about 30 mA. The same technique can be applied to matrix arrays. The anodes and grids are again used as the controlling electrodes, both being taken positive with respect to the cathode to select the dots. The lower duty factors in these displays necessitate higher drive voltages (about 25 V). The frequency of operation is high enough (60 μs line dwell time) to enable update at flicker free rates. Because of the open construction of the display there is inevitably some interaction between adjacent dots and this, coupled with reduced light output due to lower duty factors, at present limits the display size to some 240 characters with fixed character positions (see section 6.9). Grey scale modulation is best achieved by pulse width control in arrays as the use of part voltages can lead to poor contrast. Several i.c.s developed for d.c. gas discharge are suitable for v.f.d.s although an external clamping resistor is generally required to clamp unselected anodes and grids to the cathode potential.

7.7 Filament displays

Filament displays were used quite extensively in earlier display systems and consequently several custom drivers have been developed to address them. The direct view devices have the advantage of high brightness and low voltage operation. Against this we must put the question of reliability and difficulties of addressing them in a matrix form.

The basic filament has a low 'cold' resistance and this means that in an array it appears to be a near short circuit. By addressing them with a high frequency drive (1000 Hz) it is possible to overcome some of this effect by running the panel in

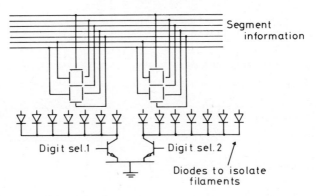

Fig. 7.26 Filament drive using i.c.s

a 'warm' mode. Very little information is available as to how the display is driven in practice, but claims of 40 x 40 matrixes have been made.

The display drives are generally of the open collector single-ended variety. If digits are being multiplexed, it is necessary to incorporate isolating diodes to eliminate any sneak paths. A standard arrangement is given in fig. 7.26. This diode arrangement can also be used to simulate a threshold and hence create a small dot matrix although the end result is not particularly cost effective.

7.8 Cathode ray tubes

The cathode ray tube has been employed in several novel ways to produce alphanumeric display panels. Here we shall consider the two principal techniques of addressing namely raster and vector scanning. The raster scanned c.r.t. is the most familiar as it is the technique employed in video displays. For alphanumeric displays, a dot matrix is created by relating dot information stored in a refresh memory (chapter 8) to points on the screen. The resolution can be as high as 1200 x 1000 points with high resolution tubes. The three control points in this system are the x/y deflection plates or coils and the z modulation grid which enables or disables the passage of electrons onto the screen phosphor. There are two advantages in addressing the display in this manner. Firstly, the subsystem electronics are fairly simple. It is easy to use existing video circuits by creating the requisite drive waveform. Secondly, the interface between the user who is creating the text and the display memory is straightforward as dot information can be created using standard character generation techniques and easily transferred to the display memory. This is the approach which is common in the personal computer and small office terminal.

The problems arise when complex high resolution shapes have to be reproduced. To obtain very high resolutions, a large display store is required and the c.r.t. bandwidth becomes a limiting factor. Special character fonts (italics, Chinese characters, etc.) appear grainy, even if rounding techniques are employed. The vector scanned c.r.t. makes better use of the deflection bandwidth by building up the information algorithmically from vector information; in other words it writes the data to the screen as one might with a pen. The only difference is that it has to do this repeatedly to maintain luminance. The display memory now holds a set of vectors. This is a better concentration of display information but the subsystem electronics have to be much more intelligent in order to convert the data to a meaningful screen representation. Vector c.r.t. controllers are realisable in a handful of i.c.s. Their internal operation is very complex and the reader is referred to any of the manufacturers' applications sheets for further detail.

Vector scanning is only one aspect of the improvement brought about by very large scale integrated (v.l.s.i.) circuits. The intelligence embodied in these devices can also be used to overcome intrinsic defects in the c.r.t. and its drivers by compensating for deflection errors intelligently. This is useful in conventional displays, but the area of real interest must be in the production of a feasible flat panel c.r.t. where the electron gun can be placed to one side as achieved in the Sinclair flat c.r.t. The divergence errors caused by this have, in the past, made an acceptable alphanumeric display impossible. If the beam deflection is controlled intelligently, then these can be nulled out. Such displays are in their youth but it is very likely that this will be an important area in future display technologies.

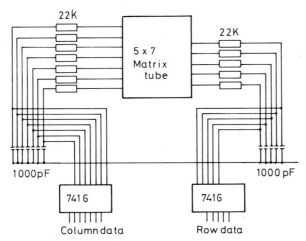

Fig. 7.27 E.E.V. character tube drive

The other cathode ray tube application worth mentioning is the character tube, as developed by E.E.V. There are no deflection plates in these displays but instead the electron gun floods the display and grids are used to select various portions of the display. The grid drive is low voltage and the high voltage is generated internally from a 12 V source. A circuit for a 5 x 7 character tube is given in fig. 7.27. As can be seen, this makes use of standard logic devices.

References

1. Alt, P. M. and Pleshco, P. (1974) 'Scanning limitations of liquid crystal displays'. *I.E.E.E. Trans.* **ED-21**, 146–155.
2. Jackson, R. N. and Johnson, K. E. (1974) 'Gas discharge displays: a critical review'. *Advances in Electronics and Electron Physics*. Vol. 35, Academic Press.

Chapter 8

Encoding and data organisation

8.1 Introduction

Although the impact of integrated technology on display drive circuitry has been important, the really significant advances have been in the display subsystem encompassing the encoding and data organisation, where integrated techniques have reduced the size, cost and power consumption of the total system package and offered considerable improvements in display servicing, yielding a much more attractive end product.

One of the consequences of integrated technology has been to package the expertise in such a way that only the input and output are defined and the operation of the display electronics within the package is not readily apparent. On the one hand this is an advantage, because it greatly eases the design of standard systems. However, when we wish to adapt or modify a display package there is a need to have a much clearer understanding of the total system than can be gleaned from the 'black box' approach generally associated with integrated technology. We have considered the various display interfaces in chapter 7 and in this chapter the principal elements of the subsystem are discussed to complete the picture. We need to explore several methods of data encoding, both in terms of hardware and software implementations to encompass the latest generation of display systems.

8.2 The display subsystem

Most displays have drive circuitry which is unique to their particular technology. However, when we move further back into the system, the differences become less important. This universality in subsystem architecture is very useful. Not only does it make the various systems simpler to understand, it also means that general purpose devices can be used reducing the cost of system development.

In chapter 3, a clear distinction was made between scanned and multiplexed displays as their operation was quite different. It is only in a very few examples that these differences are apparent in the subsystem electronics, especially if we confine ourselves to the use of these displays for the presentation of alphanumeric information which is the principal interest of this book.

Except for a few special exceptions most subsystem electronics is now implemented using digital techniques. This is quite compatible with matrix displays although the use of a grey scale may introduce other circuit elements, some of which may be analogue. With many scanned displays, especially those displaying video information, an analogue approach is more common. Even here, the display of character type information is more frequently tackled digitally.

8.2.1   Subsystem requirements

We define the display subsystem as that part which allows the outside world to communicate with the display drive. The subsystem has many functions. Firstly, it needs to service the display by updating it when changes are required and, in the case of a volatile display, refreshing it when necessary. Secondly, it has to receive external information and decode to a form suitable for the display drivers. Thirdly, it may need to perform ancillary tasks such as cursor control, graphic commands or other specific tasks. In its simplest form the subsystem can be represented as shown (control) in fig. 8.1. The three principal functions of interface, storage and data interpretation, update and refresh are covered in the interacting units, shown servicing the display. The decoding function will require a data input interface, a data store and a control handler. Similarly, the control function must be accessible and must act upon the data store. The nature of the display control depends on the information being displayed. If the information is principally character based then it is likely that a cursor would be employed to determine where the next character would be placed or where editing is required. A quite different set of control requirements are imposed when displaying graphics information. Intelligent display systems, which we discuss later, can have a very complex set of control commands, the object being to relieve the host system of the bulk of the work associated with display servicing.

8.2.2   Subsystem interfaces

Information has to be passed from the user of the display. The communicating channel may be intimate, with no defined boundary between the host system and

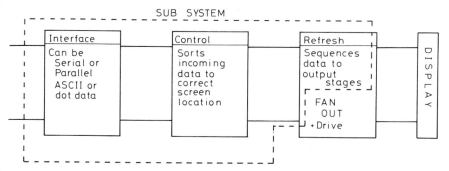

Fig. 8.1 Basic elements of the display system

the display electronics, or it may be interfaced through some standard remote connection such as the C.C.I.T.T. serial data bus, V24. In both cases the need is to transport data rapidly and reliably into the display system.

Small numeric or alphanumeric displays are generally intimately coupled to the host system and in many cases the host system and the display electronics belong to the same integrated circuit. The larger display systems usually require a 'looser' connection and it is here that a more elaborate method of data transfer is required. To illustrate the point, consider a character display capable of displaying 300 alphanumeric characters and consider the requirements or constraints which may be imposed.

The display needs to be updated rapidly, perhaps so rapidly that the observer must not be aware of the updating process. This would mean that the new information would have to be transferred in a few milliseconds. We need to consider the nature of the data. We could send 'dot' information relating the state of each element on the display. With a 300-character display and a 5 x 7 matrix this would mean that we should have to send 10 500 binary bits of data to build up one display image. Although, as we shall see in section 8.2.3, an encoding system will be preferred, the number of bits will still be large.

Only new information need or indeed should be sent from the host system to the display. It would be wasteful to continually send information from the host system when all that is actually needed is notification of any changes. Updating every character in a 300-character display remotely would cause several problems, especially in that the host system would have to spend a considerable amount of time performing this function. The display subsystem should incorporate sufficient capability to obviate the need to do more than send update information.

Finally it might be useful to relieve the host system of such tasks as display 'clear' or other display oriented commands. The need to send 'control characters' would also exist as part of the interface requirement. These characters would instruct the display electronics to perform any of the predetermined special functions. In general the more complex the display, the more likely such facilities would be desirable.

8.2.3 Data presentation

Several different data encoding standards have been evolved to cope with particular display requirements. The most commonly used are ASCII, binary coded decimal to seven-segment and, more recently, limited resolution graphics standards as used in the information services Prestel, Ceefax and Oracle.

Each of these is designed to minimise the number of bits required to convey a message to the display. A character display without the facility to represent pictorial information will generally only require about one hundred different codes — the letters (upper and lower case), numerals and punctuation. Additionally, some codes are required to control the display, their precise nature depending on the application. The ASCII character set is specifically designed to cater for these requirements and is reproduced in fig. 8.2. Because the whole character set only occupies 128 different code slots, each character can be represented by a seven-bit binary word which offers a considerable saving over transmitting a dot-by-dot representation. Although several codes have been allocated to special control codes, these relate to earlier display systems such as teletypes and simple c.r.t. based systems and as such do not offer the range of control commands required to service the more complex display systems. Consequently it is quite common to see some of these codes reallocated for special applications.

Data encoding not only saves time by reducing the number of bits of information needed to build up a message, it also provides a standard, independent of the display itself. The host system need not concern itself as to whether the display is based on

				D6	0	0	0	0	1	1	1	1
				D5	0	0	1	1	0	0	1	1
				D4	0	1	0	1	0	1	0	1
D3	D2	D1	D0		0	1	2	3	4	5	6	7
0	0	0	0	0	NUL	DLE	SP	0	@	P	`	p
0	0	0	1	1	SOH	DC1	!	1	A	Q	a	q
0	0	1	0	2	STX	DC2	"	2	B	R	b	r
0	0	1	1	3	ETX	DC3	#	3	C	S	c	s
0	1	0	0	4	EOT	DC4	$	4	D	T	d	t
0	1	0	1	5	ENQ	NAK	%	5	E	U	e	u
0	1	1	0	6	ACK	SYN	&	6	F	V	f	v
0	1	1	1	7	BEL	ETB	'	7	G	W	g	w
1	0	0	0	8	BS	CAN	(	8	H	X	h	x
1	0	0	1	9	HT	EM	)	9	I	Y	i	y
1	0	1	0	A	LF	SUB	*	:	J	Z	j	z
1	0	1	1	B	VT	ESC	+	;	K	[	k	{
1	1	0	0	C	FF	FS	,	<	L	\	l	|
1	1	0	1	D	CR	GS	-	=	M	]	m	}
1	1	1	0	E	SO	RS	.	>	N	^	n	~
1	1	1	1	F	SI	US	/	?	O	_	o	DEL

Fig. 8.2 ASCII character set

a 5 x 7 dot matrix or a multi-segment character format. The task of sorting that out is left to the display electronics.

Other encoding standards have been evolved to provide a low redundancy representation of seven-segement numeric information (fig. 8.3), limited resolution graphics based on existing information services (fig. 8.4) and several other less standard representations. All of these strive to relieve the burden of data transmission by limiting the number of bits required. Some information, principally graphical, is data intensive and an encoding standard would offer only a slight saving; one example is in displays used for printed circuit board design which require a very high integrity in the reproduction of the computed information.

'Remote' display systems are much less common than even a few years ago. It has become so much simpler to design very intelligent subsystems whose cost is comparable to that of the display itself, that quite new techniques of information transfer are used in these more intimately coupled systems. To understand these developments we are going to look at several examples of real display subsystems making use of the range of currently available devices.

8.3 Non-multiplexed displays

As we discussed in chapter 3, non-multiplexed displays are usually fairly simple, comprising a few digits or characters. Accordingly, the supporting circuitry is not

No.	Digit	D	C	B	A
1		0	0	0	1
2		0	0	1	0
3		0	0	1	1
4		0	1	0	0
5		0	1	0	1
6		0	1	1	0
7		0	1	1	1
8		1	0	0	0
9		1	0	0	1
0		0	0	0	0

1 – Logic one
0 – Logic zero

Fig. 8.3 Seven-segment code

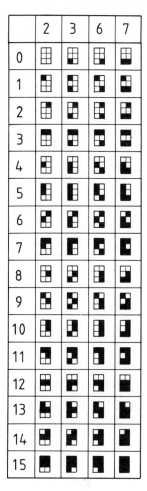

Fig. 8.4 Viewdata graphics set

usually complicated unless some special control of the display is required such as compensation for ageing. Fig. 8.5 describes one commonly used method which uses a multiplexing technique to provide the necessary fan-out to the display elements. It comprises four latches which serve as storage elements. Information is transferred from the data bus which interconnects the latches by routing it using the appropriate latch select line. If the information is encoded (e.g. binary coded decimal) then these latches would have to incorporate decoding circuitry. This arrangement is commonly used in microprocessor systems because of its inherent compatibility with the processor bus structure. The use of storage elements such as latches makes display maintenance very simple. It is only necessary to update when the display has to be altered.

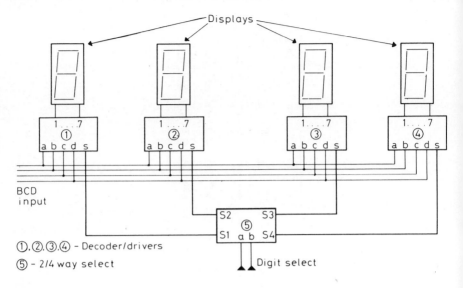

Fig. 8.5 Digit drive

8.4   Matrix displays

As we have seen, alphanumeric information is most frequently represented using one or other of the dot matrixes. This applies equally to scanned displays. Fig. 8.6 gives a block representation of the front end of most alphanumeric display systems. The interface collects information from the outside world and in the case of control character based systems a check would be made for any control characters. These characters control such elements as the cursor counter and the character generator and are not displayed. Display characters are passed to a local display memory under the control of a cursor counter which points to the destination of the data in the display memory. This memory is the local store from which the display is updated. The updating process involves reading the memory sequentially, decoding the information (if it has been encoded, as would be the case with ASCII) and passing it to the output circuitry. The output circuitry varies depending on whether the display is scanned or multiplexed.

8.4.1   Data memory

The heart of fig. 8.6 is really the display memory for it is here that refreshed displays (which cover most displays in current use) require a continuous updating process. The refresh process is generally cyclical, i.e. it follows a well defined sequence which is repeated regularly. Disturbing the refresh process can have many repercussions. Firstly it could cause the display to flicker reducing readability. Secondly and more importantly it could actually damage the display by causing

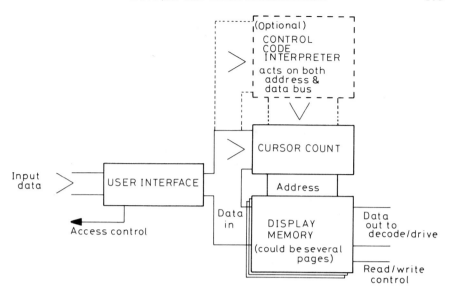

Fig. 8.6 Display front end

elements to be selected for a long time with the high currents required to maintain luminance when multiplexing. Therefore the refresh process should be disturbed as little as possible. The display memory, however, has to be accessible to the host system or we could not update the information being displayed. This requirement for two-way access is accomplished by using a circuit similar to fig. 8.7. It is important that the host system has access to the memory only when the display refresh circuitry does not require it if the effects described above are to be avoided.

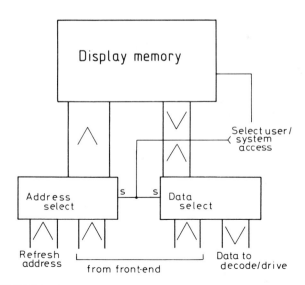

Fig. 8.7 Two-port access

The usual technique of display memory access is called time division multiplexing. Access to the display memory can only be granted to the outside world when it is not required by the display. This is usually during the period when the display outputs are active (in line-at-a-time multiplexing, during the line dumping time). This access time is short in most systems and some method of synchronising to this time period is necessary. The simplest method is to latch incoming data and admit it to the display memory in the correct phase. Some form of 'handshaking' may be required if the incoming data is not synchronous to the display refresh rate.

8.4.2   Control characters and memory mapping

Several references have already been made to control characters as a method of organising the display information. The principle is to transfer some of the responsibility of data handling to the display system thus easing the interface process. ASCII control characters treat the display as a piece of paper. Each incoming data character is written into the next screen location unless a control character is sent to modify this procedure by forcing a jump to a different screen location. With this arrangement some tally of the position of the next character space has to be kept. This is the function of the 'cursor counter'. Control characters act directly upon this counter and modify its value to determine the position of the next character. In a real system this cursor counter may be a discrete binary counter or it may be a memory location used by a microprocessor. By way of an example fig. 8.8 shows how the cursor counter is used in a software system by giving a simple flow chart of the effects of the ASCII characters. Several other control characters exist which perform operations not involving the modification of a cursor counter.

Memory mapping is another way of passing data to the display memory and is

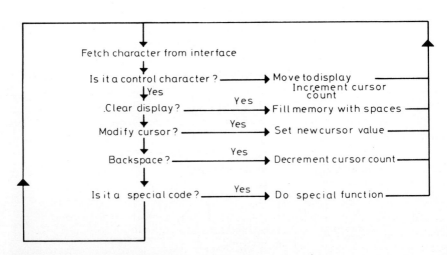

Fig. 8.8 Software cursor control

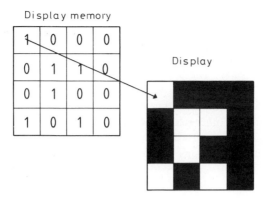

Fig. 8.9 Memory mapping

commonly used in microprocessor based display systems. Essentially the data memory is directly accessible to the host system and it may both write information to it and read it back. The display 'housekeeping' becomes the responsibility of the host system as no local cursor control is available. This is usually no problem for most applications. Fig. 8.9 shows how the memory is 'mapped' in this way.

8.4.3 Refresh circuits

Having a memory with the appropriate data is only part of the story. Next we need to see how this information is passed to the display. The first thing to bear in mind is that the display data generally pass from the memory to the display sequentially, usually under the control of a refresh controller which simply cycles through the memory and allows the data to be passed onto the next stages in the system.

The rate at which this refresh counter cycles through the memory is a function of display size, the drive output requirements (pulse width, duty ratio, etc.) and the arrangement of the scanning stages of the system. For many applications it is vital that the refresh operation is continuous (which is an important point if the system is implemented using software techniques) with a field refresh rate fast enough to ensure a flicker free display.

If the information in the memory is encoded in some way (e.g. ASCII) it will be necessary to decode it into a form suitable for output to the display. The circuit element responsible for this is generally referred to as a character generator and takes the form of a read only memory. This device is programmed to contain all the display characters in a dot form. Unlike most other parts of the display system, the character generator must be selected for the particular display in question, that is, factors such as dot-matrix size and whether the display is scanned or multiplexed column or row-at-a-time need to be taken into account.

8.4.4 Interfacing with the display drive

To complete the picture, fig. 8.10 gives a circuit representation of a typical interface to a matrix display. The character generator and refresh counter are shown for completeness. In this example we have chosen to show the sequence for a two-line display, each line containing thirty-two characters on a 5 x 7 dot matrix. The principles hold true for other sizes although some of the figures will change. As was shown in chapter 3, the most efficient way of addressing matrix displays is either row-at-a-time or column-at-a-time. We shall arbitrarily choose to address this display row-at-a-time. The refresh circuitry must therefore prepare one row of information before passing it to the display.

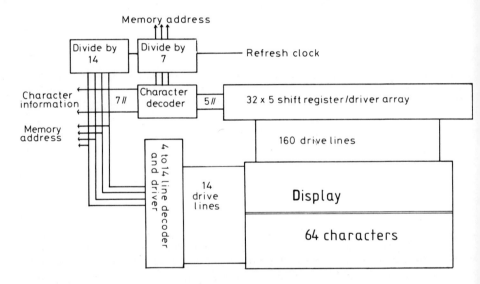

Fig. 8.10 Output via shift register/decoder drivers

The sequence of operation is as follows: The first line memory is read through by sequentially accessing the first thirty-two memory display locations. Each piece of information is decoded (if necessary) by the character generator and the first row passed to the row storage buffer (fig. 8.10). Once the complete row has been passed to the buffer it can be displayed. The whole process is repeated for the other rows pertinent to the first thirty-two characters. The next line of thirty-two characters in the display store are then read.

It is important to remember that seven rows (because we are using a 5 x 7 dot matrix in this example) have to be displayed before one character line is displayed. This means that some care has to be exercised in the arrangement of the decoding circuitry.

Scanned alphanumeric displays are addressed dot-at-a-time. There is no need for

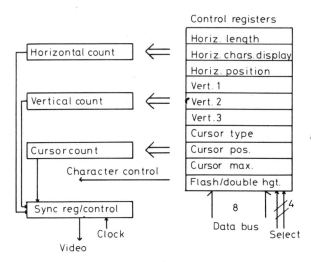

Fig. 8.11 C.R.T. controller: typical internal organisation

a line buffer as with matrix displays. C.R.T. circuits for this application are profuse. A fairly typical example is given in fig. 8.11. This shows the simplified output stages and most of the extra circuitry discussed above.

8.4.5 Software versus hardware

One of the more important considerations when designing a display system is whether the system is best implemented using hardware, software or a combination of the two. It would not be worthwhile going into too much detail as many factors only indirectly related to the display will probably decide the final design. In this section we will, however look at the major considerations and derive some idea of the overheads in servicing a display using software techniques.

Microprocessors are very much at home in the display system. The tasks of display refresh and character manipulation are sufficiently simple to ensure compact coding which keeps the cost of software development to a minimum. Before the design engineer even considers designing a display system from scratch, it is imperative that he studies the available devices. At the time of writing, display control devices were being announced with such regularity that it seems very likely that one of these would suit most applications.

Assuming that a special requirement has to be satisfied, the next stage in the development of the system would entail producing a full specification of the final system. This usually gives a fairly clear idea as to which design technique is most suitable. The more complex the specification the more likely that a microprocessor based design would prove the better option.

Most commercially available systems do not service the display with a microprocessor. There are two reasons. Firstly, the display operation is essentially 'real

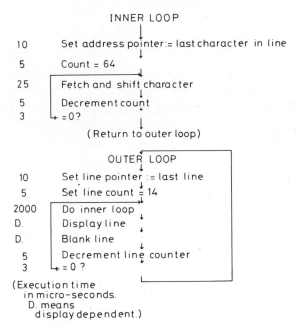

Fig. 8.12 Flow chart of refresh activity

time', which means that while the display is being serviced the microprocessor is unable to do much else. Secondly, there is always the danger that the refresh process can become disturbed (by a software fault or an unanticipated interruption) which could have disastrous consequences due to overdriving the display and its drivers. Most other display operations do not impose this real time constraint and are amenable to software control. To illustrate this, fig. 8.12 is a flow chart of a fairly standard display servicing routine with times to execute each program segment given in milliseconds. This should give some guide as to the amount of time left for other computing functions.

8.5   Other facilities

There are many adjuncts associated with displays. One of the more interesting is the so called 'light pen' used for updating the display directly. Light pens are not difficult to incorporate in most display systems although passive displays such as liquid crystal displays require backlighting. Light pens work by sensing the presence of light emitted by the display and relating this to a time frame. They rely on the fact that no two points on the display are alight at any one time and as such are suited to multiplexed dot-at-a-time or scanned displays. There are several points that need to be considered. Firstly, in order to recognise the position of the light pen we have to select each element of the display once. It is important that the light pen only 'sees' the element nearest to it. It is important that the light pulse emitted from the display is of a short duration and corresponds with the electrical signal generating the light output so that we can relate it to the scanning cycle and hence determine its position. Secondly, if the light pen is travelling quickly across the display we must scan quickly enough to be sure to track its progress. Displays which are scanned slowly may need addressing differently in order to achieve reasonable results. Thirdly, we have already seen that multiplexed displays are driven line-at-a-time not dot-at-a-time. Some additional decoding is required to give the effect that the display is being scanned. There are many ways of achieving this. Most of these affect the readability of the display during the pen search time.

One circuit to provide a light pen facility is shown in fig. 8.13. The circuit is the same as that shown in fig. 8.10 except that when the light pen detects a pulse as a result of being in contact with the display, the value of the refresh counter is 'trapped' in a register which may then be read by additional circuitry giving the position of the light pen. This is only a simple example but forms the basis of many current designs.

8.6 High resolution displays

In the above discussion we have been concerned with alphanumeric type displays which are limited in both the number and type of characters available. There are several ways of providing a much higher definition by independently accessing each of the display points. The 'brute force' approach is to map each screen dot in a memory. This requires a much larger store. The general scheme is very much as for alphanumeric displays but there is no need for the character generator as information in the memory directly corresponds with that to be displayed on the screen. One quite elegant compromise takes the form of a programmable character generator which can be filled with special screen patterns by the controlling system and then

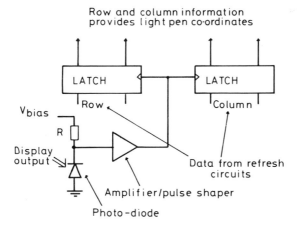

Fig. 8.13 Light pen circuitry

operates precisely as a conventional character generator, but is continuously modifiable to cope with changing patterns. It is not as flexible as a full size memory but suits many applications. High resolution displays capable of reproducing pictorial information from digital information are the subject of considerable interest in that they provide a powerful man—machine interface. The science is in the early stages and, for the moment at least, beyond the scope of this book.

Chapter 9

Applications

9.1 Introduction

In chapter 2 we saw that there was a wide range of applications for numeric and alphanumeric displays, as summarised in table 2.1, covering the 'spectrum' of displays from a few numerals, as required in clocks and watches, to 6000 or more characters for full page editors. It was clear that all these applications could not be described in any detail and five examples were selected which typified the various regions of the display spectrum. Having discussed the available technologies and drive circuits we can now reconsider these five applications and examine how far the requirements of each may be met by practical display systems.

For many applications there will be more than one technology or system which can be adapted and it is the aim of this chapter to compare the various possibilities with a view to making the choice for a particular application easier for the user. However, it is not our intention to present the 'best buy' for each application, indeed there may not be one. What we can do is to point out the advantages and disadvantages of the alternatives and leave it to some extent to the user to decide to which parameters he will give priority for his particular application. For this purpose it is sometimes better to look at the problem from the other end and consider in which applications the attribute of a particular display system can best be exploited. It must be remembered, however. that the world of display is a rapidly changing one. Improvement in both the technology and the circuitry or new discoveries can change the picture dramatically. We have seen this happen in the pocket calculator market where the liquid crystal display took over from the l.e.d. display within a period of a few years. It could happen again in other display areas and it would be a clever man who could predict when and in what area the changes might take place. We can only comment on the present state of the art at the time of writing this book.

9.2 The pocket calculator and other hand held instruments

The requirements for the pocket calculator are similar to other hand held instruments including the watch, where the main consideration is size. One of the main factors in determining size is the required supply battery. The HP7 type battery, which might be considered as the largest acceptable battery for such instruments, gives 0.6 ampere hours. Therefore for the 5 mW suggested maximum dissipation given in table 2.2 the battery would only give 200 hours continuous operation before it had to be changed and this ignores the power dissipation in the circuit. This situation could be acceptable for instruments requiring intermittent readout such as the pocket calculator but it is obviously not ideal. To achieve this level of dissipation we would still require an efficiency of 5.6 1m/W with an active display, a value which is at least an order greater than has been attained with most present technologies. The obvious solution is to use a passive display which depends on the environmental illumination. In particular the liquid crystal offers a very low powered display of about 5 μW per character for 0.4 cm high numerals which at the present state of development is reliable with a long operational life. With such displays much smaller batteries can be used, witness the watch displays which can be operated continuously for over a year without having to change batteries. The liquid crystal display is not entirely ideal. There is criticism of the contrast, especially when multiplexed, and the twisted nematic liquid crystal extensively used for these displays has a limited angle of view. In low ambient illumination they are difficult to read, and the drive circuit, although easily integrated, is more complex than required for an l.e.d. Although improvements such as the guest host colour displays are expected in the near future, for some applications where a larger or rechargeable battery can be used the small l.e.d. is still a contender. The l.e.d. display can be directly interfaced with low voltage integrated circuits. They are rugged and reliable, are very cheap and most important they are active giving an illuminated display. Although gas discharge and vacuum fluorescent displays could operate at lower powers than the l.e.d. they cannot compete on voltage, ruggedness or price, and generally small 3 mm high numerals are not available in these technologies. At present the cheap small multi-digit l.e.d. displays are red and for some people they are difficult to see and tiring to use for any length of time. Until the other colour l.e.d.s are cost competitive there is still room for the vacuum fluorescent multi-digit display with its green high brightness output in hand held instruments.

What of the new technologies in the future? The most promising for this applicational area are the electrochromic and electrophoretic displays. Both offer low power, limited non-volatile memory and superior appearance in contrast and viewing angle to that of the liquid crystal. Of the two the electrochromic display with its low driving voltage seems to be the most suited for small numeric displays. However, both technologies require further improvements if they are to compete on the operational life and reliability performance set by the present technologies. Of course they could be overtaken by some of the newer ideas such as 'dipole suspension', but a truly solid state low powered device is still sought. On this score it is a pity that PLZT displays have not fulfilled their early expectations.

On the drive circuit, the latch system of fig. 8.5 is very suitable for such a limited register of numerals, giving a better presentation than a multiplexing system at very little extra cost.

9.3   The digital meter

For the larger numeral requirements such as digital meters and clocks, only the cathode ray tube and its derivatives can be ruled out. All the matrix devices are suitable and the display engineer has the choice of at least five technologies in production, each extolled by its manufacturer, as well as a number of other technologies which are at an advanced stage of development. In table 9.1 the main technologies commercially available are listed with typical examples giving similar sized characters. The incandescent filament gives the brightest display and is of especial interest in applications where there are high ambient light conditions, for example on petrol pumps and in aircraft cockpits. It might be argued that the reflective passive display is more suited to such applications but this is not necessarily so. In the case of the cockpit display, the pilot's eyes are adapted to a high level of illumination external to the cockpit, and when tranferring to the cockpit display the lighting level appears relatively dark. Wharf *et al.*[1] have shown under these circumstances that the active display is superior in giving less reading errors in simulated experiments. Further, there is no need for subsidiary illumination for the active display when the light level falls. The main subjective objection to the incandescent filament is the narrow line width of the characters. The number of digits that can be multiplexed is limited and they are rather more expensive than other devices at this present time.

If the display is not required for a high brightness environment then there are three active display technologies which compete for this area of the market. They are l.e.d., gas discharge and vacuum fluorescence. All three have proven reliability and can be readily multiplexed. For the 10 to 15 mm high characters the costs per digit are similar and there is very little to choose on display appearance. The l.e.d. has the advantage of low switching voltage but because it is slightly less efficient than the other two it requires more power for comparable brightness. The larger numerals are packaged as single-digit devices or multiples up to four, but if smaller numerals can be accepted then multi-digit displays of eight or more numerals in a single package are available at a lower cost per digit. L.E.D.s are now available in several colours, red, orange, yellow and green. However, the colours other than red are less efficient and, at present, more expensive. The red l.e.d. is close to the limiting wavelength for visibility and some users find them difficult to see. Although the gas discharge display is also red, it has a much wider bandwidth with wavelengths more towards orange than the l.e.d. and so it does not present a visual problem. Normally gas discharge displays are packaged with several digits in each device. Their main disadvantage lies in their driving voltage requirements. The total potential across the display is typically 200 V with switching voltages around 65 V. However, because they have been popular for some time, integrated circuits specially designed to drive them are readily available. The vacuum fluorescent tube offers a similar display but with a pleasant green output at lower power and potential. They have been less popular than the other two technologies and are mainly produced in Japan. Their performance perhaps has been underrated in Europe, where they are the most expensive of the three technologies. However, prices are coming down and they are creating greater interest now that other colours also are available.

The liquid crystal consumes the least power and for battery operated equipment it has an enormous advantage. The fabrication technologies facilitate the design of custom displays combining all the required numerals and symbols in one device. The appearance is less pleasing than the active displays and auxiliary lighting is

184

Table 9.1 Data on examples of numeric displays for instrumentation

Technology	Example	Character height (mm)	Voltage (V)	Mean current to digit 8 (mA)	Mean power digit 8 (mW)	Brightness (cd/m²)
Gas discharge	Philips ZM1550 (2-digit)	15	175	2.1	367	(860) 3 mcd per seg.
L.E.D. (red)	Hewlett–Packard 5082–7750	10.9	1.6	140	224	(140) 0.4 mcd per seg.
L.E.D. (yellow)	Hewlett–Packard 5082–7660	10.9	1.6	140	224	(750) 1.5 mcd per seg.
Vacuum fluorescent	Futaba 2LT02 (2-digit)	15	18	5.5*	119†	750
Incandescent filament	Okaya FDG 5V15	15	5	105	525	15 000
Liquid crystal	Hamlin 3906 (4-digit)	12.7	5	0.01	0.05	20:1 contrast
D.C. electroluminescent		15	100	2.5	250	340

* Includes portion of grid current.
† Includes portion of cathode power.

required for viewing at low ambient light levels. The latest colour liquid crystal display using pleochroic dyes gives an improved display, which will no doubt increase their market share.

As with the hand held equipment the new technologies of interest are the electrophoretic and the electrochromic displays. However, the competition in this area of the market is much greater and unless new devices can significantly reduce cost or have real technical advantages, for example a higher efficiency, they are likely just to add to the number of choices available.

Although not strictly covered by the digital meter title of this section, there is a growing number of applications requiring a single register of alphanumerics, such as electronic games and data entry displays, for which most of the technologies discussed above have been adapted. Indeed all the technologies offer limited alpha-numeric displays either as star-burst patterns (see chapter 1) or as 5 x 7 dot matrixes. The gas discharge was first in the field and is relatively cheap. The Self-Scan® dot-matrix panel, which is the most popular device, has the added advantage of economy of drivers, requiring about fourteen drivers for sixteen or more characters. Displays in single packages with up to forty characters are available with integrated circuit drivers specially tailored for them. Incandescent filament displays offer only star-burst displays in single-digit tubes and are therefore limited in the size of the register. The limited register is also true of the l.e.d.s, although small starburst alphanumeric displays in similar packages to that of fig. 6.3 are available. The l.e.d. can also be obtained in dot-matrix form packaged with up to four characters in a single unit. The Hewlett–Packard alphanumeric display of fig. 6.4 includes the decoder and drive circuits. The cost of such dot-matrix l.e.d.s are expensive when compared with the gas discharge panel. The vacuum fluorescent tube probably represents the main challenge to the gas discharge approach particularly for the larger registers of forty characters. They run at lower voltage and give a brighter display and are now becoming more competitive in price. They do not have the same economy of drivers, requiring about fifty drivers for sixteen characters.

The liquid crystal also competes in this area with dot-matrix devices giving up to thirty-two characters already available commercially. For a single register scanned in the vertical direction the duty ratio is fairly high so that reasonable contrast can be obtained. Although the driving circuit, as described in chapter 7, is complex the low power handling makes integration fairly simple. For battery operation the liquid crystal is likely to be used extensively in these applications in the future, but where power is not a major factor the rather more pleasing emitting displays are likely to be preferred.

For new technologies, the electroluminescent panel must be included as a very competitive device. At present the manufacturers are concentrating on larger character capacity panels, but once they gain a foothold in that area it seems reasonable to suppose they will be extended to cover the more limited character capacity display market.

9.4   Low cost data terminal

For the small size alphanumeric data panel of around 500 character capacity the c.r.t. is probably the first choice. A low cost television tube with its associated deflection coils and drive circuits can be adapted for this application. It has disadvantage in size, particularly for table top equipment and there is distortion at the edges and a certain amount of jitter, but overall it represents a very low cost approach which is acceptable for most applications. The presentation can be improved by using a 'professional' c.r.t. and better design of the coils and drive circuit, but this appreciably raises the cost. The alternatives such as the gas discharge and electroluminescent panel then become very competitive in price, in spite of the larger number of circuit components and connections required. They have the advantage of being more compact (flat) and with the light elements being spatially defined, there is no distortion or jitter. They are also more versatile in their format; for instance, long thin panels can be constructed to display two or three rows of eighty characters. The gas discharge panel was the first matrix display in the field and has obtained a substantial market foothold; the market survey in the U.S.A. in 1981 showed dot-matrix gas discharge displays to have a similar market value to that of black-and-white c.r.t.s. Integrated circuits have been developed to drive them and most manufacturers supply the panel plus the drive circuit in a module which makes them relatively easy to incorporate. There is a choice between a.c. and d.c. panels although the Burrough's Self-Scan® configuration with its economy of drive circuit has the largest share of the market at present. The electroluminescent panel is just emerging as a competitor to the gas discharge panel. Again it is being marketed as a module with the drive circuits incorporated. The fact that the display is yellow is considered an advantage, but if it is to oust the gas discharge panel it will have also to be cost competitive. The gas discharge panel has been around long enough for its performance to be adequately assessed by users and it will probably take a year or two of user experience before the electroluminescent panel is accepted with equal confidence. A third active matrix display which is competitive, for the area of a limited number of characters, say four rows of eighty characters, is the vacuum fluorescent dot-matrix alphanumeric panel. The commercial panels have defined character positions, although a cross-bar panel with all dots addressable has been described (chapter 6). It has the advantages of higher efficiency and lower drive voltages with a bright green display.

A considerable amount of research and development effort is also being expended on liquid crystal dot-matrix displays for this area of application. Several different approaches have been described in the literature and panels giving up to 500 characters have been demonstrated. Clearly such panels would have great advantage on power dissipation if the problems of contrast and update rate can be overcome. Similarly the electrophoretic display has been described for dot-matrix panels with a 500-character capability.

In terms of drive circuits, purpose designed i.c.s have been developed for the available matrix alphanumeric panels and generally the cost is dictated by the number of packages required rather than the complexity or voltage values. In this respect the Self-Scan® panel has the advantage but as circuit costs continue to fall the price of the display device itself could become the controlling factor.

9.5 Graphic terminals

The type of graphic display considered here is at the cheaper end of the market
with a resolution of the order of 512 x 512 elements. Gas discharge panels, particularly the a.c. panel, and electroluminescent panels can still be exploited for this
applicational area, although some of the specification given in table 2.2, such as the
efficiency, would have to be relaxed. However, since the cost of a matrix addressed
display increases almost linearly with the number of columns plus rows, they
cannot compete on price with the c.r.t. There are a few applications where the
flatness or some other aspect of the matrix display is essential and the extra cost
can be tolerated. As an example of this, Illinois University brought out a computer-
ised educational system called Plato in which the display was augmented with back
projected slides. The most convenient method of doing this was to use the a.c.
plasma panel which is semi-transparent and their terminals incorporated a 512 x 512
element plasma panel from Owen—Illinois for this purpose.

For most graphic terminals, a c.r.t. with rather better resolution that a t.v. tube
is required. These are readily available in black and white, and are also now being
joined by higher definition colour tubes. The latter have the obvious advantage of
giving extra information with the use of the different colours which could justify
the extra cost.

The bulkiness or rather depth of the c.r.t. is still considered a problem, and there
is a large amount of effort being expended on trying to achieve a flat cathode ray
tube. If successful, the matrix displays would find it even harder to compete.

Also looking into the future, it is possible that passive displays such as the liquid
crystal and electrophoretic displays will challenge the c.r.t. for such applications
and offer the potential of battery operated terminals.

For this type of application the display unit will be either used as a peripheral to
a large computer or incorporated in a small desk-top computer. Either way the
organisation and control of the data will be 'remote' from the display unit making
use of the logic and storage of the computing section of the main frame computer
or, in the case of the table-top computer, the microprocessor. Because of this there
could be an advantage in a storage display such as the a.c. plasma panel, although
storage within the circuit has now become relatively cheap.

9.6 Full page editors

For more sophisticated graphics or a page editor for a word processor a display with
at least 1000 x 1000 pixels is required with a pitch of about 0.25 mm. Although an
a.c. plasma panel has been demonstrated with 1024 x 1024 elements and a resolution
of 80 lines per inch (0.3 mm pitch), the c.r.t. is really the only practical device
capable of fulfilling the requirements. Black-and-white tubes with over a 1000-line
resolution have been developed, but at present they are expensive. The Charactron
with its present capability of 30 lines of 132 characters may be an alternative answer
in the future, but it has a limited versatility on font. The possibility of a full page

colour display is some way off. The shadow mask colour tube, even with the improved resolution, cannot meet the 1000-line specification and the alternative approach with the 'penetron' phosphor has problems of adequate focussing with the voltage switching that is necessary.

In the meantime half page editors are being used and the c.r.t. performance comes well within the specification, with adequate margins on brightness and efficiency.

For graphics, the fast update time of the c.r.t. is an asset which allows 'real time' variation of the display (moving picture). This is particularly useful in interactive graphics where the consequences of changing parameters can be followed visually. For example, in a simulated drawing of an electron gun the effect of varying the electrode potentials on the electron trajectories can be readily seen. Also because the screen is scanned a dot at a time, the position of the beam can be determined by a light detector. This facilitates 'light pen' addressing and editing, a facility which is much more difficult to accomplish with line dumped matrix displays. This does not mean there is no need for improvement. Apart from the need for higher resolution and the extension to colour there would be great advantage in lower voltage tubes and a flat construction. There is also the worry that continuously watching a c.r.t. can cause eye strain or at least fatigue, and better presentation is required.

For some applications a larger projection display may be required. The Eidophor is commercially available and could be used for such an application. Other systems are being investigated using both electron beam and light beam scanning. It will be some time, however, before such systems with adequate resolution will come down sufficiently in price to find use in an office machine or small computer system.

9.7 Conclusions

In the above we have tried to show how the available display technologies fit the spectrum of applications. None of the display types is completely ideal; the engineer would like lower costs and better presentation. Nevertheless for the majority of applications a display device can be chosen which to say the least is adequate. Indeed great credit must go to the research and development engineers who have produced such good displays and to the electronics engineers who have developed the drive and control circuits to exploit them.

For applications where a large amount of information is required the c.r.t. is really quite remarkable. If offers a bright colour display with no restriction on font and can show graphic and 'real time' variations in the information. It needs few connections and, because of its efficiency, does not consume enormous amounts of power. Its exploitation has gained greatly from the sophistication of modern integrated circuit technique, especially from the introduction of the microprocessor. Matrix displays to give similar versatility require a large number of picture elements and consequently a large number of connections and drivers. Even with the continuing decrease in integrated circuit costs it will be hard for the matrix addressed display to compete against the c.r.t. at the 'top' end of the range.

When less information is required the matrix displays come into their own. Although they are less versatile in terms of the number of applications that can be satisfied with one standard display format, they have the advantage of a construction that can be easily adapted for custom designed purposes. For example, it would not be economical to design a display for the instrumentation in a car based on a large dot-matrix panel, but on the other hand it is a relatively simple matter to design a panel to include fixed legends, bar graphs and numerics which could fulfil the requirements. Apart from l.e.d.s and incandescent filaments, the matrix technologies can be fabricated with the electrode patterns deposited with screen printing techniques. Changing the format is basically very simple, requiring only changes in the printing masks.

For simple displays such as numerics there are a number of technologies to choose from, and the choice depends on the overriding parameter in the specification. If power is the main consideration the liquid crystal is the obvious choice. If high brightness is required the incandescent filament display is way ahead. If on the other hand the display is to be viewed in room lighting and is required to be visible at low light levels, as for example a clock, then an emissive display is required which does not glare in the dark. Gas discharge, l.e.d. and vacuum fluorescence would fulfil this requirement.

Finally, in a book of this size it is not possible to cover all devices, circuits and applications as thoroughly as one would like. However, it is hoped that the detailed descriptions in the chapters on the devices and circuits will give the engineer who needs to incorporate displays in his equipment a better understanding of the display components and make the choice of technology and drive circuit for his application easier.

References

1. Wharf, J. H., Peters, D. V., Te, R. N. T. and Ellis, B. (1980) 'A comparative study of active and passive displays for aircraft cockpit use'. *Displays* 1, 115—121.

Appendix

Luminance and illuminance conversion tables

Illuminance

	lux	phot	foot-candle
1 lux (lm/m²)	1	10^{-4}	9.29×10^{-2}
1 phot (lm/cm²)	10^4	1	929
1 foot-candle (lm/ft²)	10.76	10.76×10^{-4}	1

Luminance

	nit	stilb	cd/ft^2	apostilb	lambert	foot-lambert (f
1 nit (cd/m²)	1	10^{-4}	9.29×10^{-2}	π	$\pi \times 10^{-4}$	0.292
1 stilb (cd/cm²)	10^4	1	929	$\pi \times 10^4$	π	2920
1 cd/ft²	10.76	1.076×10^{-3}	1	33.8	3.38×10^{-3}	π
1 apostilb (lm/m²)	$1/\pi$	$1/(\pi \times 10^{-4})$	2.96×10^{-2}	1	10^{-4}	9.29×10^{-2}
1 lambert (lm/cm²)	$1/(\pi \times 10^{-4})$	$1/\pi$	296	10^4	1	929
1 foot-lambert or 'equivalent foot-candle' (lm/ft²)	3.43	3.43×10^{-4}	$1/\pi$	10.76	1.076×10^{-3}	1

Index

About the Authors

G. F. Weston is a Group Leader on opto-electronics at Philips Research Laboratories in Surrey, England. He obtained his MSc in physics from London University. Mr. Weston is the author of several papers and two books, *Cold Cathode Glow Discharge Tubes* and *Glow Discharge Displays*.

Richard Bittleston is employed as Senior Research Scientist in the Applications Laboratory at G.E.C. Hirst Research Centre.